Today I have reached the Grand Canyon.

Over the course of the past month, I have been taken back by the vast array of splendor our country has to offer. From the Atlantic to (soon enough) the Pacific, the foothills of the Appalachians to the snow-covered peaks of the Rockies, the great high plains of the Midwest to this spectacular view of the largest crater on earth, America certainly has it all!

We are a hospitable people who have withstood financial hardships, social injustice, racial prejudice, war and peace. We are the face of America, you and I, striving to make this world a better place.

For just a second today, while standing out on the edge of the earth, amidst the beauty of this canyon surrounding me in practically all dimensions, I was able to accept that you have gone on to a better place, one even more beautiful than where I stand today, where you no longer feel pain, endure suffering, injustice or cruelty. For just one second I was able to accept this.

I will take what I can.

~Jennifer

Leaving Virginia

A Bike Ride across America in Memory of Jeremy

Jennifer T. Herbstritt

Joan + Bud —
I'll always remember the
good times spent at your house
around the holidays.
Thank you for all your love &
support throughout the years.
All my love,

Hardcover: ISBN-13: 978-0-615-34972-5 ~ ISBN-10: 0615349722
Paperback: ISBN-13: 978-0-615-34901-5 ~ ISBN-10: 0615349013
LCCN: 2010901928

Inquiries regarding *Leaving Virginia* should be directed via email to:
leavingvirginia@gmail.com.

Book cover and design by Janice Phelps Williams

Herbstritt, Jennifer T.

Leaving Virginia : a bike ride across America in memory of
Jeremy / Jennifer T. Herbstritt. -- [S.l.] : Jennifer T. Herbstritt,
c2010.

    p. ; cm.

    ISBN: 13-digit, cloth: 978-0-615-34972-5; 10-
    digit, cloth: 0615349722; 13-digit, pbk:
    978-0-615-34901-5; 10-digit, pbk: 0615349013
    Includes bibliographical references.

    1. Herbstritt, Jeremy, 1979-2007. 2. Bereavement--
Psychological aspects. 3. Virginia Tech Shootings, Blacksburg,
Va., 2007. 4. United States--Description and travel. 5. Bicycle
touring--United States. I. Title.

BF575.G7 H47 2010   2010901928
155.937--dc22   1006

To my big brother.
Never will you be forgotten.

Jeremy and Jen, circa 1987, Alliance, Ohio

Table of Contents

As you lay dead, skin cold and eyes shut, I stood tall,
frozen in time: voice silent, soul screaming inside.

Confused, I reached my hand toward your shoulder.

Alone, in a room full of unfamiliar faces, I lay silently,
eyes sewn shut, mouth stuffed, whispering your name.
Seeking comfort, human touch, scattered, my thoughts
wandered.

Who are these people, what names are they called? Why
am I here? How did this happen?

The events of the past ten days are unclear. Perplexed,
sadness overwhelms me, my tears pour like rain.

I will be fine — an explanation must draw near, breathe
deep.

Jeremy relaxing over Christmas break 2006 ~ Jennifer, Salida, Colorado, June 2008

Preface. Before the Trip

"Life is either a daring adventure or nothing."
~Helen Keller

When I made the 375-mile long drive from Bellefonte, Pennsylvania to Yorktown, Virginia on May 12, 2008, I was surrounded by a sense of sadness I'd never before experienced while beginning a vacation. The explanation for my sorrow was obvious. I'd made a similar trip at least a dozen times before to visit my elder brother, Jeremy, who attended Virginia Tech in Blacksburg, Virginia. A little more than a year prior, on April 16, 2007, Jeremy, along with thirty-one others, was killed while sitting in class making an attempt to become a more well-rounded person, someone noteworthy, someone who could contribute to society and make this world a better place. The world lost thirty-two unique and precious individuals that day. But I lost my big brother.

The first half of the trip to Blacksburg and that of the trip to Yorktown follow exactly the same roads, up until shortly after arriving in Breezewood when the routes take on separate paths. From Breezewood the route toward Blacksburg traverses through Berkley Springs, West Virginia, before arriving on Interstate-81 in Virginia; I-81 leads one almost directly to Blacksburg.

Each time in the past when I'd made the Bellefonte-to-Blacksburg journey, I had to travel nearly 185 miles on this mind-numbing interstate before arriving at Jeremy's apartment in Cardinal Court. Time and again, this seemingly endless section of road, combined with my excitement to see my older brother, made the six-and-a-half-hour long drive seem to last an eternity. Yet the drive home always seemed so much shorter.

Now, as I made the trip to Yorktown on May 12, I was reminded of the worth of our memories. What I remembered of my previous drives amazed me as my mind filled with the type of detail I had initially been so afraid of losing. Each exit, twist in the road, and aggressive driver brought back a memory unique to itself: a rain storm, a wrong turn, a problem thought to be flat tire, a phone call to inquire for directions, and a stop at a convenience store late in the night made simply to purchase a caffeinated beverage to finish the trip. I replayed each memory over and over wishing for nothing but to go back in time and be present in the moment at which these memories were formed.

Still, I knew this was impossible. When you lose someone whom you truly love all you are left with are details of memories. These are what you choose to hold on to. You relive them over and over again in your mind, day in and day out, in an attempt to provide the mind with, sadly, a far-too-brief break from the grief it will never be able to escape. Even the smallest objects, phrases, or gestures present in everyday life can act as triggers that resurface these memories at sometimes the most inopportune times, like during that car ride when I was "supposed" to be taking back control of my life, the exact control that I'd lost through Jeremy's death.

From the beginning we had the media knocking on our doors. They snuck through our fields just a day after his death in an attempt to get their hands on the perfect picture of a grieving family. The local cops were sitting at the bottom of our driveway in an attempt to blockade their entrance onto our property, but they were heartless and seemingly smarter than the police. They knew the woods would lead to a good story.

News reporters called our house repetitively, asking for pictures of Jeremy, information regarding his character and hoping for nothing other than a good story. I didn't want Jeremy to turn into a story: news one day, then soon replaced by the next big tragedy. He was (and still is) worth far more than that to me.

Major television networks and celebrity newscasters were so bold as to ask if it would be acceptable to attend his private funeral and viewing services — of course not. And beyond the fact that their actions ranged from insensitive to just plain heinous, they made it all the more difficult for me to grieve.

I wanted the phone to stop ringing. Just for a minute. Along with so many other variables, the interference and hounding of the media distracted me from what should have been my focus all along: the death of my big brother.

Throughout the days and weeks following his murder, the focus wasn't on Jeremy's death; it was on the media, the university, my parents, our extended family, the killer, the community, and, well, you get the point.

Eventually, the media found other stories to focus on and then the pendulum swung the other way.

Our family, along with other victims' families, was in the middle of forming a settlement package with the State — not because we are covetous people but because we were looking for accountability and change. The shootings at Virginia Tech had been the largest mass murder ever on a U.S. college campus; the event and response of the university demanded close examination, as well as steps to prevent anything like it from ever happening again. Perhaps only those who have lost a loved one in a mass-murder situation can understand the implications of the legal proceedings that almost always follow such events.

When articles were published regarding meetings being held with the State, folks would comment, blatantly stating for the umpteenth time, that we should "move on" not only for our sake but "for theirs as well." Virginia Tech was so "last year."

People often seemed cold-hearted and cruel; they stated there were more important things to focus on: the state of the economy, a different murder trial, or an upcoming election to name a few. I thought to myself, *If their big brother had been killed, would they feel the same way? Would they want to move on and would they actually be able to do so?* I hope they never have to suffer through something this tragic to find out. I wouldn't wish this nightmare upon anyone.

In any case, every individual variable combined together into an equation that culminated in my need for an escape.

So, a little more than a year since Jeremy's death, I found the familiar drive to Yorktown incredibly distressing. Every aspect of it reminded me that my brother was, is, and always will be *gone*. I wanted him to be with me, but I knew this wasn't possible, even in the most abstract of scenarios. His life was over.

I remember everything there is to remember about Jeremy. Not only the color of his hair and the sound of his voice… I remember the most minute details of events, entire conversations we enjoyed, and the humor and love embedded in dozens of ironic situations that the two of us had been placed in during our lives.

During this, what I was sure would be my final drive to Virginia, I remembered more about Jeremy than I had ever expected to remember. All memories of my previous visits with him surmounted. Christmas, Easter, Thanksgiving, elementary school plays, family vacations, and races run all swamped my mind. As these memories surfaced, the ride became more painful with each mile marker that passed by. The pain his death inflicted in me in those moments was still all too raw within my flesh for even me, a person who felt she'd gone to hell and come back, to manage.

Although this statement may seem obvious, it was through Jeremy's death (and in those hours sitting in my car) that I recognized that the relationship siblings have with one another is often the longest relationship any of us will have throughout our lives. Siblings arrive at birth, as do parents, but often parents die prior to our siblings. Friends and spouses come later in life.

For Jeremy and me, we had twenty-five years. When you lose someone who has played such a significant role in your life since the time of your birth (whether it be negative or positive) you can't "just forget" and it is absolutely impossible for you to "just move on with your life." A relationship of this length is simply too full of worth, too long and detailed to ever let go of, particularly so abruptly. Death might take a person away from us in the physical sense, but the relationship continues on, often for the remainder of our lives.

By the time most of us reach young adulthood, we don't yet know what it is like to experience the death of a loved one, let alone that of a big brother. I know I didn't. In our twenties, death often remains a very foreign concept. It is an event that only the elderly must face.

From left to right: Jeremy, Steph, Joe, and Jen, Joe's high school graduation, June 2006

But the truth is, eventually we all will face death.

Death is what drew me to the point where I gave up everything I'd known simply for the chance to leave it all behind. Let me explain...

When Jeremy died my world spun out of control. He was one of my very best friends. I admired him, wanted to be just as he was, hoped he'd find success and happiness, and loved him for the person he was. Many others felt just the same. In turn, I wasn't the only person affected to such a degree. My parents were devastated. My younger siblings were just as confounded. His best friends were horrified. Thinking I could erase the pain from any one of them was simply naïve. But I did think that.

I tried my best to be supportive of what was left of my family but my attempts were meaningless. Taking them to therapy wouldn't necessarily solve anything. Force feeding them wasn't the answer. Showers don't cleanse people of the ramifications of death.

Still, with Jeremy's murder I'd become the eldest living child. The torch had been passed to me. In the blink of an eye, I elected myself to a position I knew nothing about. It was my *duty* to care for my family.

From day one, rarely did I allow my true emotions to surface. I had to be strong.

Yet I needed to sob.

I needed to grieve.

During Jeremy's viewing I greeted the masses. While he lay dead in a casket placed in front of the altar, I read his eulogy, pretending (no, hoping) he was floating around in that church listening to my words. Proud, he would have been!

When guests came to our house to offer their condolences, I organized the food they brought, smiled, and greeted them like welcomed company, asking them how their families were doing, if they'd like a snack or even a cup of coffee. I was courteous and polite, never allowing my true feelings to surface.

I taught myself not to cry. I learned to be stoic.

In public settings, when asked about my family, I answered quickly, dismissively, even at times untruthfully, and then I would change the subject of the conversation to a matter I was far more comfortable discussing. This was how I acted right up until May 12, 2008, when I embarked on a trip that I hoped would teach me, sadly, how to live without Jeremy.

During what might have been labeled as the "grieving process," the year following Jeremy's murder, I felt as if nothing was ever about me or my emotional needs at the time. In retrospect, I can see that my behavior supported an environment that prevented whatever healing a young person can find when their loved one has been taken away from them in such a violent, public way.

I took on full responsibility for everything related to my brother's death: getting my dad back to work, helping to salvage my parents' relationship, ensuring my younger siblings returned to school and received proper counseling, and on and on...

My parents became increasingly distraught and engrossed in their own individual grief. They couldn't make it through a minute without being reminded of the horrific death of their son, let alone a whole eight-hour day of work; so I did what I could to lift their burden (if even only in the most minuscule fashion) — washing dishes, attending meetings, taking care of bank statements, taxes, litigations, Jeremy's estate, etc.

Eventually things started to settle down. As you will soon learn, this phase was incredibly short lived.

Because of my parents' profound grief, from the beginning the focus of our community was on their well being. Even within our extended family, rarely did anyone ask how *I* was doing. In retrospect, perhaps I should have been more understanding. My parents were fairing horribly — it was obvious to everyone. On the contrary, I appeared to be doing just fine. Nevertheless, my big brother had just been murdered in a very public fashion and, in my mind, I was hurting just as badly as our parents.

I felt alone and helpless but, just the same, I felt I didn't have the right to feel the way I did. After all, I hadn't "lost" my son.

In a sense it seemed that indirectly everyone around me, including my parents, was sending a message my way that I didn't deserve the right to grieve the death of my older brother. This was not intentional but the statement is true: he wasn't my child, my spouse, or my parent. He was simply my big brother and it seemed (at least on the surface) that in their eyes my loss wasn't all that significant. I was young. I should be able to eventually move on.

People who'd never experienced a real tragedy in their life told me, over and over again, "You've got to move on, Jen, you still have to live." I hated such statements as this was the last thing I felt I *needed* to do. I hated when people told me what I *had* to do, or *should* do, or *couldn't* do. They had no right to tell me how to cope with my brother's death, and I just wanted to escape. No, I *needed* to escape.

I needed to take my life back, make something of myself, continue my brother's legacy and allow myself the necessary time to grieve. Thus, I came up with the idea to endeavor on a bicycle trip with my younger brother, Joe, our sister, Stephanie, and my boyfriend, Brad Updegrove. We would travel from Virginia to California. I planned on keeping a journal documenting my experiences and sights seen, as well as my emotions and journey through grief.

The trip began in Yorktown on May 13, 2008 and ended in San Francisco on June 24, 2008. On average we biked ninety-three miles a day with our longest day being 171 miles and our shortest being

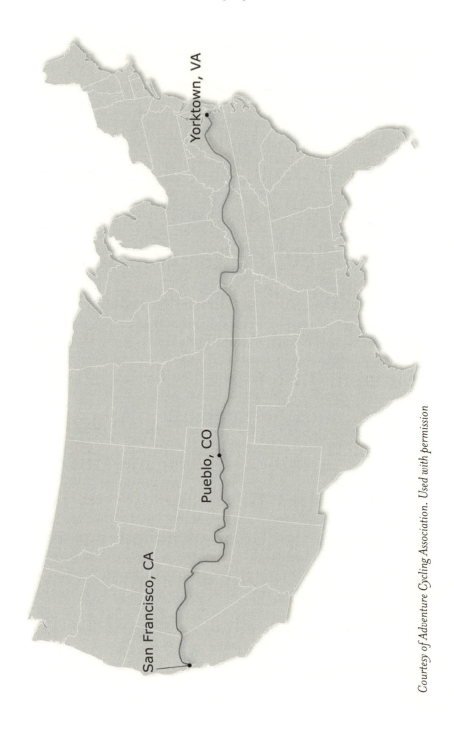

Yorktown, VA

Pueblo, CO

San Francisco, CA

Courtesy of Adventure Cycling Association. Used with permission

fifteen. Our trip was fully supported, meaning we had a support vehicle filled to the brim with all of our gear, driven primarily by my younger brother, Joe, who met us each night and oftentimes throughout the course of our ride to refill water bottles and provide emotional support and encouragement. Therefore, we didn't have to carry panniers or a trailer attached to our bikes. Some may call this cheating. I'd have to disagree. This adventure was mine to design.

In Chapter Two, you will find a detailed itinerary of our trip including mileage for each day. The total trip was nearly 3,700 miles in length. Once we made it to the West Coast we spent some time there celebrating and enjoying the culture of San Francisco. From this hilly city we drove south down the coast all the way to Big Sur, slowly making our way back home (this time) in our support vehicle with the bikes on their racks.

This journey was the best possible thing I could have done in my life at the time. Before the ride, I couldn't find anything good about this world. I lost my religion, became bitter and resentful. I no longer saw a purpose in this life for me. I was sad, scared and alone. I lived in a constant state of anxiety relentlessly anticipating the next horror-filled, life-changing event.

After the trip, life didn't suddenly become bliss. You'll have to read through my journal entries to find out the truth, and the process of transformation. I hope that along the way you'll also remember why I went on this trip. The real purpose of my journey was to give something back to a forever twenty-seven-year-old man named Jeremy Michael Herbstritt who wasn't given a fair chance at life like so many others of us in our society. This trip was intended to be my gift to him. I hoped, deeply, that he'd follow along in the spiritual sense. The places we visited were places I'm certain Jeremy would have loved to have not only witnessed but experienced for himself.

I know that my big brother will never have the opportunities that I've had in my life following his death, so this trip, in every aspect, was done for him, in his memory, in an attempt to find some form of peace about both life and death.

Jeremy Michael Herbstritt
November 6, 1979 — April 16, 2007

From left to right: Jen, Joe, and Steph posing outside a diner in Eads, Colorado

From left to right: Joe, Jeremy, and Steph, Baltimore Harbor, Summer 2005

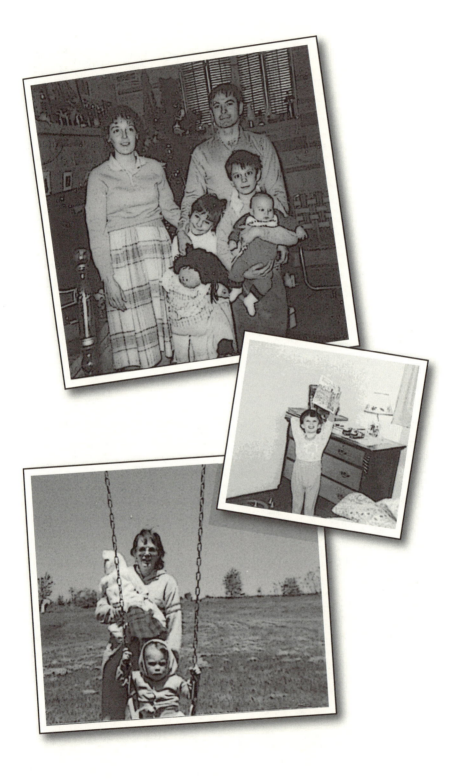

1. Jeremy's Story

"Life's a voyage that's homeward bound."
~Herman Melville

A *good story always starts from the beginning, so it seems I should rewind. I won't lie. I don't consider this to be a good story whatsoever. Last thing I ever wanted to be was a "story." So maybe I should rephrase that and say a good lesson must have meaning behind it.*

I was born during the early morning hours of November 6, 1979 to Margaret Ann and Michael Thomas Herbstritt, ages twenty-three and twenty-five respectively, in a small, simple, and white obstetrical room at Andrew Kaul Memorial Hospital in St. Marys, Pennsylvania.

St. Marys is a small, predominately Catholic town located in northwestern Pennsylvania, just about twenty miles north of Interstate 80's Penfield exit, also the highest point on 80 east of the Mississippi. (Forgive me for the trivial details, it's just that my siblings and I always made a point to mention this fact every time we passed over that summit and abruptly exited the highway.) It was founded in 1842 when fifteen families from Baltimore settled on 30,000 acres of wilderness and forest, on land purchased by the German Catholic Brotherhood of Baltimore and Philadelphia for only seventy-five cents an acre.[1] It was here that my Great-grandfather Herbstritt dreamed of a better world for his wife and children.

I lived in St. Marys for only two years until my dad was offered a job in Waterloo, Iowa with John Deere. Mom and Dad had never ventured far from St. Marys (outside of Kersey) and this was the opportunity of a lifetime for them. Young, scared, and with little money, they were hesitant as to how they would make ends meet. Somehow, this variable didn't deter them.

Dad had been working at a factory in St. Marys where his father-in-law, Rich, (you guessed it) was his boss. Dad was a trained engineer with a degree from The Pennsylvania

State University in electrical engineering. He knew the National Electrical Code better than anyone in his department and was a genius when it came to calculus, physics, statics and dynamics and anything even remotely related to electrical engineering. He didn't want to settle in this life.

Mom, she was a registered nurse, with a degree from the Indiana University of Pennsylvania. At the time of my birth, she was still working nights on the Med/Surg. Floor at Andrew Kaul. My mom knew nursing like she knew the back of her hand. This knowledge, combined with a heart of gold, made her one of the best nurses in town.

So I am sure you can understand why, when my dad got that offer from John Deere the two barely blinked an eye. They couldn't resist the temptation to find something better in this life and so they set sail on the adventure of a lifetime.

Mom was pregnant with my little sister, Jen, at the time of Dad's offer and didn't want to leave home until she gave birth. It was too stressful to move to a foreign place, find a doctor, and give birth alone. So, Mom and I stayed in St. Marys while my dad went to Iowa and started his career. We joined him with my new baby sister a few months later in the dead of a typical Iowa winter. I'll never forget that snow. It was so deep at times that it buried our front door handle as well as the basement windows. Did it ever pack well!

Mom and I formed a bond that winter that only a mother and son can form while Dad worked diligently day in and day out. Jennifer got sick with pneumonia and was hospitalized for nearly a week. I'll never forget the fright in Mom and Dad's voices during that time. I never was jealous of Jen, just happy to have a companion for life and grateful for the opportunity to be a big brother. I wonder how she's fairing today…

Times were rough during those four years in Iowa as we were living in the recession of the early 1980s. Dad had to work diligently at his job, as each week board meetings were held and subsequently employees were laid off. I'm sure he felt as if he were sitting on a time bomb, ready to explode at any moment…never knowing when that might be.

Additionally, (believe it or not) race was still an issue even at that time in our country's history. Dad was harassed many times by colleagues, told the only reason he still had a job was because he was Caucasian. Segregation was evident in his workplace and even within our own community. White people lived on one side of the city, African Americans on the other. The same held true in regards to the employee lunch room and company picnics. Dad tried to befriend everyone possible, regardless of their race. This was just him. But this character trait created animosity among him and his less progressive coworkers. Eventually, a certain individual couldn't take Dad's kindness anymore. He threatened his life.

Truth be told: he came to our house with a gun. Dad and Mom decided enough was enough. They made the difficult decision to leave. Initially this decision was solitarily Dad's. Mom had started to make very good friends over the course of those four thorny years. Jen and I had formed friendships with the neighborhood kids, and we weren't ready to say goodbye either. We were content in our own little world. But Dad was homesick, Mom as well, and times were all too rough in every dimension to remain.

Dad was fortunate in that while all of this chaos was erupting he was simultaneously offered a position in Alliance, Ohio, with Babcock and Wilcox. He turned in his resignation to John Deere and the keys to the first home he and Mom bought together, to the bank, and off we all went on our slow journey "home" toward St. Marys, Pennsylvania.

Mom and Dad never did make it all the way back home, but they sure did come close.

Ohio was lovely. We lived in a fixer-upper: a quaint, faded white farm house situated on a few acres of land. We had a rusted old barn filled with pigs, cows, and chickens and a lovely rose garden. That garden was perfect: surrounded by red roses but filled with plentiful harvest. Jen and I loved every aspect of Ohio: from Sunshine, our dog, to rides on the lawn mower with Dad in the summers. It was where I started school, and Jennifer too. It was where I learned to ride a bike without training wheels then quickly excelled at riding my mom's blue, ten-speed Schwinn (the old-school type with the long curved-style handlebars).

Jen and I learned a lot about life and death there by witnessing our dad butcher chickens in the back yard and discovering Ernie and Bert had turned into our delicious Easter pork dinner with family and friends. Our rabbit had a heart attack in front of our very own innocent eyes, and (worst of all) Mom lost a baby late in the night in that very farmhouse. We were all sad in regards to that miscarriage but Mom was understandably devastated most. We were too young to fully comprehend what this meant.

I'll never forget the taste of unpasteurized milk from the farm up the road. Mom and Dad rewarded good behavior with this very divine treat.

Ohio was also where I found a lump in my groin and (ashamed) didn't say a word to my parents. When Mom noticed this lump for herself, she took me straight to the pediatrician's office, not wasting a minute. I was diagnosed with a simple, benign hernia that my doctor recommended be removed so as to avoid the possibility of enlargement or, worse yet, strangulation. Soon enough, I was scheduled for surgery. The operation went well, only I didn't wake up! I had a reaction to the anesthesia or maybe an error was performed in regards to the dose. Who knows? Regardless, for nearly two weeks I lay still in a coma, remembering nothing from those days or the many days thereafter except for the sound of my parents' voices praying by my side for my survival. I made it. I had to learn to perform a number of tasks all over again from running, playing whiffle ball, talking, and so on, but I survived.

In fact, the truth is I made it so far past that minor obstacle in my life that I became a civil engineer. But before I earned my degree, we moved back to Pennsylvania where Dad landed a job at The Pennsylvania State University as an electrical engineer in design services. Penn State was his alma mater and he was happy to return to "Happy Valley." Who wouldn't be? Mom was pleased as well; Penn State is located not even two hours away from St. Marys, Pennsylvania. Weekend visits home would now be more feasible.

For a year we lived in a rental house in Boalsburg where my little brother, Joe, was born in September of 1987. And then we moved to Bellefonte, just ten miles down the road, when a fifty-acre farm was posted in the paper for sale. This place was exactly what Dad had always dreamed of; Mom not so much. She was more the type to enjoy living close to her neighbors in a subdivision. Dad wanted land and animals, a tractor and a combine. He wanted to bale fields of hay, sow seeds of corn, soybeans and grain, raise beef, breed sheep, and ride on horseback under the stars. Mom agreed upon the move mainly to fulfill Dad's ambitious dreams.

Mom gave birth to Stephanie in February of 1989. Out of all my siblings, Steph was the one who most closely resembled me.

Eventually, Mom ended up loving the farm and actually made some of her very dearest friends there: neighbors who moved into newly built houses structured on the main road set below us not more than a few years following Mom and Dad's closing date. Over the course of the past two decades, that entire area has grown into a community of people, all with common goals and aspirations, who've formed very close friendships with one another. Sadly, many of the original members of our community have died off, including me.

Mom and Dad's dreams were fulfilled on that farm. They had four beautiful, healthy children, a strong love for one another, a lovely home close to family, with dear friends a short walk away. Their life seemed to have turned out just as they'd hoped.

I grew up on that farm from the third grade on. I raised sheep there, which I showed at the county fair annually in the fall, just as school was about to begin again for the year. I sheared those sheep in the summers and delivered their lambs in the cold, dry air of the Pennsylvania winters. I baled hay with my dad, planted an apple orchard, and a massive garden each spring from which I harvested sweet corn, peppers, tomatoes, cantaloupes,

Morning sun at Herbstritt farm, Bellefonte, Pennsylvania

pumpkins, watermelon, green beans, and anything else I felt like planting. I worked hard. I dug the holes for the fence that surrounded our pasture with nothing more than my bare hands and the help of Dad, Mom, and my two youngest siblings. I kept that barn in working order, rebuilt the suspension wall when it collapsed, and made sure the animals were vaccinated properly and fed the appropriate nutrients. Dad and I made that farm into a home. We renovated that house inside and out. It never turned into a mansion, but we never wanted it to. It turned into our home.

I never wanted to leave the farm. I wanted to buy some dairy cows and start a business. But Mom and Dad saw something else in my future. They sent me to college at Penn State in the fall of 1998. I was always a bright kid but never really knew what I wanted to do as far as an education. I was content simply farming and was angry with Mom and Dad when they suggested college. I filled out my application only because I was forced to do so, and actually I didn't speak with either of them for a week or more after I moved into my dorm in Geary Hall. I did this out of spite. But when I met my very best friends at Penn State and found for myself the challenges of college, of growing up, and becoming a man, I knew my parents had pushed me to do the right thing.

Dad wanted me to make something of myself and suggested I become a doctor or even a lawyer. I started out in pre-med but graduated with a degree in biochemistry and molecular biology with a minor in chemistry. I was good at my studies but I had to work hard to perform well. The Dean's List didn't always come easy. I just didn't have a passion for this specific field of science. To be frank: I hated it. So, after a lot of soul searching I decided to pursue engineering just as my dad had done. This decision didn't come easy and not without reservations, but in the end it resulted in my lifelong passion. I wanted to make this world a better place, structurally sound, environmentally friendly, with safe roadways and securely constructed bridges. I was a designer interested in alternative sources of fuel and energy.

I went back to my roots, got a second B.S. from Penn State (this time in civil and environmental engineering), and then turned down an offer to get my graduate degree in engineering from my alma mater. I needed to do like my parents did some twenty-six years prior and go out on my own and find my own path. I didn't want to settle for just anything in life.

I accepted my place in Virginia Tech's Civil and Environmental Engineering Graduate School. I worked closely with my advisor, demonstrating my drive and ability, passion and determination. Additionally, I worked as a Teaching Assistant for one of the entry level engineering labs. It was here where I found my passion for teaching; I loved helping the younger students learn to be not only quick thinking, analytical engineers but also talented writers whose writing made sense and displayed the results of their hard work both efficiently and proudly.

I considered becoming a professor or possibly a consultant. I wanted to make money. I wanted to find love, start a family, buy a car of my own choosing, a house, and maybe someday a farm of my own. I wanted all of these things but knew that I first needed to complete my education. I was excited with my place at Virginia Tech. I loved that university. Honestly, I did. Their tailgates prior to football games couldn't quite compare to Penn State's but I was finding my purpose in life there. I kept in touch with my best friends from college, who were like brothers to me, but I also started to form new relationships. I knew my roots and wouldn't forget them. I took friends without vehicles to the grocery store when I went and befriended the elderly woman in the basement of my building over cookies and milk.

I never forgot my roots. I was proud of my family. I missed them dearly but kept in touch with them often. I told everyone I met of my parents and three siblings: Jennifer, Joe, and Stephanie. Stephanie, a senior in high school, and a Joe, a freshman at my alma mater, looked up to me. They were about to begin on their own journeys through college. I worried that they would make the same mistakes I had. I kept in touch with them on an almost daily basis, supported their decisions and provided them with my advice. I hoped they would become engineers like me. Trust me, they knew my opinion. I missed running with Jennifer, but we kept in touch over the phone. I hoped to continue our running relationship by meeting her in places like New York City or Boston for marathons.

If only I had gone to Boston...

In April of 2007, I was a graduate student pursuing a master's degree in civil and environmental engineering. I had recently been granted a scholarship that would pay for the remainder of my graduate education. I was seriously contemplating pursuing a PhD as well as a masters and maybe someday working for a university, teaching students like myself the backbone of the field of engineering. Like I said, I couldn't make up my mind between this career path and consulting. But none of this seems to matter anymore as I no longer am a part of that world.

Mom and Jeremy, Virginia Tech, fall 2006

How and when I left does not matter. The fact is, I'm writing this letter in hopes that my family will come across it. I have spent the past year and a half trying to figure this place out. I have returned to the earth numerous times, sending anything I could possibly come up with as a sign to my family to let them know that I am alright. I have rung their doorbell more times than I can remember. I ran that marathon: confused as to how I had even found my way there; I ran it with my sister. I have broken chairs, flickered lights, made animals run in front of their houses and walk down their sidewalks, introduced them to people whom I hoped would remind them of me; but to my dismay they have not picked up on a single sign. They have lost all hope.

My heaven is lovely. It is wooded, a large forest, but at the same time a cornfield of gold, dreams and desires. I live in the same house I grew up in with my sister's leather couch to relax on and the biggest TV I could find, on which I watch the best football, baseball, and basketball games a man could dream of. I play backyard football with friends and family. I've met many inspirational people. I play Five Hundred, a card game, nightly with Grandpa, his brothers, and sisters. I still drink beer when I feel like it, yet I never overindulge. And yes, Lager is still my favorite. I feast on the most perfectly made Buffalo wings and Greek pizza I've ever devoured. My heaven is easy to travel around. I just wish it, or think about it, and it happens. If I want to travel to Europe, it takes me only a brief pause in time to get there; Asia, no longer.

My heaven is perfect, except for one very important detail. My family — Mom, Dad, Jennifer, Joseph, and Stephanie — are not here with me and from what I can see they have lost all faith that one day they will see me again. Life as they knew it is over. Not only have I been unfairly robbed of my life, but they have been robbed of theirs as well. I cannot enjoy my heaven knowing that they are so immensely sad, feel so alone, so helpless and have lost all hope of a place far better than that of earth itself. I cannot rest here knowing their sadness. Therefore, I have written this very simple note both as a reminder to myself of who I will be reunited with for all of eternity when their day comes to make the transition from the world of the living to that of the dead, and also in hopes that maybe my family will somehow come across it, or simply sense it and finally understand and appreciate that I am okay. I still do exist, and they will see me again. Nothing will ever make sense. It still doesn't make sense to me. But one day we will be back together and none of this nonsense will matter anymore.

I am building for you a bridge. It runs high, across mountains of tall pine trees, oak, and maple. In the distance are cornfields of gold and peach trees with peaches so ripe that when you bite into them the juice just drips to the ground beneath you. There are fields covered in wildflowers of more colors than you ever knew to exist back on earth. The sun shines brightly here even when I'm skiing and the snow is light as air. One day this place will be ready for you — it will be yours to enjoy just as it is now mine. It truly is magnificent. You won't be disappointed.

But for now, I beg you to try to understand that although I am dead, I am still Jeremy Michael Herbstritt, son of Michael and Margaret, brother to Jennifer, Joseph, and Stephanie; civil engineer, Penn State alumni; best friend of Jim, Jacques, Phil, Justin, Vicky, Brian, Tony, Scott, Patrick, and more; cousin to Katie, Heather, Eric, Vince, Jason, Brandon, Breanna, and more. I am a Catholic, with roots dug deep in Bellefonte and St. Marys, Pennsylvania, Waterloo, Iowa, and Alliance, Ohio. I bleed blue and white. I crave Bonfatto's "fire in the hole" Buffalo wings. I love black olives, my mother's sugar cookie dough, my sister's boyfriend's homemade salsa, and a good haircut accompanied by ridiculous conversation from my Aunt Mary.

When I died I was searching for something better in life; I wanted to make something of myself. I was on a hunt for love and for life. I still am. And I still am Jeremy Michael Herbstritt. I may have made it to heaven but I have not forgotten my beginnings.

Please know, all that is missing in my heaven is my family, built on the basis of love alone, and I am searching for peace. For me to achieve this, I need you to do so as well. Peace, hope, and love: this is all I desire. Please give me this.

(Back row from left to right) Brad, Jeremy, Jen; (Front row from left to right) Dad, Mom, Steph and Joe at Aunt Chris and Uncle Chuck's house, Christmas break 2006

Left to right: Jen, Joe, Steph, and Jeremy at the Baltimore Harbor, Summer 2005

Jeremy playing backyard Frisbee, summer 2005
Photograph taken by Stephanie Herbstritt

Brad leisurely riding to Sausalito following our arrival in San Francisco, June 2008

Joe standing along a railing atop the Golden Gate Bridge, June 2008

2. The Beauty of My Dream
San Francisco

"The future belongs to those who believe in the beauty of their dreams."
~Eleanor Roosevelt

June 24, 2008

Dear Jeremy,

So I made it to San Francisco. You better believe it: I arrived here on the firm seat of my bicycle around three o'clock this afternoon.

Nope, you're not dreaming — I actually rode this carbon frame as far west as I possibly could.

"Bessie" and I sure have gotten to know each other quite well over the course of the past month and a half. A beauty she is! She might be young and I, an inexperienced cyclist, but we've been a good team. I have to believe her twenty-seven-inch tires and thirty gears displaced amongst three rings could have taken on any terrain. And, well, my mental stamina could have somehow figured out how to plow us both through a wall of solid brick if for some reason we'd had to!

Shhhh, don't you even say a word! I'm quite aware of San Francisco's distance from central Pennsylvania. No, I didn't do this for the exercise and of course I'm out of my mind, but that's far beyond the point. Just let me have my moment in the sun.

I just can't believe it! I've arrived at the Pacific, today: June 24, 2008! Today, I saw water: clear, blue, pure, refreshing water, saturated with salt. And I wasn't hallucinating!

Just a few short hours ago I was in Vallejo, California, and, believe it or not, forty-five short days prior I was in Yorktown, Virginia, almost 3,700 miles away. Bessie and I were just getting to know one another back then. She was just about ready to leave us both lying in a line of heavy traffic when I finally did figure out how to unclip my feet from her pedals without falling over.

That's when our journey westward began.

Well, actually, first we had to get all of us down to Yorktown. I was pretty darn adamant in regards to beginning biking from the most eastern body of water I could find in Virginia. Between the battle of the Chesapeake and that of the Atlantic, the Chesapeake won.

So, with Bessie and a few of her "friends" planted on top of the Pathfinder, Joe, Dad, Brad, and I traveled south to Yorktown where our adventure officially began.

As we drove down our lengthy gravel driveway then surrounded by fields of fenced-in green pasture in a direction away from our home, I took one final glance into those rolling fields of green. The winter might have been mentally challenging for me but to the land, evidently, it had been kind.

We were traveling toward our black plastic mailbox still marked "311" and still situated where it has been for the past two decades: at the end of our lane. That mailbox looks exactly the same as it did back on April 15, 2007, but we all know it doesn't mark the same home it addressed at that point in time.

As our house disappeared within the horizon, I knew this possibly would be the last time I'd see the white farmhouse with black shutters in which we grew up in. As well, I knew I might never see that run down, red barn situated adjacent to our house. The truth is I didn't care. I had no desire to remain within the confines of that property any longer. It had already generated too much sorrow in me. If I never returned, I was fine with this prospect. Change was imperative. Plus, Bessie and I had made plans.

It certainly was a typical dark and dreary mid-May afternoon in central Pennsylvania but the car's engine was warm and amidst our sorrow excitement was plenty. We were all looking for a better life and this was our definitive ticket out.

As I looked down at the mileage posted on the odometer within the dashboard I was taken back by the number: 68,000. I realized I'd put nearly 40,000 miles on that car since I purchased it with your guidance a short three years prior. All too often I feel stuck in a time warp, but in that moment I was beginning to recognize that time traveled by far faster than it ever had before. It was in that moment that I realized while I lay dormant, saturated in sadness, for practically thirteen months the world around me continued to prosper. Nausea swept quickly all the way from my gut to the back of my throat. I hate the reminders.

Abruptly, I forced a smile onto my face.

I'd just taken that silver SUV into the shop for a tune-up. At the time, the oil was changed and the engine was prepared for a ride to the ocean. The car's exterior was shiny from a recent car wash and the interior was immaculate as I'd recently vacuumed every square inch of it myself in preparation for this trip.

Activity sure does occupy the mind.

The car certainly didn't remain clean for long but its spotlessness undoubtedly added a flavorful touch to our "fresh start."

With no more than $400 total dispersed amongst our pockets and a credit card, a few pairs of clothes, three bikes and the same number of helmets, we began our journey.

We could have been considered the "wealthy homeless." Indeed, for an undetermined number of days we would be without a secured structure, not because we had no choice other than to succumb to this all-too-sad, almost always undesirable ultimatum, but because we chose this lifestyle for ourselves on a quest for adventure.

What was brought certainly was not ample but we hoped it'd be enough to get us across America in search of the West.

We were to live out of my car as well as a nine-by-four, four-person tent. Hotel stays were to be limited and chain restaurants would be eliminated, or so we thought. (You know me and my obsession with one certain chain's divine breakfast sandwiches!)

The guests of our trip would vary but at most times there would be four of us total embarking together into the unknown. Initially included were Dad, Brad, Joe, and I. Stephanie was to join us in Bowling Green, Kentucky, as was Mom. After visiting with us in Kentucky, Mom and Dad were to return home to Bellefonte together.

Jen and Brad posing in front of the Golden Gate Bridge, San Francisco, California,
June 24, 2008 ~ Photograph taken by Joseph Herbstritt

I was the brains behind the mission (cue the laughter). And the organizer. My attention focused on the details while I struggled to learn to live life again.

Joe was the musician, a voice of reason and the wizard of misadventure. His energy was spiritual and his nature contagious. He was happy to take a road trip and be our SAG wagon while simultaneously searching for meaning in life.

Brad was in competition. If I were to do this, he dare not be left out. Throughout our trip he was the most practical and rigid of us all. He seemed to be in search of a purpose in life far greater than the accumulation of financial wealth.

Dad was our comedian. Although he wasn't with us for the entire span of the trip, his presence brought laughter throughout our journey. He simply wanted a vacation, so took two weeks off of work and initiated our journey with us.

A libertarian displaced from the 1970s and the apple of your eye, Stephanie was searching for love, laughter, and a life far better than what she had come to know over the course of the past thirteen months.

Other than for the few short days that she spent with us in Bowling Green, Kentucky, Mom remained at home in Bellefonte searching for reason. In Kentucky, she was an unambiguous voice of reason. Her thoughts focused mainly on our safety.

Conflict did arise often amongst all parties involved, but I'd expected this as the journey was real and life happens while surrounded by chaos and drama. Even Bessie and I got into a few quarrels of our own.

There was very little planning involved. I simply purchased maps through an organization that specializes in creating maps, organizing trips, etc. for people who are crazy enough to consider such a quest.

I quit my job and packed my car. That was it.

From the beginning, I had plans of leaving from Virginia as I felt this would be symbolic. I'm not sure how many times I heard, "You're traveling east to west? Have you not heard of the prevailing westerlies?"

I had, but chose to ignore these comments as I wanted to leave from Virginia. I didn't want to bike home. And so we didn't.

Out of that familiar gravel driveway, we ventured south to the Chesapeake in Yorktown, Virginia. We'd seen this sight many a time before but, like I said, we were determined to depart from Virginia. We all had our eyes set on the Pacific and couldn't wait to leave from the Atlantic (or as close to it as we could get) so the quest could begin.

The drive to our prospective first and last hotel of the trip proved to be rainy, tiring, and long. When we finally did arrive at our hotel late in the night, we walked our bikes into the lobby past the receptionist and into our rooms. The next morning came all too early as sound sleep was impossible that night due to our thoughts and the depth of each of our imaginations.

We awoke to the smell of coffee in the hall and the sight of frost blanketing the windows. After dressing and devouring our feed as if this were our last scheduled meal, we walked our bikes through the hotel's entrance with a smile hiding each of our faces.

After witnessing the glory of the sunrise above the Atlantic for one final time before setting our sights on the Pacific, we departed on our journey, that of a lifetime.

The weather here in San Francisco is beautiful. The sun is shining. The air is cool and humidity is absent. The ocean is spectacular. The waves here are so much more intense compared with those of the Atlantic. And the drop off into the water from some of these look-out points is breathtaking.

Of course, the wind is strong! It's San Francisco after all. But this doesn't seem to bother me as I've made it to California on my bike. For once, I've accomplished something of value worth telling you about. I'm definitely proud but something is missing.

I was certain once I reached the Pacific I'd be ecstatic. I was certain things would change. The water would cleanse my soul. Instead, I find myself staring blankly into the ocean with a piece of my being stolen, taken away.

Possibly the pain will never fade.

All my love,

Jen

Steph (l) and Jen (r) on the top story of Coit Tower, Telegraph Hill, San Francisco, June 2008 ~ Photograph by Joseph Herbstritt

3. Choosing Life
Yorktown to Ashland, Virginia

"Don't go around saying the world owes you a living.
The world owes you nothing. It was here first."
~Mark Twain

May 13, 2008

Jeremy,

*I*t's really a shame you couldn't have been with us this morning, or even right now. We really were a sight to see as we biked away from the Chesapeake under the sunrise. The only one of us who had any idea what he was getting himself into was Brad. I was far too excited about taking my first few strokes to even consider how difficult it might be to ride my bike 105 miles. Someday, we'll all look back on how today started and just roll in laughter. This is my hope.

One of my favorite characters in history was General Robert E. Lee. I bet you set your sights on Kennedy, Reagan, or George Washington himself. Nevertheless, I will explain.

Of course, I liked Lee because he was one of the most celebrated generals in American history. He was an idol of the south, General-in-Chief of the Confederate forces during the Civil War, President of Washington College, graduate of West Point, a soldier in the U.S Army for thirty-two years and a proud engineer.[2] But I didn't like him because of these facts, nor did I like him because of his victories at the Seven Days Battles and the Second Battle of Bull Run.[3] The truth is I never was one to gain excitement over victories and defeats. And if I'm going to be completely honest here, you should know that I actually never was one to care much about history. Math made more sense.

41

Map illustration by Janice Phelps Williams

Date	From	To	Daily Miles	Total Miles
5/13/2008	Yorktown, VA	Ashland, VA	105	105
5/14/2008	Ashland, VA	Charlottesville, VA	85	190
5/15/2008	Charlottesville, VA	Lexington, VA	67	257
5/16/2008	Lexington, VA	Catawba, VA	70	327
5/17/2008	Catawba, VA	Damascus, VA	96	423
5/18/2008	Damascus, VA	The Breaks, Va	63	486
5/19/2008	The Breaks, Va	Hazard, KY	86	572
5/20/2008	Hazard, KY	Berea, KY	80	652
5/21/2008	Berea, KY	Bardstown, KY	105	757
5/22/2008	Bardstown, KY	Salida, KY	51	808
5/23/2008	Bowling Green, KY	Bowling Green, KY	0	808
5/24/2008	Bowling Green, KY	Bowling Green, KY	0	808
5/25/2008	Bowling Green, KY	Cave In Rock, IL	140	948
5/26/2008	Cave In Rock, IL	Murphysboro, IL	76	1024
5/27/2008	Murphysboro, IL	Farmington, MO	93	1117
5/28/2008	Farmington, MO	Alley Spring, MO	101	1218
5/29/2008	Alley Spring, MO	Marshfield, MO	104	1322
5/30/2008	Marshfield, MO	Pittsburg, KS	85	1407
5/31/2008	Pittsburg, KS	Toronto Lake State Park, KS	97	1504
6/1/2008	Toronto Lake State Park, KS	Wichita, KS	70	1574
6/2/2008	Wichita, KS	Larned, KS	102	1676
6/3/2008	Larned, KS	Scott City, KS	125	1801
6/4/2008	Scott City, KS	Ordway, CO	171	1972
6/5/2008	Ordway, CO	Pueblo, CO	15	1987
6/6/2008	Pueblo, CO	Pueblo, CO	0	1987
6/7/2008	Pueblo, CO	Salida, CO	112	2099
6/8/2008	Salida, CO	Gunnison, CO	65	2164
6/9/2008	Gunnison, CO	Telluride, CO	130	2294
6/10/2008	Telluride, CO	Delores, CO	65	2359
6/11/2008	Delores, CO	Natural Bridge, UT	120	2479
6/12/2008	Natural Bridge, UT	Capitol Reef, UT	140	2619
6/13/2008	Capitol Reef, UT	Escalante, UT	76	2695
6/14/2008	Escalante, UT	Panguitch, UT	70	2765
6/15/2008	Panguitch, UT	Panguitch, UT	0	2765
6/16/2008	Panguitch, UT	Milford, UT	117	2882
6/17/2008	Milford, UT	Great Basin / Baker, NV	86	2968
6/18/2008	Great Basin / Baker, NV	Ely, NV	69	3037
6/19/2008	Ely, NV	Eureka, NV	83	3120
6/20/2008	Eureka, NV	Middlegate, NV	137	3257
6/21/2008	Middlegate, NV	Carson City, NV	110	3367
6/22/2008	Carson City, NV	Placerville, CA	115	3482
6/23/2008	Placerville, CA	Winters, CA	98	3580
6/24/2008	Winters, CA	Vallejo, CA / San Francisco, CA	63	3643

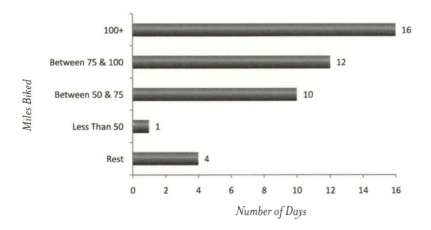

*(Left to right) Brad, Jen, and Joe, Yorktown, Virginia,
Yorktown Victory Monument, May 13, 2008*

What fascinated me about General Robert E. Lee was what I perceived as a sense of mystery about him. Possibly I felt this way because it's who I wanted him to be. I wanted him to be an abolitionist at heart. I wanted him to recognize slavery as inherently wrong. I wanted him to be misunderstood: not just by the North, but by the South, and even himself.

I created in him a man he (in all probability) wasn't: one who rejected slavery for all the right reasons but lived out his character for a reason unbeknownst to me.

I always hoped if I read further through my history books I'd learn that Lee eventually agreed with African American's scripted rights. The imaginary character I created in my mind would have done this.

Unfortunately, I never read precisely what I desired.

With time, I realized the only person who will ever understand Lee in all totality is Lee himself. Not even his wife, his parents, or his children could clear up any potential misconceptions regarding his character.

The same fact is true for you and for me. At the end of each of our lives, we may all end up being a bit misunderstood. No longer will anyone be able to answer for us. We will be gone. At such a time, only speculations will be made as to our feelings, beliefs, and persuasions.

Because of this plain and simple fact, in life there end up being some things we will never understand. For me, Lee is one of them.

Virginia reminds me of Lee, which brings me back to my journey. I'm south of the Mason Dixon line and feel as if I have taken a step back in time right into the history books.

From the beginning, today's ride was filled with history and fascinating facts. But what I realized as I biked away from the waters and a very noteworthy monument was that today was a day of historical significance of far more momentous importance than even such facts for me as a person who had experienced firsthand the ramifications of murder.

Today will forever mark the date where I chose life for myself amidst death.

From the Chesapeake, we traveled through historic Yorktown where I remembered what I'd learned was essentially the end of the American Revolutionary War. It was here that General Cornwallis and his countless men surrendered to George Washington at the Battle of Yorktown in 1781.

From Yorktown, we continued to follow the pages of my high school history books all the way back to Colonial Williamsburg where we returned to the eighteenth century and met a multitude of faces, many familiar, just as many not. The streets of this area were made up of red brick. Buildings were old fashioned, many still with dirt floors. The people were dressed in a Victorian type of apparel with large wigs of white for the men and puffy dresses for the women made from delicate textiles of fine colors with a complexity of textures.

From Williamsburg we followed winding country roads perfectly shaded with tall draping trees dressed pleasantly with fresh, flowing

Chesapeake Bay, May 2008 ~ Photograph taken by Joseph Herbstritt

green leaves for miles on end. By the time four o'clock arrived, my legs were exhausted. I had never ridden my bike this far before in my life and as a result it seemed I didn't have an ounce of energy left in my being. Still, I couldn't help but notice the smile hiding my face. I was free.

With just the perfect timing, Dad and Joe drove by waving bags of fast food out the Pathfinder's passenger side window, "Pull off at the shopping plaza located on your left about a half mile up the road!"

Starving and eaten up by exhaustion, Brad and I didn't bother to question what was present in either of those bags.

As soon as we spotted that plaza, abruptly, we pulled our weary bodies off of the road and immediately laid them down atop the warm pavement of that random supermarket parking lot. Meanwhile, Joe and Dad just stared at us appearing to be grateful they weren't in our precise predicament. As my teeth bit through that sandwich while I continued to lie still on the ground, I could hear their silent thoughts:

"These two must be nuts!" In that moment, I truly enjoyed my reclining position. Still I was bothered by myself that I gave into fast food.

I wanted to step out of my element. I wanted to experience America: small, family operated diners, real people and see history unravel before my very own eyes. I didn't want to settle for routine, so in that moment I swore off fast food for the remainder of this trip. We'll see how long this devotion lasts.

After this late lunch was consumed, I thought I had enough energy to complete ten more miles; it turned out to be fifteen. Brad sure was jacked.

I followed my directions spelled out clear as day on my map. Additionally, I had my GPS situated directly in front of me on the handlebars of my bike. I shouldn't have gotten us lost, but somehow I did. I purchased these maps for this reason specifically: so as to avoid getting lost. Yet, I am inept at reading maps. This was your job.

We are following the TransAmerica Trail (a collection of back country roads from Yorktown, Virginia, to Astoria, Oregon, that a group of cyclists rode back in 1976 to celebrate the Bicentennial[4]) to Pueblo, Colorado, and then we'll be taking the "Western Express" to San Francisco.

From today on out, a collection of nearly fifteen maps will be our guide west. Modifications will be made when deemed necessary (or when I inadvertently guide us off-path). Clearly, today marked the first of these "off-route excursions."

Nearly fifteen miles following the consumption of that divine crispy chicken sandwich, I landed Brad and myself at a gas station located nowhere on our map. After inquiring for directions to our campsite from the cashiers, those pumping gas, and those purchasing food, we were still lost. No one had heard of our destination.

After a "small dispute" amongst the two of us bikers as to whose fault it was and why we were lost, I called Joe and Dad from my cell phone and begged their help.

Not more than a half hour later, they arrived at our beck and call and graciously transported us back to our campsite located not more than five miles up the road. We had passed this exact campground ten miles from that fast-food joint. I can't tell you how we missed it. It was marked with a neon green sign. We must have been tired, our minds distracted. This is my only explanation.

I was embarrassed with our necessity for the SAG wagon but glad to have our driver's "just in case" of situations like this.

My feet aren't very sore, nor are my knees. My shoulders feel heavy and my body is tired, but other than this, physically, I don't feel too bad. We'll see how long this resilience lasts. My spirits are high; my smile is incredibly warm.

As I write this to you, I'm sitting by our campfire in Ashland, Virginia. I'm down $15 for our lodging and am slightly discouraged to discover that our campsite is located directly adjacent to a major interstate, separated merely by a rickety wooden fence no taller than my waist; but the sun is about to set and my marshmallow is golden. The air is cool and I'm reclining in a folding chair surrounded by a perfectly lit fire.

As an ash touches my forearm, I can't help but think this couldn't get any better. I'm enjoying my new life, at least for the moment. Not my new life tarnished with death: I hate that life. But my new life: unemployed, homeless, and on the road.

I biked 105 miles today. No, *we* biked 105 miles! Unbelievable! It may have taken us all day but we did it. I biked my first century! I'm proud of this accomplishment but faintly worried for my stamina. I hope I can keep this up to get me across.

I am fully aware that today is only day one and this trip could take months for all that I know. The conditions today were easy. Hills were absent, as were mountains. Traffic was light. People were kind and my emotions were high, high in a good sense.

Additionally, for the moment this journey doesn't seem all so unusual. At the monument in Yorktown we ran into a few other groups of bikers beginning their own journeys across. Some were carrying their gear in trailers and panniers. Others were supported just like us by family and friends in a SAG wagon, meeting them at night at a campsite or hotel. No one seemed to think our quest was all that unusual. This was slightly disheartening but also comforting as it demonstrates that we're not alone with our goal.

We're sleeping at a campground with showers and warm water, laundry, and a game room. There are even vending machines, so I can't say we're roughing it, at least not yet. I look forward to that day, but for now this will do.

Our tent is set on a pile of mulch. There is no rain, but if there were, it is waterproof with a floor. The bathrooms are approximately a quarter mile away, cleaned daily, with soap dispensers and even hair dryers.

I doubt we'll see any wildlife tonight other than for the typical chipmunk or squirrel scavenging for food as this place is fenced in and (like I said) located no more than ten feet from the byway.

The sky doesn't look any closer than it did back at home in Pennsylvania, and the scenery isn't all too unfamiliar to me as I've been to Virginia a time and again.

Our food is far from exotic. In fact, the frozen chili that I packed has long been perfectly thawed. In addition to this leftover award-winning chili, for dinner we ate "foil packs." Although they aren't the healthiest of meals, they certainly are divine. Made up of a half cup of olive oil and two teaspoons of seasoning salt, diced potatoes, peas, carrots, and beans all wrapped in foil and cooked within a campfire, this meal certainly would steal any outdoorsman's heart.

I'm not too worried about dropping crumbs on the ground tonight, but I can't wait for the day that we have to fear for what might happen if one of us does.

It's about 9:45 P.M. and the sky just recently turned a very dark shade of black. As I'm exhausted, I've deemed it's time for me to draw to my new bed: a four-foot long blow-up sleeping pad that requires only four puffs of air, a sleeping bag, and a travel-sized pillow surrounded by three other bodies.

I hope to sleep well tonight as tomorrow it's the same thing all over again; the only elements that will change are the mileage and destination.

From Virginia, goodnight!

Jennifer

Spring view of the Appalachian Mountains, May 2008
Photograph taken by Joseph Herbstritt

4. Remembering April 16, 2007
Ashland to Charlottesville, Virginia

*"Do not dwell in the past, do not dream of the future, concentrate
the mind on the present moment."*
~Buddha

May 14, 2008

Dear Jeremy,

*F*or days prior to our departure I fantasized your presence in this journey. Regrettably, logic has spoken and I now both know and understand you are on a journey very much your own. You can't be here. You are dead.

Just like me, I suspect you've been searching for a solution as to how to live life again, if indeed life truly does exist after death. I beg, hope, this is the case. Otherwise, what's the point in this life?

Our journeys may be unique to our individual situations, but I hope in the end we both find our perfect reward. Peace will be mine.

Death is complicated. People don't *just* die and those who are left behind don't *just* continue on. This is a far too simplistic observation.

One of the hardest aspects of losing you is that when you left I didn't only lose you (as if your absence hasn't been horrible enough). In addition, I lost myself and everyone and everything I'd ever known. As your world crumbled, so did mine.

I hope this journey provides us both with the opportunity to learn to live again. I know life will never be the same, and I know you'll never be able to return from the dead but I hope somehow (through this journey) I am able to place the pieces of my life back together and return to my place in this world.

I wasn't expecting the mornings to be so frigid, not this time of year. We left the campsite around 5:30 A.M. dressed in typical biking apparel. For me it was padded shorts, a jersey, and clip-less bike shoes. Because it was so cold (it couldn't have been more than forty degrees in calm air, not to mention how cold it felt when I stepped into a head wind), I had to dress in multiple layers. On top of my base layer, I wore two long sleeve t-shirts, one being the red Steamtown Marathon shirt we both received after completing our first marathon together. I also chose to wear leg warmers, arm warmers and long-fingered gloves. If one didn't know any better, at first glance an observer might have thought I was in Alaska or Iowa in the middle of winter. Initially, I felt quite comfortable clothed in all this apparel but by noon I had to shed off most of these layers so as not to swelter.

We biked quite a distance from Ashland to the Charlottesville KOA, all on back country roads. The terrain was mainly flat although a small amount of climbing was required. I'm not sure if we've made it to the foothills of the Appalachians yet but something tells me we haven't. After all, it *is* only day two!

As we biked through these lovely, rustic, country roads of eastern Virginia through small towns with names like Palmyra and Mineral, my mind simply wouldn't allow me to escape the events of *that* day and the many thereafter. Often I wonder how you were able to be so strong.

Realizing the pain that death has brought to all of us, throughout this day I wanted nothing other than to wipe the smile from my face. I felt I had no right to be gleeful especially within the confines of this very state.

In the beginning (right after your murder) guests suffocated us with their company. I certainly was appreciative of good company, but we weren't permitted a second alone from the minute we heard the news until long after the funeral.

That entire weekend before our lives changed forever had been bliss. From the food to the shopping, time spent with family and friends, I couldn't have asked for anything more. The weather was terrible but it was Boston in the middle of April; nothing a rain jacket and umbrella couldn't fix. I was on top of the world and understandably so; I had qualified for the event all marathon runners (young and old) dream of participating in.

For three days I experienced the time of my life exploring Boston, touring the marathon expo and preparing to run. While I did so, a certain chapter of our lives was concluding. Little did I know that you were living out your final days.

Due to a previous shin injury, I was ecstatic when I finished (even if my time wasn't all that impressive). I was even able to walk in excess of two miles in order to meet up with Mom, Dad, Stephanie, and Brad.

One hour following that finish, the minute my eyes met with our sister's, all elation turned to sheer terror. When I saw Steph's eyes welling up with tears I knew something was incredibly wrong. Of course, at first I assumed Dad had had a heart attack (or possibly something had happened to Mom), but when she mouthed the words "shooting," "Virginia Tech," I just knew there was bad news concerning you.

They didn't yet have official confirmation that you were dead. Still, for hours on end our parents and siblings frantically searched for you, calling not just your cell phone but every hospital, police station, and news station possible; not once hearing your voice, that of a doctor stating you were in surgery, that of an officer stating you were in questioning or that of a friend stating you had walked out of that building alive. We all knew you had class in Norris Hall at that exact time. Rumor had it your classroom was the first one hit. Your phone was called at least two hundred times without a response. Everyone knew you were gone — deep in their guts, they knew. Still, our family refused to believe it. And, while all of this chaos played out, I was focused solely on myself, on the race, not having a clue anything was wrong.

You lay dead in a classroom for six hours while I ran a marathon.

While I complained about standing in that frigid Boston rain, waiting in line for a bus to transport me to the start; as my rain jacket failed me and subsequently bled red dye onto my new, white, dry-fit shirt worn beneath… While my body chilled as a result of the moisture encased in that now, ironically, red shirt (during the precise minutes in which your clothes were turning that exact wretched color I never want to see again)… While those school bus windows steamed up from all of the wet bodies present inside and I considered calling you while sitting in that slick green-colored seat reminiscent of our childhood days to tell you I was soon about to begin my race… While my teammates and I (like children) wrote both silly and encouraging phrases in permanent ink all over our bodies awaiting the start of our big race, and I somehow started to write "Running for my Brother" when indeed I'd intended to write "Running for my Grandpa"… While I rushed to the start not realizing it was nearly a half mile away from where those buses had dropped us off… And finally while I began that race… The "biggest" race of my life, or so I thought…

While all this minor drama played out, your life was coming to an end.

You were shot.

Killed.

Murdered.

And left to lie dead, helpless, and alone.

The thought still provokes nausea. *How could this be?*

You were a good man.

Upon our reunion, Mom, Dad, Steph, Brad and I continued the relentless calls. We called friends, professors, hospitals, hot-lines, morgues, funeral homes, more hospitals, police stations (and the list could go on) probably thousands of times, all without a definitive answer as to where you were.

As midnight drew near we lost almost all hope that we'd ever see you alive again. Then, I couldn't tell you who, but someone phoned Brad stating that he saw you walk out of a hospital alive. "You refused treatment…were incredibly shaken up." We got hold of the police, relayed this information, and were told they'd (immediately) check in on you at your apartment.

Holy God, you were going to be okay! I couldn't wait to hug you. Everything was going to be alright.

While Brad was obtaining this information, I was on hold with the school's emergency hot-line. I wasn't completely convinced the information he received was totally accurate and wanted confirmation.

When the woman on the other end of the line heard mention of your name, she asked me to hold…

"The proper authorities are trying to get in touch with Jeremy's next of kin."

"What does this mean? Does that mean he's dead?"

"He could be injured."

"But he could be dead?"

And then, one hour later, we got that terrible call. A little after midnight the call we'd anticipated (yet dreaded) all day long rang. The truth is Mom, Dad, Steph, and Brad knew a little after ten A.M. Joe knew just around the same time. And I knew the truth the minute my eyes laid on Steph's. I felt it in my gut. You were gone. We all felt it. The world had changed.

The words spoken were simple, frank, and to the point. Pronounced clear as day was nothing more than: "Are you Jeremy Michael Herbstritt's next of kin?" And when Dad answered yes, he was informed of the presence of your name on their list. I couldn't tell you who was on the other line. It didn't matter. They had done their job. Your fate had been told.

From that moment on, I didn't know what to do. What I did know was that I had to make a pivotal decision as to how to proceed. I called a local Catholic Church begging for the aid of a priest. What is one supposed to do after her brother is declared dead? You can't just give up searching, for it cannot be true. But when you have nowhere left to search because the fate of the person whom you've been searching for hours for has already been pronounced, sometimes actions occur in spite of good judgment. All I wanted was to get to you and bring you back to life. Surely, there was something I could do. You hadn't been gone long. I was convinced they didn't provide you with the best possible medical care. How could they have, with all of the other victims whom they needed to tend to? If only I could get to you, I'd fix you, and you would be alright. I'd insert a chest tube, shock you twice, and do something, anything, whatever it took to bring you back.

I frantically told our family to breathe calmly, everything would be alright. I tried to reassure everyone present, but my attempts were nothing more than a disappointment. I couldn't get to you for hours, and it was the middle of the night. I wasn't thinking logically and was about to vomit. So, I proceeded to the hotel desk and informed the female receptionist that my brother had been killed, at that horrible place, and inquired if she could please direct me to the nearest Catholic Church for my family needed the comfort and solace of a priest.

I called the church's "emergency hotline." This was how it was written in the phone book. Possibly this is when I lost my religion, possibly not. The priest had just returned from overseas and "needed his rest." I told him my brother had been murdered, and this was the response I was given! This would only be the beginning of my experience with learning what it is like to be the family member of someone who has fallen victim to murder.

The priest did eventually show up at our hotel room door, but only for a few minutes and his words were a far stretch from comforting. He told us that things like this "just happen" and that "this is life." I wanted to hit him. His words were nothing more than a joke. I wanted to strip him of his title and throw him out for the dogs (no, the wolves), but this wasn't an option.

So, I knocked on Kim's door (our good friend who ran Boston for Centre Volunteers in Medicine alongside me) and informed her of your death. From that minute on (and, in fact, to this day) she has stuck by our side. A true friend, a true Christian; the woman should be named a saint.

Then, long after midnight, I called Grandma Meier and belted out those dreaded words: "Jeremy is dead." I will never forget her response: "No, not our Jeremy!' I wanted to die, right then and right there. I wanted the world to come to an end. But this wasn't an option, so I attempted to draw to my bed, in a hotel room, alone, filled with a void, helpless, in terror, in shock, and full of fear. My life had changed drastically for the worse in the blink of an eye. I wanted to awake from the nightmare but it wasn't a dream; this was reality and there would be no awakening, not then and not now, not until the day of my death.

Prior to bed, I called Joe at home. He was comforted by his friends, but alone and away from his family. His brother was dead and we, what was left of his family, weren't even able to be there by his side, tell him we loved him, were sorry, sad, devastated, and in shock, just as he was.

I listened to his voice. I am unsure what words were exchanged, but my heart fell to the ground just listening to him: a young man, just starting off his life on his own, in a college dorm at Penn State, now without a brother, left alone to face death straight on, eye-to-eye.

Mom was in shock, "not her Jeremy" — he "could be fixed." And Dad was devastated, throwing objects at the wall, fisting his pillow and screaming out loud with tears flooding his eyes.

What a nightmare it all was, but I can't say it was worse than yours. For while all of this drama played out, you lay dead on a floor, a cold floor, on a campus, at a university that had failed you, drenched in the blood of you and many more — soiled and rigid, shattered, with tears, I am certain, in the corners of your eyes. My heart broke and still does for you.

The following morning I found myself in the corner of the bathroom, barely dressed, hysterical, phoning my boss to inform him of my absence. It was then breakfast, where I didn't ingest a thing and then home, back to Bellefonte, a place now far different than when I had left it just a few short days prior. It was Kim, her mom, or a dear friend who drove Mom and Dad's car home. Brad drove mine. We were chauffeured home like celebrities, members of a new club no one in their right mind would ever want to be a part of.

Mom and Dad caught a flight out of Scranton to Roanoke on our way home from Boston. It was one of Mom's brothers who purchased the tickets for them. Neither had flown on a plane in years; for Mom it had been decades. She had refused to fly anywhere but didn't think twice about jumping on a plane that day.

Brad drove me and Stephanie home to Bellefonte where Joe was waiting impatiently for our arrival. I honestly don't remember much of that ride home as my mind focused mainly on your death and the birth of my new life now without you in it. Whereas initially I was in shock and emotions were hard to find, during that ride I couldn't stop my tears from falling. I sobbed uncontrollably for hours on end.

When we arrived in Bellefonte it had been over twenty-four hours since I last consumed anything, including water, and I had just finished a marathon. I was clearly dehydrated, although at the time I didn't realize it. I was consumed by your murder. My world was frozen in the moment I learned of your death.

I was taken to my office and given IV fluids, antiemetics, and quick-acting anti-anxiety medications. Throughout all of this, Joe and Stephanie sat at our house, surrounded by friends, our family and neighbors.

I hated that I couldn't fix the situation. It was the second time in my life where I felt totally helpless, completely out of control. The first time was when I was hospitalized for anorexia following the sixth grade. At that time, I simply succumbed to the doctors. When they asked me to eat, I simply did what they asked. I knew that if I listened to their commands, I'd be discharged far sooner than expected.

This was similar in that I had no control left, but this time there was absolutely nothing I could do to fix the problem. I couldn't take the pain away from Joe, Stephanie, you, Mom, or Dad. I couldn't take the pain away from myself. I couldn't make you breathe life again.

When I finally arrived home to Bellefonte, people were everywhere. There were those who tried to tell me that you were in heaven, a believer, your day in paradise finally had come. There were those who told me that no matter what I did, there was nothing I could do to change the situation. If you were in heaven, then great; if not, what did it matter? For the situation was out of my hands. But of course, you were in heaven! And if there is nothing after this world, none of us knows, not even you, and my worries could change nothing. I would have to accept what had happened, maybe not then, but soon.

My favorites were the people who tried to explain the grieving process to me: I would feel angry, sad, and depressed. I would face denial, try to bargain with my god, and then finally accept your fate. It would take time, but it would get "easier."

There was not one person who didn't mean well. They simply wanted to help. But there were times I became incredibly frustrated. They were alive and their loved ones were as well. They could not possibly understand my pain as they'd never been in my shoes on that day before. I hated the priests and the clergy as their theories were nothing more than a mound of empty promises to make me feel better about both life and your death. And even more so, I hated my god.

The company of people was wonderful. The last thing I wanted to do during those awful first few days was be alone. I hated being alone. Worse yet, I hated being alone with the remaining members of our immediate family. I feared for what would be the topic of our conversation. I didn't want to talk about your death, not with them. The subject was too painful. I didn't want to face the truth. Around others I could put on a front but around our family, initially, I could not.

The house felt haunted. I thought that maybe you were visiting us. Possibly this is why I refused to leave Mom and Dad's house for nearly six months following your death. My apartment simply sat vacant. In all actuality, I believe I didn't return for a multitude of reasons but this certainly was one of them. This sounds nuts, but I thought you'd be more likely to haunt Mom and Dad's house than my apartment so I remained there. Although I was scared to see you as a ghost, I wanted to. Death creates all sorts of bizarre, often unlikely, scenarios within the mind.

I thought you might be confused as to what had happened to you. You would check your email and wonder why your account had been closed. You would panic when you saw all of us in your apartment. How did we get in? Where did your keys go to? Where were your clothes? How would you dress? The list of ridiculous questions that fluttered my mind could go on for pages.

I prayed for you to appear to me as a ghost, yet I was scared of this possibility. I was scared of every little thing, and I really can't explain why. Possibly, it is because your murder was a violation of my security, my assumption that my world was safe and secure. Regardless, I was plainly petrified.

I didn't want to do anything alone: not eat, sleep, shower, talk, walk, or even cry. Because of this and a multitude of other reasons, I didn't shower for ten days after that marathon. It wasn't until the date of your viewing that I actually showered and I only did so then because I didn't want to see you for the very last time, or have you see me for the very last time, as such a mess. That day I showered while Aunt Mary and Nancy took turns holding my hand firmly through the curtain. Like I've said before, unfortunately, showers don't cleanse people of the ramifications of death.

I didn't want to sleep upstairs alone, nor did I want to sleep in any bed alone, so we all slept on the same pull-out sofa, together, a whole bundle of us. It was the most bizarre of situations. We appeared like the children in many a Christmas movie or story book sleeping side by side in a line all together on Christmas Eve. The only contrast was our demeanor. We were anxious for a very different reason than the appearance of Santa and gifts, and our souls were overwhelmed with melancholy, not thrill. Joe had no part in our bed sharing and I don't blame him one bit!

People were constantly gifting us with sufficient food to cover all meals for our day. We certainly shouldn't have gone hungry as we had pastries in the morning, sandwiches for lunch, barbeque, baked beans, casseroles of an endless variety, pizza, and desserts for dinner and the list could go on for days. Our best friends even brought alcohol, I kid you not.

Our house looked like a continual party. Guests were never absent and food was abundant. Our two refrigerators were packed to the brim. But during those first ten days, I dropped at least a solid ten pounds. The thought, and to be honest even the sight, of food was nauseating. I didn't crave food. No, rather, I craved your return.

Mom and Dad remained in Blacksburg fighting for your body for over a week, and then finally you were brought back to your home to be placed to rest in the soil of our town.

What a disaster your funeral turned out to be and your viewing as well was no different. The sight of your corpse was absolutely atrocious. Your clubbed fingernails were the only definitive evidence available to confirm the body as yours. As kids we always used to measure hands: "No, my hand is bigger." Sadly, those hands undeniably were yours because of those nails. I'll never forget them. If I hadn't seen them, I wouldn't have been sure.

Now I understand why so many who grieve pass on seeing a loved one's body; for the sight was not closure for me; it was sheer horror.

Joe and I stood by your side for more than eight hours. Mom, Dad, and Stephanie were not there the entire time, and I didn't blame them. It didn't seem right that you were enclosed in a casket. Though made of oak, it was truly revolting. No casket is beautiful, for it signifies death. My stomach gnawed in agony the entire time and that sensation, even now, returns immediately when I take myself back to that time.

We stood there because someone had to. I listened kindly to guests' condolences, shaking each person's hand, and forcing a smile. But no words could ease my pain in even the slightest fashion. My brother was dead.

No more than twelve hours later your funeral followed and amidst rain and dark skies, your body was carried by the hands of your very best friends and brother to the altar where the priest spoke an assortment of words regarding your death, the senselessness of it all, and how you were now happy because finally you had arrived in your heaven. Your day in paradise had come. I wanted to scream out, *"How do you know?"*

Mom was tired, angry, and broken. She simply wanted to scream but instead made an attempt to escape. She tried to avoid detection as she walked out the back of the church, but as the sanctuary overflowed with guests, and as voices started to whisper, a friend gently escorted her back to her seat.

We followed your body to the cemetery, but we couldn't watch you be dropped into the ground. It simply wasn't right. That day had come far too early for all. I will never forget the words of your brother when our cars took on separate paths, yours to the grave and ours to the church hall for a feast that none of us could taste. His words were: "This is the saddest day of my life. He must be so lonely."

I'm sorry we didn't go. I'm sorry we left you. I'm sorry you're dead. It all isn't fair.

The media wanted to be at your viewing, and — I'm not sure what's worse — at your funeral as well. I wanted to kill them. For the first time in my life, I was beginning to understand how people are drawn to the point of murder. Not a murder like yours, but murder out of revenge. I also wanted to kill your murderer. And, if he were alive, I am sure I would not have been alone in seeking out his blank stare. And on the day of your funeral, did I ever want to kill the ruthless media! What nerve they had! Not only were you given no choice other than to die without dignity, but now they wanted to take away your right to have a dignified funeral and viewing. Where were their hearts, their souls?

Throughout all of this, I learned a lot about death, life, and people. Death is not decorous. No matter how you look at it, death is despicable. When one dies, all bodily functions are lost. Feces are released. Blood is excreted. Urine is leaked. It is a disgusting ordeal.

Brought into this world not by our own choice, we are also forced to face death, straight-faced eye-to-eye. Some of us are allowed to die in a more dignified fashion than others, possibly in old age, after a long battle with cancer, surrounded by loved ones holding our hands until the very last breath, controlled with medicinal substances so that our pain is minimal, diapered, with soft music playing and a pleasant aroma filtered from the most perfect candle. But, it's still death, the end of life, the end of the body that houses the essence of who we are. And for those who love us, it's never pleasant or easy.

I resent the priests and religious elite who assert that they can't wait to die. They must be nuts, because the experience doesn't sound pleasurable to me whatsoever. And the pain death leaves behind for our loved ones is something that I would never, ever wish upon anyone.

I hate death, and worse, I hate that you are dead. But I did appreciate greatly our friends and loved ones who hovered by our sides from the day of your death until more than one year later. These people deserve more than a medal. They are good people, and proof to me that amidst everything that happened there is still good remaining in this world.

There are those whom I haven't heard from since the day of your funeral. There are those who still hover, perhaps needlessly, but I appreciate their persistence. There are those who continue to send cards just to check in on us, simple reminders of the good remaining in a world full of iniquity. Some of these people I never knew existed, but I am glad that I now know of their worth. Nevertheless, I'd rather have met them for a reason other than for your death.

There are those who sent cards and a few who chose not to. I'm embarrassed to admit that I remember those who didn't, but cannot name all who did. If I could weigh the good and evil deeds of this world on a scale, the good certainly would outweigh the evil in quantity of deeds done, but the evil that took you on April 16, 2007 surpasses, in my mind, all of the good when analyzed by its eminence. And for that and so much more, I hate that evil. I would give anything to make it all go away.

When my mind takes me to this place of anger and hatred, I try to focus on the good that remains here with me on earth. Though sometimes good seems almost impossible to find.

The trees here sway softly as the wind blows ever so gently. The birds chirp a heavenly tune, and I wonder if each knows what the other is saying. The streams flow swiftly and the squirrels are plump.

The beauty here is surreal, yet I am surrounded by poverty, unemployment and despair. I am less than two hundred miles from your apartment, and you are nowhere to be found. I hope to get out of Virginia soon.

All my love,
Jennifer

P.S. It is at night when I miss you most. When there is nothing around me but darkness and the faint sounds of nature present in the distance, distraction is quite hard to come by.

Tonight, I'm having one those nights.

During the day, thoughts of you never leave my mind. In fact, I expend a great deal of energy actively trying to focus on happy memories of our family, goofy things you used to do, and silly phrases only you could have come up with. I spend a tremendous amount of time hosting make-believe conversations with you. While listening to a ridiculous song on the radio, often I swear I can hear you rolling in laughter right next to me just like you used to. I try my best to focus on these pleasant memories but often I get consumed by the circumstances surrounding your death. Continuously, I'm trying to create a scenario in which you are able to come out of this nightmare alive. I can't help but be consumed by what I believe might have gone through your mind when that monster entered your classroom and opened fire. I can't help but dwell on how scared you must have been, whether or not you had time to register your thoughts and whether or not you physically suffered. During the day, these thoughts never leave me, but it is at night, when I just cannot sleep. Dark thoughts overtake me. I place myself in your shoes, not at the exact minute of your death but in the minutes prior and following, and as your body must be now, in the grave.

Your body has decomposed, your skin decayed. Bone shows through the surface, though you are dressed in a suit that fits you perfectly — tie and all, shoes polished, with a beard cleanly shaven and hair recently cut.

By now your fingernails have probably lengthened for I know they continue to grow after death. Your face, however, would be unrecognizable.

For the moment your grave is without a headstone. For some in our family, we simply aren't ready to fare you well.

In my head, I know you are gone. My heart is taking longer to catch up.

I walk through the motions of grief day after day. I face death head-on every morning I awake, but it is at night when I am hit hardest by your absence.

Uncontrollably, images of you dead, buried, and decomposing, screaming with fury in your eyes, trying to escape from the horror of your own death are flashing in front of me.

I'm trying to imagine you alive: running ahead of me, me chasing after, you laughing and that smile, your hand shake, the way you used to talk with your hands when out grabbing a drink with friends.

In this moment, you're ending a ridiculous sentence with your thumbs and index fingers positioned just like a pistol. You're flashing your hands in the air, elbows are bent, and ever so quickly you're demonstrating that, your trademark gesture.

I just want the pain to go away.

Please help me sleep.

Joe and Jeremy, Grange Fair, Centre Hall, Pennsylvania, August 2004

Location of Jeremy's annual garden, Bellefonte Farm, spring 2008

Cousins posing at the Herbstritt Farm atop Dad's truck cab
Back row from left to right: Katie Meier, Jen, Jeremy, Jason and Brandon Meier
Front row from left to right: Steph, Joe and Nathan (Meier)

Jeremy and Brad, Grange Fair tent, August 2004

Jen, Joe, and Brad at Charlottesville, KOA campsite, May 2008

Odd-shaped tree hovering over green valley, Virginia, May 2008
Photograph taken by Joseph Herbstritt

5. Gertie and Lexington
Charlottesville, Virginia, to Lexington, Virginia

"Unbeing dead isn't being alive."
~e.e. cummings

May 15, 2008

Jeremy,

*A*fter *awakening around five o'clock to the sound of birds chirping, the smell of fresh air and the sight of frost blanketing our tent, our journey toward Lexington began.* Just as I'd noticed yesterday, I was shocked to have awoken shortly before sunrise without any help from an alarm clock. Perhaps this occurs as a result of my enthusiasm to experience the unknown. It's funny how we as humans enjoy experiencing certain aspects of the unknown such as visiting new places and meeting new faces. Nevertheless, death is an off-limits aspect of the unknown, which most of us would like to keep just as that.

I brushed my teeth in a lovely bathroom situated a quarter mile away from our tent-site, dressed in layers, packed my belongings back into the car, and carefully pedaled along the KOA's gravel driveway up to the main road. Here, I looked at our map, confirmed a right turn and directed Brad farther west.

Before I continue on, I feel it's appropriate to mention to you that Brad has (possibly foolishly) decided to leave me in charge of the directions for the course of this trip. As well, he always bikes behind me. Although, I give him a hard time for both his rigidity and practicality (and the fact that I'm always breaking the wind for him), the truth is I am beyond fortunate to have him in my life. He's given me probably the best gifts anyone could have given to me since your death: an open road ahead of me, the opportunity to feel as if I still have some control left in my life, and arms that will always be open.

Seven and a half miles after that right turn I realized it should have been a left. Thanks to my inherent inability to read maps, today's ride quickly gained fifteen additional miles. This seems to be a trend.

Take two.

As I biked those extra miles downhill in the wrong direction, my GPS (a.k.a. "Jill") repetitively indicated to make a U-turn. While the wind blocked out all other sounds, I kept Jill's obnoxious beeping to myself. Being as stubborn as I often am, I plainly refused to listen to this intelligent device (nor did I pass on Jill's advice to Brad). Unfortunately, by the time I was willing to admit my mistake (and verbalize it to Brad) I had already landed us into a terribly deep ravine. We had no other choice but to climb out of it if we were ever going to get back on track. Possibly there was another route, but at this time neither Brad nor I was interested in searching for any further misadventures for the day. He was irate. You should have seen his nostrils flaring! As you might remember, he's not one who enjoys taking the scenic route.

The air blowing in my face as I made that mistaken descent was incredibly frigid on my skin. As we stopped at the bottom to analyze our location on the map, my hands proved to be numb. I noticed my teeth were chattering as well. Fortunately, none of this lasted very long as once we started to climb the effort required of my body was sufficient enough to warm me up to the point of near perspiration. I guess I'll end my complaining tangent here. It was my mistake; Brad would be sure to tell you that. All I can say is, after all, all exercise regimes are supposed to start with a warm-up, aren't they? Brad didn't find that comment all so amusing.

After this unexpected yet congenial climb, I was mistakenly convinced we had hit the foothills of the Appalachians. Wow, was I ever off to a bad start!

The grades at this point were simply far more intense than I had ever imagined they'd be. It seems I'll be in for a big surprise over the course of the next few days, as it wasn't until the end of the day that I realized what we experienced today was only a snapshot of what the Appalachians will soon have to offer our already fatigued quadriceps.

After this mishap, the ride finally "began" (as it was intended to) with an enduring three-mile climb on grades exceeding eight to ten percent. Possibly by the time I reach San Francisco, grades like this, covering this distance, will seem trifling. For today this climb was a challenge, to say the least.

For three continuous miles there were absolutely no sections of flat terrain, and, of course, there wasn't an ounce of downhill present. The climb seemed incredibly steep both for me and motorized vehicles passing by. As I passed by a couple each carrying both panniers and a trailer, I pitied their legs. I could hear trucks downshifting rapidly, both as they were ascending and making the descent. I'm almost certain I didn't travel more than three miles per hour up that mountain. I could have walked quicker. But, truth be told, I made it to the top without a break (I wasn't sure I'd be able to start all over again if I stopped). There's something to be said about the strength of one's mind.

Once we reached the summit, I stepped as far away from my bike as I could, prayed someone would steal it and took a long, well deserved break while getting lost in the view that surrounded me. The valley beneath me was wide and deep, full of trees of green; the scene truly was exhilarating.

As my brain re-oxygenated and I returned to my bike while continuing to watch eighteen-wheelers make the ascent to the summit in their lowest gears, I smiled at my accomplishment. I was proud to have conquered such a great climb, but couldn't deny that I was glad it was over. My legs were becoming increasingly fatigued even as I walked. Still, I decided to keep my bike. The journey was mine to continue.

As I clipped my feet back into my pedals, I realized it had taken me a good fifteen minutes to catch my breath. At the same time Brad was running all around the summit gaining insight on how horrible the remainder of the ride would be. I thought I was in fairly decent cardiovascular shape prior to my departure on this trip; however, this ascent proved me wrong. I worried once again for my stamina.

The ride today was lengthy and after this climb the majority of the remaining miles were ridden along the Blue Ridge Parkway. For seventy-five miles it seemed we were traveling primarily uphill. In all actuality, we were biking along what was supposed to be the ridge of the mountain. I knew we were on the ridge because the view was brilliant, but the grades didn't seem to agree. Although it felt as if we were climbing for the majority of the ride, this actually wasn't the case. The descents most likely made up an equivalent distance.

There were absolutely no cars along the Parkway so I found myself hugging the central yellow line. The shoulders of the road were abrupt, and I worried I might fall off the edge while gazing into the distance (go ahead now and laugh at my silliness). There was absolutely no litter or debris on the sides of the road. The only noises I heard were those of the sounds of nature, my heavy breathing, and the shifting of my gears. Although civilization wasn't far away, I felt totally isolated. This ride was one of my favorites of the trip thus far.

Brad became a little lightheaded and queasy during this section. It seems neither of us is in as good of shape as previously thought. I had an energy "gel" pack in my saddlebag that I'd been hoping to discard since long before the trip began. I think I got it as a free sample at a marathon some time ago. I absolutely hate the consistency of this type of energy snack but I knew Brad was totally naïve to it. Therefore, I figured having him consume it in his current state of suspected hypoglycemia might be an easy means for me to get rid of it. Unfortunately, for both him and me, he almost vomited upon the taste. In the moment his lips met that frosting like slime, I felt terribly guilty for my behavior. I'm not sure if it was Brad's anger or the "gel" that made him start pedaling, but boy did I have to work to keep up with him after that snack! "I thought you said these were good!?"

After we exited the Blue Ridge Parkway we approached a three-mile steep decline into a small, cozy, little town called Vesuvius, home to a charming little sandwich shop called Gertie's, where we ate lunch.

Initially, I was grateful for the decline into Vesuvius, a well deserved treat after a long day of climbing, but the downward grade was so intense that I believe going uphill might have been less of a physical challenge. The grade had to have been twenty-five percent. No joke. By the time I reached Gertie's, my triceps were on fire and quivering with exhaustion from clenching onto my brake handles.

My mind couldn't have been more relieved to have made it down that mountain. All the way down, all I could think about was how I was going to stop if I lost grip of my brakes or if my triceps gave out. I'd ride straight into a tree and hope for the best: that was my finest and *only* solution. Luckily, I never found out.

Engulfed with fatigue, I placed my lunch order with Gertie, a petite, gray-haired woman a few years younger than our grandparents. As she fried onions atop a large metal grill, I stood in silence at the bar subconsciously reflecting on my current whereabouts.

I was enchanted by the fact that there appeared to be absolutely no businesses in this town except for a small post office and Gertie's. I wondered what kept the owners from leaving town. I'm sure, if desired, they could leave and set up shop in a far more developed section of the state. These were people with flavor — intelligent and witty. Their conversations were fun to listen to, their clothes spelled out a style of their own, and the stories of their lives compelled me.

I am now in a section of our country completely unfamiliar to me. There are no shopping malls, movie theaters, or chain restaurants; at least not in my field of view. The residents of Vesuvius appear on the surface to have nothing other than their families and friends. Many work in coal mines.

I listened as a local woman spoke with Gertie about child care. She questioned why certain women choose to work outside of the home rather than care for their children full-time. Just the same, she spoke of how long she pictured her days would become once her own children were enrolled in all-day kindergarten. She wondered if she should consider working part-time outside of the home. I wondered where.

I listened to the radio and learned of a conflict between the mayor and police chief of a small nearby town where a few seventeen-year-old boys were recently arrested for underage drinking. The mayor felt that punishment should be the responsibility of the boy's parents; the police chief disputed. There was debate over whether or not the chief of police should be fired for arresting these boys. In my family, this question never would have been raised. Breaking the law is just that.

Lunch was ready. I paid my bill and walked outside to an area in back of the store where some old patio furniture was awkwardly placed in an open field of green grass. I thought of the people of Vesuvius and other small towns in America. From a financial standpoint, many of these folks may not be considered by most to be rich but to me they are, primarily because I can see such happiness when I look into their faces. It is present in the twinkle of their eyes, and in the tone of their voices. You can see it in their smiles. These people have so much to teach me.

I tried my best to obtain as much knowledge from the locals at Gertie's as I could, but I simply am not as good at small talk as you, Jeremy.

There was a group of motorcyclists eating lunch, too. They were from Canada and biking south. They were full of life and happiness, continuously laughing and joking throughout their conversation, and, as much as I wanted to converse with them, for some reason I was unable. I became shy and timid, embarrassed of my past, and not looking to disclose any information. I thought about what type of conversation you would have enjoyed with these men.

I thought about the conversation you would have evoked with Gertie while she stood behind the bar making your sandwich. You would have told her your entire life story. She would have listened intently, laughing along the way. You made people happy. That was just you. Then, you would have talked about her life. You would have spent an hour or more, not just making small talk, but really getting to know her and the other people present. You would have eaten inside at the bar, right next to Gertie and the motorcyclists. You probably would have even exchanged emails or, if email was not an option, then a plain old address. You would have promised Gertie a postcard from California. I wish I'd done just that.

But I, on the other hand, introduced myself only briefly and ate outside with Brad, Joe, and Dad. I doubt I even made mention of the fact that we are biking across America to these friendly people. I didn't want to make a big fuss about our trip. The truth is I didn't want anyone to ask me why I had decided to engage on such an adventure. This question is typically the first question asked when I meet a new face. I didn't want to have to experience the pain of telling yet another person that my brother was so brutally murdered in such a public fashion. I didn't want their sympathy. I just wanted to be that girl who passed through a cozy little town, nestled in the heart of Appalachia, and so I was. I hope you'll forgive me for this.

On April 16, 2007 I wanted nothing other than to return to April 15, 2007. I would have given anything to simply hear someone say the events of that day were all a prank, a false alarm, an overreaction, anything — that you were okay.

It had happened once before, about a year earlier in 2006.

I was still living at Mom and Dad's house in Bellefonte, as were you. It wouldn't be another few months until I'd move out into my own apartment with Brad as I was trying to save some money. From my full-time job I earned a fair wage; still, I was taking advantage of the perks of having two incredibly wonderful parents who weren't ready to experience the pain of an empty nest. You were finishing up that second bachelor's degree from Penn State and in no more than a few months would be endeavoring on your own journey through graduate school (the third time around...that thought itself still makes me smile).

I went to work that day as usual but, before I left, we made plans to meet at my office after hours. You were half asleep when this arrangement was made, but I thought you'd remember — you always did. We'd run the "Triangle of Death" that evening in State College. You always hated that run, hence the name that you created.

As my day drew to a close, I phoned to see where you were at and when you'd arrive, but you failed to answer. I left a message and proceeded to finish up whatever it was I was doing, possibly dictating charts or returning patients' calls.

No more than a half hour later I exited the building expecting to see your smiling face. I figured you'd simply forgotten your phone. Unfortunately, you were nowhere in sight.

By this point in time I had probably called you at least a dozen times, each time not receiving an answer. We had made plans and it was unlike you not to follow through when an agenda was set.

I started to worry as I knew you had plans that morning to kayak with a friend down the Juniata River. You had never before kayaked this particular section of the river, and I worried for your safety. Possibly you weren't thinking and attempted to kayak over a waterfall or something dangerous like that. Maybe you'd drowned.

Fortunately, I was far more logical (and untouched by violence) then than I am now, so I disregarded these irrational thoughts and drew to the more likely conclusion that you got caught up in whatever it was you were doing, left your phone in your car, and unintentionally disregarded our plans.

I went about my business completing that run on my own. As soon as I finished, I made what seemed like (and probably was) my twentieth attempt at getting in touch with you, but once again, to my dismay, you did not answer.

I drove my car home to Mom and Dad's house, yet you were still nowhere in sight. There was no indication that you had been in the house since you left that morning. The dishes were done and all food was put away. If you had returned to the house certainly you would have cooked yourself some dinner. The kitchen would have been a mess. The television was off and Lizzy, our dog, was resting comfortably in the basement. You definitely hadn't returned since you left that morning.

At this point in time, I was beginning to get a bit nervous as I knew your kayak adventure had been scheduled to begin around eight o'clock in the morning.

Mom and Dad were away with Joe and Stephanie at 4-H camp. Mom was the nurse and Dad, adult staff. Joe and Steph were both counselors. I gave them a call, and they told me not to worry. But when they called back nearly an hour later and you still were not home, I became frantic.

I drove over to our neighbor's house and explained the situation to her, seeking out her advice. We drove together into Bellefonte in search of your car. At the time you were driving the red Jeep (as you had just settled a deal to sell that beloved, white Chevy Blazer). We went to the local kayak shop thinking maybe you were wading in the water behind the shop playing around with friends in the slalom course set up there. Still, you were nowhere to be found and the sky was now a very ominous shade of black. Night had set in.

We decided it was best to stop over at the police station and obtain an officer's recommendation as to what to do at this point in time. No one was at the station but a number was posted to call "in case of emergency." Logic told me your twelve-hour absence was not an emergency but I needed some practical and professional advice. I called the number provided and my concerns certainly were not taken lightly. The officer immediately started a search party for you in five separate counties. Announcements were made on the radio, filled with descriptions of you, your car, its make, model, and license plate number.

By ten P.M. I was growing hysterical. I came to the premature conclusion that you had drowned in the Juniata River while attempting to kayak over some sort of class five rapid even though I don't believe the Juniata has rapids in any section considered this treacherous. I became so emotional that I made Mom and Dad upset. Our neighbor was crying and so was one of our aunts whom I informed of your absence. What a disaster I created!

When the officer called me stating he had come across some information he didn't want to explain to me over the phone, I was certain my assumption was true. I prepared myself for the worst.

And then, as the officer drove up Mom and Dad's driveway, to everyone's surprise, you led the way. I never did find out what the officer had to tell me for it no longer was of importance. You were fine. You had just gotten caught up in kayaking, hanging out with your friends, and having a good time. You had forgotten our plans, just as I initially had expected. You were embarrassed and couldn't believe I had become so upset over something so "trivial." I gave you a hug, but not before throwing a few girlish punches your way.

I explained to the officer that "this" (as I pointed toward your thick brown hair) was you, and thanked him for his kind help. He rolled his eyes and left, no further words were required.

Now, how I wish we could go back. I wish this was all a misunderstanding, a mistake, a cruel miscommunication.

Lexington is lovely. You would have loved it here.

Love always,

Jennifer

Joe, Appalachia, May 2008

6. The Home Place
Lexington to Catawba, Virginia

"Call it a clan, call it a network, call it a tribe, call it a family.
Whatever you call it, whoever you are, you need one."
~Jane Howard

May 16, 2008

Jeremy,

*T*hese past few days of biking have provided me with ample time to spend simply thinking. Prior to your death, if I wasn't running with you or somebody else I would combine running with my time to think. It was almost like therapy, only I was the one conducting the session (go ahead and laugh!). A troubled patient running her own clinic; sounds disastrous if you ask me. I'd think about the events of my day, relive arguments and conversations, make decisions, and even pray. I did the same while I swam. And now, I do the same while I bike.

In all seriousness, when upset about something if instead of spontaneously addressing the issue I went for a run, once I was finished with my workout the problem almost always seemed trivial in retrospect. Individual sports have always been my thing. They keep me sane.

I never was one to really enjoy group sports when I was growing up. Perhaps, because I wasn't all too coordinated. Combine clumsiness with an introverted personality and you get a recipe not exactly conducive for group activities.

In reflecting on these thoughts, I've recognized that life during those days, when I could just get up and run and think my biggest worries were that of whether or not I'd have to work New Year's Eve, really were quite simple.

Jeremy, about 6 years old

I miss hearing you say things such as: "Jen, it's not all about you!" "Get down and do a few push-ups; you'll warm up real quick!" I'm fairly certain I heard both of those phrases at least a thousand times in my life when I'd complain about something or another, going somewhere, doing some sort of chore in the barn, or how cold the house was.

Life back then really was perfect. I can't think of a thing I would have changed.

Now, it's hard to spend time alone as my thoughts always return to your absence.

When you died, initially I stopped running. I just didn't have the energy. Then, I didn't want to run without you by my side. In September of 2007, I decided it was time for me to learn to run without you present in the physical sense. I registered for a marathon (with minimal training) one week prior to the race date and ran that race in one of my very best times. I couldn't stop sobbing during the last five kilometers. All I wanted was for you to be there. Since then, I've been running in an effort to sense your presence.

What has been different about running following your death when compared with running while you were alive is that now I don't allow myself time to think about anything deep. This may sound pathetic but thinking is sometimes simply too difficult. Possibly this is why now it is a challenge for me to complete long runs. I can't run more than twelve consecutive miles anymore without feeling completely drained. My constant need to count the mileage (one quarter mile, one half mile, one mile, etc.) from the beginning of a run straight through to the end is probably why. There is absolutely no distraction from the physical stress of running itself.

So it seems when I began biking in Yorktown, I finally started to think. I must have subconsciously decided it was time to focus on myself. I deserved the right to grieve your death. And the right to remember.

I love replaying memories, surfacing memories buried deep within the cobwebs of my brain. If only I could return to that first kayak trip you took me on! I'd relive that scare all over again if only I'd be guaranteed one final glimpse of you.

Or how about the time Mom forgot to put the car into park at the bottom of our steep lane, obliviously proceeding to get out and collect the mail? In the moment they occurred, these events seemed to be so trivial. But these are the things we will never forget.

Jeremy driving away from our Uncle Chuck's house following a day of construction, spring 2006

Lately, I've been thinking a lot about your murder and why it resulted in a loss of my religion as well as my sense of security. Previously my world felt safe. Of course it wasn't. Our country had been invaded by terrorists back in September of 2001. Then, we were engaged in a war in Iraq. Murders, robberies and rapes were occurring in many communities in our nation, sometimes on a daily basis. Children were starving within the borders of our country. The U.S. wasn't, and still isn't, safe. But I thought my world was.

Early on in our lives Mom and Dad rightfully sheltered us from the truths this world held secret. They wanted our childhoods to be precious, filled with fond memories and void of chaos and havoc. They loved us dearly and wanted only the best for us.

In my childhood misconception, America was protected solely by the president, and our house, toys, and siblings were protected by our parents. Although bad people were in existence in the world, I was fortunate enough to grow up in a place where they didn't harm me, you, Mom, Dad, or anyone else I loved.

Our parents' teachings on religion were certainly no different than this distortion of security.

When we grew old enough to talk, brush our teeth, and comb our hair, Mom and Dad also started to instill in us the values of our Catholic faith. Prior to meals, we said grace. Before bed, we knelt alongside our beds and recited our prayers. At the culmination of these memorized prayers, we'd then express our own concerns, worries and hopes which developed throughout the day.

We'd follow the same routine each morning when we awoke, and when I was old enough to attend grade school I'd periodically glance up at the cross placed on the wall in the front of the classroom and thank God for His greatness, for suffering for my salvation, and for each of the gifts He had given to me, including our family.

Fortunately, when Mom and Dad taught us about God and about prayer, they also made an educated but conscious decision to inform us that God wouldn't and couldn't answer all prayers. People around us, in our communities and on TV, were being diagnosed with cancer,

AIDS, and other life-threatening conditions. Classmates were diagnosed with leukemia and, regularly, we delivered canned goods to the food bank so those less fortunate than us wouldn't go hungry. It was evident that God wasn't answering the prayers of these people. In response, Mom and Dad told us that billions of people around the world were offering prayers to just one innate being. It was impossible for Him to answer all of our prayers. God had to be carefully selective. Because of such, I avoided being selfish with my prayers. I knew others had more important requests and, frankly, God wasn't a wishing well. I couldn't throw a penny at Him and expect a baby doll in return.

If only one good thing has come out of our parents' teachings on religion, it is that I gained empathy and compassion. For this, I am grateful.

Yet, I wish I understood more about this god I used to have total confidence in. If only as adults we could become undamaged and take that childhood innocence back.

I used to believe God had a plan for each and every single one of us. He knew the day and hour of both my birth and death. Of course, free will existed in the world He created, but He would never present me with anything I couldn't handle. Through the path of this life, we walked together.

Still, God abandoned both you and me on that horrible day. He allowed you to die. So it is that everything I was taught as a child about religion seems erroneous now. If God happens to be so powerful, I just can't figure out why he allowed that monster to commit such a heinous crime. Why didn't he answer my relentless prayers? I realize this may sound blasphemous, but I just don't want to believe in a god that kills people or at minimum just sits on the sidelines and watches the curtain close. In my opinion, God is just as responsible.

And so, my religion is lost.

Death might have been nothing to be scared of back in the days of the early Church, but today we're walking in a totally different ballpark. And, eternity is forever; a long time to not know *if* or *when* I'll ever see you again.

I've just been reminded today marks exactly thirteen months since your death. I am so terribly sorry.

Last night we stayed in a hotel outside of Lexington. So much for banning hotels! And to make matters worse, we ate at an Old Country Buffet. There were strong thunderstorms all night long. According to our maps, after today we shouldn't come within a hundred miles of a hotel for days. I didn't want to drench all of our gear, so with the projected forecast in mind, I opted (or possibly demanded) for us to stay here at the Best Western outside of Lexington.

As the others already have, please place the blame on me! I know a campsite along the side of the road would have provided more of an opportunity for misadventures (trust me, I was given this lecture more times than once), and looking back, I should have welcomed this idea, but as the saying goes, hindsight is 20/20. I thought we might melt!

At the breakfast buffet this morning, I met up with a PSU alumnus who was in Lexington for the Virginia Military Institute (VMI) spring graduation ceremonies. It turns out that we arrived in Lexington on the weekend of VMI spring graduation. This is ironic to me because you were scheduled to graduate with your master's degree in civil and environmental engineering this month. This gentleman was looking forward to watching his nephew walk across the stage to receive his undergraduate degree in engineering.

I wished that Dad and Mom would have had the opportunity to attend your graduate school graduation during your living years. Instead, a year ago almost to the date, we walked across a hollow stage to accept a posthumous degree for you in your place.

When you and I graduated from Penn State together back in 2003, Mom threw a huge party for the two of us, but we didn't even attend the ceremony for your second bachelor's degree (in civil engineering) in 2006. You were adamant that you weren't going to attend;

Lexington, Virginia, May 2008

you didn't want to make a big fuss about it as you'd already earned an undergraduate degree a few years prior. "Been there, done that." That's what you said. You told us that we could attend your graduate school ceremony in just a few years.

We should have told you we were going; *you* were going, like it or not. We should have thrown you a party. You deserved a celebration.

As I reflected on these regrets, I prayed for the students at not just VMI but all universities who are graduating this year; that they not take for granted the privilege it is to earn a college diploma and job in the United States of America, the land of the free.

Our bike ride today took us through the heart of Appalachia. If one drives the main highways and bypasses these communities he or she would think these areas are simply desolate. Nevertheless, if one takes the road less traveled, as we did today, they'll find the people of Appalachia. We biked up and down the steep, narrow, winding hollows where the people of these communities reside. These are hardworking folk who truly earn their keep. Their faces are sunken and their skin wrinkled. Most appear years older than their actual age, evidence that they do not live easy lives.

My legs are becoming stronger and my cadence is quickening. Today, I had to endure many very steep, yet quick climbs, often with a dog on my tail chasing me to the top. I'm hoping the Appalachians prepare me for the Ozarks as I hear their grades are far more intense. But before I get there I'll have to arrive at the Knobs of Kentucky. I guess I shouldn't get too far ahead of myself. Just like with grief, I have to focus on one day at a time, sometimes, one minute at a time, attacking each climb individually and not as a cluster. Otherwise, I doubt I'll ever make it across.

Not long after we left Lexington, we were surrounded by nothing but feral terrain. My definition of civilization abruptly altered as I was presented with a picture in front of me boasting nothing but the enchanting Appalachian Mountains covered in trees and filled to the brim with an array of wildlife. I can't say the view was all too hard on the eye.

Although the image was picturesque, anxiety provoked my heart to race as I contemplated the possibility of an accident: What if I fell off my bike four hours into the ride and broke my leg or my arm? What if I was hit by a hit-and-run driver? I'm not sure what Brad and I would have done as I couldn't have told you where the nearest hospital was let alone the nearest home. There was very poor cell phone reception in this area and not a pay phone in sight. Traffic was light. I guess if we ran into an emergency we would have had to hitch-hike. That, or Brad would have left me stranded as he sought help.

All I can say is: "And I thought Bellefonte was rural!"

As the day drew to a close, I thought about where our ride tomorrow intended to take us. According to our maps, tomorrow's route would traverse us through Blacksburg and Christiansburg. I knew from the start of this trip that I wasn't about to step foot in either of these communities just yet. This is not because I have anything against the people of these communities. These are generous, compassionate and empathetic people, many of whom came to our beck and call, even without us asking for their assistance, simply out of the kindness of their hearts following your death.

I loved Blacksburg. I loved Christiansburg just the same. I loved running on the Huckleberry Trail, connecting the two, with you by my side. Though it's hard to admit, I even loved Virginia Tech. Heck, I once went to a football game there and enjoyed every minute of it. The tailgating prior didn't compare to Penn State's, but it was fun in its own right. I even once thought of moving to the area myself. I loved the scenery. And, after all, you were there.

A town nestled in the heart of the Appalachian Mountains provides an atmosphere that is simply serene. Still, I never understood why and how you came to leave Pennsylvania for such a prolonged period of time. Only now am I beginning to appreciate your decision.

As much as I now loathe the administration of *that* university and the name "Blacksburg" still leaves a sour taste in my mouth, that area had you written all over it. The accessibility of trails for hiking, rivers with swift rapids for kayaking and dark, moist soil for farming made that town your type of place. This, combined with a world-renowned university with ethical standards based on an honor code of conduct, situated in the heart of Appalachia and the Shenandoah Valley, both prominent with southern hospitality — this was your paradise.

Graduation day in Blacksburg was mortifying. Following our acceptance of your posthumous degree, I listened to others in your class, alive and eager to graduate, speak of their accomplishments and successes. Then, I proceeded to watch them accept their own degrees. I wasn't happy for any one of them. I was angry. In that moment I found life to be very unfair.

During that same weekend I attended an event where I listened to other students discuss the circumstances surrounding your death. These details were private; they were all I had left. They weren't up for display, or for sale, and I was frozen with horror at the sound of their words. I cried in private for hours until I had no tears left.

With all of this said, I simply cannot go back to Blacksburg again. I've done it before. Every time I go back, I think I'll find you there. I know this is silly, but it is too painful to return with hopes of finding you there, yet knowing I never will. I am not ready to return, not now, and maybe not for many years to come.

This bike trip is about taking my life back and spending time with your soul. It is not about touring a place where happiness turned to sheer terror in a split second. I do not want to return to the place where our lives changed forever in the worst possible way.

Therefore, I made a definitive decision today as we rode our bikes to Catawba to bypass this section of the trip completely, even though it is a section of the TransAmerica Trail, the trail that I had hoped to complete in all entirety.

I have too many memories of running with you, hiking the Cascades, rafting the New River, touring the campus, eating, laughing, and existing with you *there*. I want these memories to stay as such and not be destroyed by a single memory formed in that community without you in it.

We arrived in Catawba around lunch time expecting to see a typical small town. You know, the typical All-American town made up of a few blocks of houses all with perfect fences, kids playing hop-scotch or four-square at the end of a cul-de-sac, a few churches, a local diner, post office, bakery, and grocery store all situated surrounding the town square, where everyone knows your name? Okay, so possibly I'm the only one who's ever dreamt of the "All-American" town appearing just like this! In any case, what we found was a post office and a solitary, painted white brick building large enough to house a gas station, convenience store and take-out restaurant. At first glance I was a bit disappointed by what this town had to offer, but don't be amiss.

I soon learned Catawba is home to the infamous Home Place, situated about a half mile down the road from the town center.

Until today, I never did know where the Home Place actually was. I just knew that you loved it. You always wanted to eat there during our visits; we just never got around to it. I remember your stories of the immense portions served here following hours spent hiking the Appalachian Trail (AT) with friends.

Around mid afternoon, Brad and I met Dad and Joe at what we thought was the only restaurant in town: the take-out section of that white brick building. After ordering our lunch, we proceeded out to the back patio where we sat beneath the warmth of the sun, devouring our food directly across from a man in his late twenties attempting to open a bottle of wine without a corkscrew. He asked if we had a corkscrew for him to use and with this our conversation evoked. He was just granted his PhD in biochemistry and intended on spending a few months or more hiking the entire AT in exchange for many years of hard work and determination, hours spent at the library and behind the microscope. He desired to give his physical stamina the same challenge he offered his mind. The section of the AT he just completed was precisely the section you used to speak of hiking regularly on weekends with classmates and friends.

He was waiting for his parents, whom he was expecting any minute. They would be visiting him for a few short days while he rested his body and tended to a multitude of blisters. He pondered if we knew where the Home Place was. My heart stopped. Of all the towns we could have stopped in, we stopped in this town, home to the infamous Home Place, and ran into this man in search of one of your favorite restaurants.

It is the thirteen-month "anniversary" of your death.

I felt your presence.

I wished *we'd* gone.

From Catawba, we'll drive past Blacksburg to our starting point for tomorrow morning: Claytor Lake State Park. The name sounds charming.

Love always,
Jennifer

Jeremy (right) and Dad, skiing, circa 1999

Joe, Steph, and Jeremy hiking the Virginia Cascades, fall 2006

Natural Bridge, May 2008 ~ Photograph taken by Joseph Herbstritt

Jeremy, Joe, Jennifer, and Stephanie skiing, circa 1999, Holiday Valley Ski Resort, Ellicottville, New York

Another view of the Natural Bridge, from below, May 2008
Photograph taken by Joseph Herbstritt

7. Damascus
Catawba to Damascus, Virginia
Claytor Lake State Park

"Life isn't fair. It's just fairer than death, that's all."
~William Goldman

May 17, 2008

Jeremy,

*T*he ride to Claytor Lake was heart-wrenching. Passing by road signs for your town and Virginia Tech ripped my heart. It's not fair that you are dead. You were too young. You were a good person. I just can't figure this world out. My soul is tarnished with anguish.

When we arrived here the air was bitter. How fitting... We changed clothes, set up camp, started a fire, devoured dinner, and played cards while sitting around our campfire roasting marshmallows. My eyes watered as I thought of how much you would have enjoyed this adventure.

Before I knew it, the day was completed. Unlike previously when I returned home from work, now I can't just open up the refrigerator, take out a head of lettuce, a few tomatoes and a pepper, move to the lazy susan, take a pan out, travel to the pantry, pull out a can of Campbell's, light the gas to the stove and heat up some soup while slicing the vegetables; then plop down on the couch, and eat my dinner of soup and salad while watching my favorite television sitcom.

Now, I have to set our "house" up, locate the stove in the Thule box, and create my own bed. If I want to be warm, a fire has to be started. Wood doesn't just magically appear. All of these simple tasks take time, which makes the minutes fly by. Often, time for thinking

Mom and Dad on their wedding day, St. Marys, Pennsylvania
August 19, 1978

about anything other than what I'm doing in the moment is lacking the minute I get off of my bike. This must be why I think as much as I do while riding.

Still, never once does the thought of your murder leave my mind, nor does the gnawing in my gut ever fade.

At Claytor Lake, the sky appeared incessantly dark rather quickly in the evening. The campground was fairly well wooded and definitely secluded far from society. By half past nine, excluding the light created by a few campfires surrounding our site, all light was absent.

We didn't have the luxuries of a KOA, such as hair dryers and showers, present here. In fact, our site was described as primitive. Water had to be accessed solely from the bathrooms and electricity was absent from our immediate site. Fortunately, the woman's bathroom did offer an outlet. God knows I need that GPS!

As darkness set in, I didn't even bother to take a sponge bath as I was too cold to expose my raw skin to the air once again. Changing into dry clothes was sufficient. The dishes: I cleaned them with a bucket of cool water and a hand rag above the fire. Or was that Joe?

After the fire was put out with the water that remained, predictably, almost immediately, I fell asleep.

Thankfully, this morning I woke up feeling refreshed. All of this activity sure is physically draining. So much that I'm not bothered by sleeping on top of the ground. The truth is there's something about falling asleep zipped up in a sleeping bag laid on the ground inside of a tent in the middle of the woods, particularly when the air is so cool. It's calming to me. I think I sleep best in this type of natural environment.

Not surprisingly, this morning was violently cold. I just don't remember May being so frigid. Then again, I never did live outdoors in a tent in the month of May before. How would I know?!

Today's distance was an even hundred miles. Our destination was a small town, once again nestled in the hub of the Appalachians, called Damascus. As I write this letter to you, I find myself sitting on the damp ground around eight o'clock in the evening next to a telephone pole in the midst of a massive crowd. A hundred feet or so in front of me a band is performing. The song is Bruce Springsteen's "Born to Run." I am in the center of a festival. People are socializing, dancing and singing. I'm surrounded by the aroma of a combination of pulled pork, candy apples, hot sausages with fried onions and peppers, French fries topped with vinegar, corn dogs, and anything else under the sun that could be fried.

We hadn't planned on staying in Damascus. In fact, we actually planned on staying in a town twenty miles back where, tonight, there was absolutely no activity taking place. We were going to stay in a hostel there, run by members of the local Baptist church. I'm sure this place would have had flavor of its own. I'm sure we would have met some very fine people there, but am I ever glad we decided to bike the extra twenty miles to Damascus!

We heard about Damascus from another biker whom we met earlier in the day over lunch. Jesse is traveling the same route as we are, and his brother did exactly the same thing one year ago. His brother was lucky enough to find himself in Damascus on the weekend of Appalachian Trails Days and so recommended that Jesse make it to Damascus this weekend as well. He passed on the word to us and thank goodness we took his advice. Something tells me we will be talking about "that night in Damascus" for years to come.

Damascus can't sit but a few feet off the Appalachian Trail. It is the perfect location for the festival, as by the time hikers who started on the trail back in March or April get to Damascus, they have been hiking for two to three months and haven't seen this type of entertainment in that same amount of time. This festival draws hundreds of people off of the AT, and thousands more from small surrounding towns and areas as remote as California, to spend three days in this town, which any other day out of the year has a population of only eight hundred.

The people of Damascus are friendly, down-to-earth folk. They love hikers and bikers. Heck, their entire town's focus is hikers and bikers. A local man has a phone situated on his front porch with a sign that reads "free long distance calls" placed perfectly above it. The local physicians have signs on the doors of their offices welcoming hikers to come in and have corns and blisters evaluated and treated. All of the locals ask: "So you are biking across?" It is just understood that you are biking across America.

When you bike through this town, you realize you are not alone on your quest. Each and every one of these bikers and hikers wants something more out of his/her life. They are sick of the norm. They don't want to settle for a nine-to-five job in a large city where all anyone cares about is what type of car you drive and what Fortune 500 Company you work for. These are people who suffered through adversity in their lives. They may have lost loved ones suddenly. They may be trying to overcome poverty. They may just want something more. But every single one of them has a common desire, and that is for something better. We're all out here looking for it. Hopefully we will find it. In any case, the atmosphere that is created when five thousand people with a similar mindset get together is just spectacular.

The last twenty miles of the ride into Damascus were all downhill. The road winded perfectly while following a stream engulfed with a multitude of large rocks, many covered in moss. As we entered the town, a bike path presented itself about two miles back where people were present in mass numbers biking its course. A bus transported young children to the beginning of this path situated slightly higher in elevation than the end. Repetitively, the children rode down the hill on their bicycles, many with training wheels, accompanied by their parents. A soft-serve ice cream shack was present at the end with the most delicious ice cream of variable flavors. I had a cone of peanut-butter-flavored soft serve. It was delectable. My mind brought me back to the days of our youth as I sat in the grass devouring this treat surrounded by family and our new-found friend, Jesse.

What I would give to go back in time and eat a cone of soft serve from Gheen's in Bellefonte with you, Mom, Dad, Joe, and Stephanie.

After this snack, we continued our ride to an area in town designated as "tent city" no more than a mile away. It is here where most of the party-goers set up their tents and camp out for the night, many for the entire weekend. I have a feeling there won't be too much sleeping taking place here tonight. But we chose to set up our tent here anyway.

There must be a thousand tents set up side-by-side. Many guests are sitting in Crazy Creek chairs around their campfires roasting marshmallows and engaging in conversation. Others are playing songs on their guitars, banjos, and harmonicas. Some are humming, still others are sleeping. The noise level is loud and the energy is contagious.

Not far from tent city, where I am now, under white tents there are a ton of mountain gear/outerwear venders situated in a park where one will find any type of food he or she could ever desire, live entertainment, and an opportunity to meet some of the most amazing people one could dream of meeting. These people may not be Hollywood celebrities, but they are certainly celebrities of the trail. Generations of stories have been

*Joe calling Brad and me from a pay phone about 20 miles outside of
Damascus, May 17, 2008*

passed down by the mouths of these folk, and future generations will
tell of their legacy, you can count on this.

As I tour the town, I notice there is a young man standing in his,
or someone else's, front yard, sporting nothing more than a Speedo
with swimming goggles placed strategically on his head. There's not
a pool or ocean in sight. He's in front of me, in this moment, as I
write. Of course, he has a beer in hand. The atmosphere reminds me
of college and fraternity row. How I miss Penn State!

I've spotted a guy with legs about as long as I am tall, and he is
not on stilts. He's standing directly ahead of me. I'm sure the two of
us could hold an interesting conversation but I will continue walking
and focus on my matchless thoughts for the moment.

Downtown, all of the local businesses are open. There is a live
band on each street corner. The locals are ecstatic. You can tell that
the high school seniors wait for this weekend all year round. It may
be bigger than Christmas or New Year's Eve. The energy is electric.

As I purchased some chips and soda at a downtown venue, I noticed a "wanted" sign placed by the register. A man who was known to be hiking the trail is a suspect in the murder of two young hikers. He'd been previously arrested for another crime and detained, but the police are now seeking more information in regards to his alleged involvement in this particular case. Anyone who might have come across this man's path was being asked to contact the local police to assist in the investigation.

I couldn't help but be taken aback. We live in a very sad world, one filled with violence, horror, poverty, and despair.

It is now morning.

Night came all too early last night. We attempted to lay our heads to bed a little after one. I would have stayed up longer but biking sure does take the energy out of a person (i.e. me).

Sometime during the wee hours, Dad awoke to the sounds of someone fooling around by our car, parked about a quarter mile away from our tent. God knows how he heard such activity! He grew concerned we might be in the process of losing our SAG wagon and, in turn, walked over to scope out the scene. I'm not sure what he planned on doing when he arrived at the scene of a robbery (or car-jacking for that matter) but he sure seemed to be on a mission.

When Dad arrived, he ran into a few local (under-the-influence) adolescents goofing off, socializing, and just plain having a good time. As they began talking with Dad, the volume of their voices escalated, and I could hear their entire conversation all the way back at our campsite.

They reminded me of us on football weekends back in our college days. They talked to Dad about his life, college days, how he and Mom met, and, of course, you — how Dad's soul yearned to see your face once again.

They conversed for awhile, philosophizing, and then Dad returned to the tent to make a second attempt at falling asleep. I'm sure he wasn't successful, as every five minutes or so one of the neighbors would howl like a wolf and another would scream, "Can I get a yee-hah?" Then, someone else would yell "Shut-up!"

Between this and the laughing and partying around the numerous campfires there was no sleeping to be had last night. I'm not sure why we even tried!

Throughout all of this entertainment, I stayed inside the tent, laughing.

For now, Jeremy, I am living out of a tent. I fall asleep each night in a sleeping bag. My head rests on a travel-size pillow. When I require a bathroom in the middle of the night sometimes I have to walk quite a far distance to find one. Often, I just go in the middle of the woods. I awake each morning by the light of the sunrise rather than the sound of an alarm clock. My tent is often moist on the inside from the night's frost, so it is not uncommon to wake up inside of a damp sleeping bag. I wash my dishes in a bathroom sink or bucket above my campfire. I cook my meals on a portable propane stove or above the warmth of a campfire. I change my clothes in broad daylight often by hiding myself between two opened car doors. I drink water from wherever I can get it, sometimes even from a stream. I no longer have a job. I don't earn a paycheck. I don't own a house, and I have no current bills to pay. In a sense, I feel worthless. I suspect some might say I've turned into a nonproductive member of society. This may be true, but for now, I enjoy my place.

As I mentioned earlier, it is now morning. Almost all other community members of tent city still are asleep; that or they're still awake sitting around a lit campfire smoking a bong.

I just awoke and am preparing for our (tentative) final day of biking through Virginia. I'm reminded that Mom and Stephanie will be meeting us in Bowling Green, Kentucky, in just a few days. Once we arrive there, we will take a few days off of biking and visit Mammoth Cave. If possible, we will simply relax and enjoy the precious time we have been granted together, sadly, without you by our sides. Then, Mom and Dad will return home together, a trip including just the two of them, one which for them seems to be long overdue.

As I sit here in preparation, oiling the chain of my bike and packing my pouch with food, I am reminded of the transition I will make over the course of the next twenty-four hours. I will leave Virginia and enter Kentucky. A new chapter in my life will unfold. I will leave behind the place where your murder took place.

Amongst the horror of your death, I have witnessed the beauty of this place that you so dotingly treasured. It may be years before I return, but my memories of Virginia (both those formed over the course of the past few days and those of my lifetime prior to your death) will never fade.

Virginia stole a vital piece of my soul. Throughout the remainder of this journey, I wonder if ever I'll be able to fill its place. My gut tells me not.

The prospect of traveling through states reminds me of a similar transition you and I made as children when we left our yellow and red split-level home in Waterloo, Iowa, and moved into that run-down old farmhouse in Alliance, Ohio. It was a slow transition, as it didn't occur overnight. I recall we moved, initially, into a Howard Johnson on the outskirts of town where we resided for nearly six months while we waited for the structure to be remodeled by Dad and transformed into a home.

Over late nights spent staring into the flames of a number of campfires, I've recently learned that Dad and Mom actually turned the keys of our Waterloo home back in to the bank due to financial difficulties. Because of such, they weren't granted a loan to purchase that farmhouse. In exchange for a cut in rent, Dad remodeled that Ohio house. He had hoped to "rent to buy," but as we both know, our family ended up in Boalsburg a few years later and this dream never became a reality.

As a child, living in a hotel, particularly a "Ho Jo's," was tremendously fun. What kind of kid (or adult for that matter) wouldn't have enjoyed a daily continental breakfast buffet and free use of the pool most hours of the day! We probably drove Mom crazy in that eleven-by-fourteen-foot rectangular box day in and day out while Dad was at work. In fact, I know that we did, so I'm quite certain she was grateful when we moved into that spacious old farmhouse, regardless of the color of its walls.

When we finally did make the move into that farmhouse, I was still very young. I must have been just ready to turn five and you were seven years old. You'd already attended kindergarten while we resided in Iowa. I had barely experienced pre-K there.

In Ohio, I enjoyed riding the school bus with you, both of us always sitting in the front directly adjacent to the driver "where the little kids sat." It now seems odd that Mom often accompanied us on that bus as well. These days, lunchroom aides transport themselves to school in vehicles of their own. I still remember the friends we made.

Iowa had been fun. Don't get me wrong! The mounds of snow we received each winter were perfect for sledding. Our friends lived directly across the street and that lovely Cinderella Park sat not far down the road. To top things off, I never could resist those cookies from the bakery. The thought of them still provokes my taste buds to salivate.

Most, if not all, of the adults in our neighborhood there were recently married with young children our age. Their lives were very much similar to Mom and Dad's. Each was starting out in adulthood, in a world far different than he/she had known it to be while growing up.

Our parents had moved to Waterloo, Iowa, from St. Marys, Pennsylvania. From true, rural Pennsylvania they moved to an urban and developing community. Neither knew what to expect, but they had each other and were able to make the experience a success. I'm sure if they could go back and replay the events they'd do it all over in just the same fashion, not changing a thing.

The seclusion of our yard from all others is what I liked most about that property in Alliance. When temper tantrums occurred, no one heard of our screams. Situated on nearly ten acres of land, the house, barn, playhouse, chicken coup and milk house were the only structures present within plain sight.

I guess there was an abandoned house that I believed was owned by a "cat-killer." Shamefully, I'm fairly certain only I could see this man through the corn fields. Regardless, when my kittens vanished I blamed their disappearance on him. His presence, real or imagined, formed one of my first childhood memories of evil.

Summers spent on that farm were a blast. In fact, I'll never forget the day you ran me over. We were racing down the driveway. You were riding Mom's ten-speed. I was on foot, our babysitter close behind. It had recently rained and the ground was still wet. I slipped right in front of your path (as you had given us a head start) and, unable to get out of the way quickly enough, you ran me over. My purple over-alls were clearly marked with the bike's muddy tire prints. Looking back, the event was hilarious. At the time, I cried. Not from pain. I loved those pants.

Traditions were formed in that farmhouse. On the eve of Saint Nicholas's feast day (December 6) we placed our shoes outside of our rooms. Saint Nicholas came down from heaven that night and delivered to each of us a small but special treat.

Then, on our very first Christmas there Santa showed up in his sleigh, which he parked at the bottom of the lane. We were both in shock as to how Santa was able to fly his sleigh without any snow. Mom and Dad said it was magic and we innocently believed. On this very special eve he delivered to each of us one solitary gift that we were able to open twelve hours early. For me it was a Cabbage Patch doll named Ester Fiona. For you, it was a pound puppy. I'm sure you'd remember it.

We got our first and only case of chicken pox in that house and it was there that we experienced our very first bee stings. I learned to ride a bicycle without training wheels there. You soon became an

Jen, Joe, and Jeremy with Santa in Boalsburg, Pennsylvania, Christmas 1987

expert at riding Mom's 10-speed blue Schwinn. We played Slip 'n Slide, ran through the sprinkler, made snowmen and angels, ate birthday cake, and each grew more than a few inches. Our religious beliefs developed, and our minds advanced.

Although Ohio ended up being filled with all sorts of timeless memories, the transition there from Iowa was difficult for our parents. They had to leave their friends and start all over again. Worse yet, they both wanted to go home to Pennsylvania. They just couldn't. Jobs weren't available in St. Marys, outside of the factory, so they were stuck beginning all over again. They wanted to make something of themselves, just as you wanted to do when you left your roots in Belle-fonte and relocated to Virginia.

Change is difficult for everyone.

After all of our belongings were packed into the moving truck in Iowa and driven away toward Ohio, as we took one final walk through that house, all of the rooms seemed so empty. They echoed with each word that was spoken and the place we called home all too quickly gave out an eerie vibe. I gave that house a kiss goodbye when we left and my eyes filled with tears the moment we drove away. You and I were situated in the far back seat of our station wagon, facing backward away from Mom and Dad sitting up front. We saw that house for probably a mile before its silhouette disappeared in the distance.

For a few days after we left, you and I spoke of how we missed our friends and that old house. I was four years old and frightened of a new experience but knew that Mom and Dad would protect us. We were a family and nothing could ever come between us.

Eventually, we all readjusted — to the Howard Johnson and then to the farmhouse — just in time to make the move closer toward "home," to Boalsburg, Pennsylvania. This time around the events that played out, as well as the emotions, were similar to our previous moves.

Each one was an experience that helped us to become the unique individuals we grew into later on in life. Each move left behind something, possibly a toy or a blanket, dear friends and favorite restaurants. But just the same, each moving truck delivered something special with its arrival: the possibility for a new life.

Every time we moved, it was like spring had arrived. The opportunity for new experiences, new friends and a new life appeared. Following each move, old memories of our previous lives remained with us encrypted within our beings, but the opportunity to learn and experience something unique evolved. There is something about venturing into the unknown. Possibly, this is what this trip is all about: discovering exactly what this sensation is.

This is exactly what I predict will happen as I exit this state: a new spring will arrive. My new life with Virginia left behind will begin.

My chain is oiled. My lunch is packed and all of our belongings, including this tent, are packed away in the car.

As I take one final look around I speculate there were some illegal drugs consumed here last night. Memories for all were formed here last night, whether for good or for bad. What a night Damascus turned out to be! Who would have thought that in the middle of

Appalachia we would run into such a place? I feel like last night was the closet I'll ever get to Woodstock in my lifetime. I guess you can't appreciate Appalachian Trail Days completely without truly experiencing it for yourself, but trust me, it was a riot.

For me, last night's revelry was about learning to live life again, learning to take a break from grieving and just be. The people we met here were spectacular, with trail names like Green Wrench and Sky Walker — these people had flavor and stories.

This may end up being my favorite experience of this trip.

I can envision you laughing hysterically as we biked off into the heavy fog this morning reeking of incense. This is beginning to feel more like an adventure!

Love,

Jenny

Jennifer and Jeremy on Aunt Kathy's front porch,
summer 2005

8. The Breaks
Damascus to The Breaks Interstate Park, Virginia

"I must not fear. Fear is the mind-killer. Fear is the little-death that brings total obliteration. I will face my fear. I will permit it to pass over me and through me. And when it has gone past I will turn the inner eye to see its path. Where the fear has gone there will be nothing. Only I will remain."
~Frank Herbert

May 18, 2008

Jeremy,

Today we biked to *The Breaks Interstate Park*. This (as you might know) is the location of the "Grand Canyon of the South"; home to the deepest gorge east of the Mississippi. It's one of only two interstate parks in the United States; the other I've learned spans from Minnesota to Wisconsin. This particular park connects both Virginia and Kentucky where I speculate we should arrive within twenty short miles of biking tomorrow morning. Indeed, we've almost made it to Kentucky!

The ride today was a physical challenge. The rain didn't help. When we awoke this morning the weather was perfect. Although the fog was heavy, humidity was absent and the temperature was perfectly cool; not cool enough so as to induce shivering, but cool enough to ensure we wouldn't overheat. Additionally, the wind was calm. This setting (as should have been expected) was the calm before the storm. Within one hour of biking the sky emptied on to Brad and me.

Since our departure from Yorktown only five days ago, Joe and Dad have decided to follow the same roads that we bike on. This is with the exception of either the bikes or the SAG wagon taking a wrong turn. They tend to explore more of an area by taking additional off-route excursions. I suspect they take more pictures, and I know (because I've seen the footage) they videotape everything under the sun: the good, the bad, and the ugly. Obviously, they can move much farther much faster than we can. Heck, it takes them thirty minutes to drive a distance that might take us four hours to bike. Joe sure was thinking when he volunteered to drive the SAG wagon! Maybe you'd have chosen to ride with him.

Today was no different than any of our previous days in regards to the order each of us left the campsite. Brad and I left tent city around five thirty this morning. Dad and Joe left much later, possibly it was eight or nine; I can't be sure. What I can be sure of is that they spent quite some time consuming a hearty breakfast and engaging in conversation prior to departing from Damascus. And with Dad, well, you just never know what he will find himself involved in.

Anyway, this system suits each of our schedules and personalities. Joe and Dad don't have to be anywhere until early evening when Brad and I arrive at our campground. Even if by chance they wouldn't arrive right then and right there, I'm sure we'd survive. And, since Joe isn't one to fall asleep early and rise just the same, his role in this trip seems perfect.

Dad, on the other hand, loves everything there is to love about the morning. With Joe still asleep and Brad and I off biking farther west, he has plenty of time available to spend his mornings doing exactly what he loves most: eating french toast, drinking coffee, and socializing with random strangers. Goodness, I have to believe he'd eat french toast every meal of the day if someone would cook it for him.

Joe would rather stay up late at night playing his guitar, accordion, piano, harmonica, or some other instrument while watching late-night comedy routines. These days he has the same taste for humor as you once did. He reminds me more and more of you as the days pass us by: certain facial expressions, phrases, foods preferences, and mannerisms. Seems you left a piece of you behind in each one of us. The thought makes me sad. I want *all* of you here.

Appalachia, May 2008 ~ Photograph taken by Joseph Herbstritt

Stephanie has inherited your enthusiasm for engineering. No doubt she'll fulfill your academic goals.

Mom, she's taken on your love for gardening. She just needs to remember to wear gloves when canning hot red peppers!

Just as a side note, last summer Steph got some of that violent pepper juice up her nose. You would have fallen to the ground laughing at the sight of her stuffing sour cream up her nostrils to relieve the burning. It devastates me to recognize all the fun you're missing out on.

Dad, he just keeps getting goofier and goofier as the days pass us by. You were the splitting image of him. Now, he's trying to get back in shape. One of these days he'll turn into a runner just like you were.

Joe, as I said, has your humor as well as your zest for life. He's the most laid-back person I've ever met. Doubt anyone could make the kid mad.

And me, I'm learning to write. More importantly, I've learned (a little too late) that there's much more to life than lavish material possessions and unfulfilling work. You did it right, Jeremy. You knew BMB (biochemistry and molecular biology) wasn't for you, so you moved forward in life and found a new career, one which you were passionate about, before you'd wasted too much time. I wish I'd gone on this trip five years ago. Hindsight is 20/20, now isn't it?

Anyway, from what I've been told, the past few mornings with Dad and Joe have gone something like this: Joe is difficult to rise so Dad walks to the nearest breakfast diner (which by the way may be two miles away), socializes with the locals, slowly digests his meal, walks back to the campground, and by this time Joe is just about finished putting the tent and sleeping bags away. As soon as he finishes his breakfast the two start driving "west." When they run into us, all four of us typically pull over to the side of the road where Brad and I refuel — with carbohydrates that is, did you think I was going to say beer? We all spend some time socializing, crack a few jokes, take a short break and then resume our routines. A few hours later we typically meet for lunch at a local diner (this can be as late as three in the afternoon). After lunch we may not meet again until we arrive at our destination for the night. The entire experience is a tremendous amount of fun, much more than I've ever had in my life. I know it's only been five days but I feel as if I am on a continual vacation.

Usually it's around nightfall when I allow myself to remember the reality of my world. Throughout the day I know you are dead — the thought never escapes my mind. But it is as if I have convinced myself your death is only temporary.

My previous religious beliefs seem to have permanently created in my existence two separate worlds that somehow I hope will eventually connect. In one world you are dead and I am stuck: alive, alone and traumatized. I walk through the motions of this world: riding my bike every day, eating, sleeping, laughing, and crying, knowing possibly that I may never see you again but embracing the reality of a second, imaginary world. In this world you are alive, happy and healthy. You visit us often; we just can't see you. It's like a second dimension of this earth, a dimension I can't yet have contact with, none of us here on this earth can. At nightfall, I erase the sense of this new world and come to the realization that I might be stuck here on this earth for the next sixty years without you here.

At night I reflect on why I am here. It is so painful to recognize that I am here on this amazing journey because you are dead. When these thoughts arise my heart starts to cry. Even so, for quite some time now I refuse to let the tears fall from my eyes. I hate the pain crying brings to the surface. I buried that pain long ago with your body. I hate the memory of it, and I hate it even more when it resurfaces. Death is a bitch.

So I've created a system: I've chosen to live in my own fairy tale where one day you and I will be reunited again. Do fairy tales ever come true? I have my doubts.

Today Joe and Dad must have left a wee bit earlier than they usually do as I doubt we put on more than thirty miles when we first saw them. (Possibly, we're just gaining speed.) I believe it was on an intense climb up one of the hollows in southwestern Virginia when the two came across Brad and me struggling to keep our sanity. The rain was pouring out of the sky in buckets. Luckily, we had packed our rain jackets so we were at least partially shielded from the shower. And I shouldn't complain excessively as the depth of the forest blanketing this particular Appalachian mountain did provide us with a tremendous amount of relief. Nevertheless, by the time Joe and Dad found us we were completely drenched.

Not only were we cold and wet, we were becoming increasingly frustrated with our positions. Our legs were tired. Brad's knees produced an agonizing strike of pain with every stroke he pedaled. My shoulders were sore and my shorts weren't fitting me properly. I've developed saddle sores. These are far from pleasant. All of us were sick of being chased by dogs. I missed terribly my life the way it used to be (that is prior to your death) and mentally my stamina was running low. Brad's energy appeared to be dwindling as well. (I think his began to diminish the minute we left on this journey.)

As Dad and Joe passed us by, they wound their windows down only briefly. The Pathfinder never did come to a stop. They simply waved while inquiring (rather abruptly I must add) how we were doing. Before my brain even had a chance to register their presence, they passed us by.

At the time I was devastated they didn't offer us a ride to the top. I wanted to quit and hitch a ride back home to Bellefonte. But once I did finally make it to the summit I was rather grateful they didn't. They knew my weaknesses. They knew Brad's as well. They most likely heard in our voices our proximity toward defeat.

At the top of that mountain we sat in the car for what seemed like hours while the windows steamed up from the moisture within and that present on our bodies. We turned the heat on full blast but still were unable to maintain warmth. (Meanwhile, Joe and Dad were profusely sweating.) Our bodies were wet and cold, as were our souls.

Once we got in neither of us wanted to get out of that car to complete our ride. We would have been content sleeping in the damp warmth of that car parked on the side of the road for the remainder of the day. But once the rain settled, Joe and Dad practically pushed us out. "You wanted to ride your bikes across America, now get moving!" Ouch.

Freezing, we ventured carefully down the grade we had just climbed, praying we wouldn't slip. I'm surprised that we didn't as our tires are as thin as the rim of a toothbrush and the rain was flooding the surface of the road. The terrain was treacherous but Joe and Dad didn't allow us to give up.

This scenario of climbing in the rain, warming up at the summit inside of the Pathfinder, and slowly traveling downhill while praying not to fall repeated itself approximately three times. The rain never did slow down all that much (well, at least not until nearly the end of the day). Fortunately, by this time we had made it to our destination. I thought the hour would never come.

After the second climb, we landed ourselves in a valley where some sort of very large meeting was taking place. Due to the large presence of the KKK in this section of our country, I quickly began to question the purpose of this get-together. It was still daylight, although the sky was gray and gloomy. At the time, I couldn't imagine a group like this would meet during such an hour. Nevertheless, the group of possibly four hundred people was found to be congregating no more than one hundred feet from the road, nestled very snuggly together under a metal pavilion, chanting in harmony what appeared to be incredibly angry, violent phrases. Large pickup trucks blockaded all entrances into the park. I can't be certain if their words were actually violent in nature as I couldn't make them out but I wasn't about to take any chances. I realize, perchance, this might have been simply a church group chanting their memorized prayers. But after seeing at least forty signs covered in graffiti with words suggesting hatred toward African Americans, Brad and I didn't take any risks. We made a conscious effort to move out of that valley as quickly as possible. Perhaps our legs weren't as tired as we thought they were!

Today was a trial, a test of my strength. My mental strength had already been tested to the point I never could have imagined I'd be able to handle. Now, my physical strength is being tested just the same. The ironic aspect of this trip is that I've voluntarily endeavored on this journey. No one is forcing me to continue on.

Every solitary mountain we climbed today was steep, short, and vertical. Of course while we were biking I wouldn't have described any of the climbs as "short" but in the grand scheme of mountain distances, these mountains were short in length. Truth be told, even though today's climbs were short, they were not easy. There were some ascents with grades so great that I wasn't sure I would make it to the top without having to pull off and rest (that, or fall over, whichever came first). As it became more and more difficult to rotate the pedals of my bike with the remaining strength from my quadriceps, and my strokes became slower and slower, at times I was convinced I would merely fall over and land flat on my side with my feet still clipped into my pedals due to extreme exhaustion. If this scenario actually occurs, I'll let you know.

My experiences have taught me the power of my will. As an anorexic, it took me incredible self-discipline to starve myself to the point of near death. I am not proud of this truth; it is just so.

Every race I've undertaken, from my first 5K cross-country race in high school to our first marathon run together, has required incredible resolution. If it weren't for the power of my mind I would never have finished the Boston Marathon to which I long to return. I've learned that my body is only so strong; my mind must do the rest of the work.

The same has held true with grief. In learning to live my life again, I've found that often the strength of my mind and its trickery and tactical deception are often the only variable that is able to provide me with any scrap of peace. My mind knows when I simply can't think about you dead any longer. So, it re-directs my focus to something else: work, writing, eating, exercising, worrying about God knows what. When I think about your body dead in that casket, my mind takes me to a picture of you alive: running, kayaking, or simply sitting by a bonfire roasting a marshmallow and savoring a beer. When I think about the possible pain you experienced, my mind jumps to another subject. When a picture of that horrific beast enters my vision, my mind abruptly changes the slide to that of our family together at the beach, Grandma's, or even on a Christmas morning surrounded by stockings and gifts. The mind is brilliant. Truly it is.

I know that the pain I endured today was nothing. It was no more than the pain a marathon creates. But still it was difficult. I have to remind myself every now and again that if you could suffer through what you did, then really there shouldn't be anything I can't overcome in life myself.

Even though we did make it to The Breaks today, by the time I got here I was more than ready to throw in the rag for good and return to routine: a job that I loathed and the everyday grind of listening to people ask questions regarding your death: "How is your family?" "How are your parents?" "I didn't know he was your brother."

I can't help but feel that many people are just nosy and don't genuinely care about me, my feelings, or the content of my answers.

Just as I remember who didn't send me a condolence card over who did, for some reason I have a tendency these days to be judgmental and only remember the bad. I am embarrassed to admit this. Yet, these conversations are awkward and always leave me with a pit in my gut. I hate them. And that is why I cannot return home. No matter how hard it rains during the remainder of this trip, I have to continue on, for returning can't possibly be the solution.

I must tell you about something incredible that happened today.

I have to believe that just as the day was about to come to a close, you couldn't help but bring out the sun, just as you did for me during the second half of the Boston Marathon on that awful day in 2007.

When I tell Mom about this, she will probably say that you saw my despair and yearned for me to continue on with this journey. For when the sun came out, in that moment, my sadness washed away along with the rain. My body might have still been soaked, and my mind exhausted, but I had enough energy left to put forth an unprompted smile.

A smile returned to my face!

People used to know me because of my smile: "You're that girl that's always smiling." "I never saw anyone smile during mile twenty-four of a marathon." Now, people know me because of your murder.

As you might have expected, this section of our ride is proving to be the most beautiful portion of our trip thus far. Possibly you did have a hand in this discovery. I can only hope.

After biking three miles up a steep incline, just as I was about to approach the summit saturated in the warmth of the sun's rays, to the left of me, out of the corner of my eye, I caught a glimpse of the scenery present in this park.

Brad and I pulled off to the side of the road where Dad and Joe were parked. All four of us walked a short distance down a steep and narrow rock path leading to an overlook where one could view this majestic ravine. Here, I experienced the glamour of this hidden treasure. I'd never visited the Grand Canyon but couldn't imagine how stunning it must be as this was the most beautiful place I've traveled to thus far in my lifetime.

As I stared deep into the canyon, I saw a variety of trees from white pines to maples and red oaks (per Dad's description).

The wind here blew ever so softly against my skin, a complete contrast from biking into a head wind all day long for the past five days, which, by the way, has already created a rough texture and dryness about my skin and numerous appalling episodes of nose bleeds.

I witnessed an eagle soaring high across the gorge and couldn't help but hope it somehow was you. I never was much of a believer in reincarnation but sometimes my desire to see you becomes so intense that I start to believe anything is possible.

I heard a hummingbird in the distance and the squirrels below me were scavenging for food. Three white-tailed deer crossed to the right of me in the distance. No joke. I was startled by their movement amidst the sheer serenity.

I had to stand a foot-length away from the edge of the gorge. My heart pounded and my hands began to sweat. I was taken aback by my fear of heights.

Dad decided to step out and stand on top of a rock on the very edge of a cliff that dropped directly into the canyon below. He jokingly threatened to jump. I didn't find this behavior amusing whatsoever. I begged him to return to a distance at least five feet back from the edge. He continued to tease me. His position made me nervous. I am petrified of heights (as if you don't know!). My heart began to beat stronger and my hands started to drip.

Dad, Joe, and Brad had videotaped this entire escapade unbeknownst to me. I screamed at them and ran right on back to my bike just like I used to do when teased by you during our youth (only Mom wasn't there to tell on you to).

I can't be near cliffs when I am around those three, at least not when I am the only fearful person in their presence. It's too easy for them to pick on me.

As I waited at the top of the hill for my pranksters, I began to feel overwhelmed. The beauty I had just witnessed was awe-inspiring. Words simply can't give it justice. I wanted to call you and explain to you how deep this canyon appeared, as it must have been a mile deep, and inquire if you'd ever visited. I was once again reminded of the horror of the reality of our daily lives.

This will be our last night in Virginia. I am pleased for this fact.

After Dad, Brad, and Joe returned to the summit, we proceeded halfway down the mountain to our destination for the night. I would typically refer to an inn like this as a motel, as the entrance to each individual room opens from the outside rather than through a long narrow hallway within.

The building is old, two stories and musty with décor from the late seventies or possibly the early eighties. The price is steep for what is provided. Ice, soap, and shampoo are considered extras, and the sheets are thin due to what I would consider has been many years of repetitive washings; but a microwave is present in our room and the price is far less expensive than at the Interstate Park. Therefore, I will hold back on my complaints. Plus, a variety of handcrafted rocking chairs are placed in the sunlight outside of each door facing the "Road Kill Kafé" (what can I say?) situated across the highway. The delight I got from rocking in one of these chairs was astonishing. The view that surrounds this place is like a perfect painting, some of God's finest work.

As I sat in my seat, I made small talk with a group of pipe-line workers while snacking on strawberry milkshake-flavored Oreos. They expressed their elation regarding the fact that the price of gas has increased to an average of slightly over four dollars per gallon. They are prospering as a result. I am happy for them that they are thriving. I am sad for the state of our economy and for the sake of the rest of America. And, even something as mundane as the price of gasoline brings my thoughts to you. In 2007, gas was less than three dollars per gallon. What will it cost in 2017? Will you, will I, even care?

The night is now far from young but I cannot fall asleep as my thoughts are focused on the dogs of the communities we have crossed through. They arrive at the most inopportune times. Since we entered the Appalachians, I have been chased by more dogs than I ever thought existed. These dogs are nasty. They come with plans of attack. Sometimes there are three in a pack. They eye me up from a distance, probably camouflaged somewhere within the forests. Once they catch me at what appears to be a weak moment, like halfway through the ninth Hail Mary of my decade on a challenging uphill, they come out of nowhere and startle me with their advance. All three dogs come at me from the same side, but one aims at my front tire, the other at my back, and the third at my foot, which is logically attempting to pedal as fast as it possibly can. They try to push me off of the road and into the grass, a ditch, or off of a cliff. These dogs are cruel.

I question what type of owners they have. For all I know their owners are the nicest people in the world, but by the way these dogs behave one would think they were taught to attack from an early age. I've seen dogs that have come from abusive homes and this is how they have behaved. Unfortunately, we often learn to behave how we have been treated. For all I know, I should feel sorry for these dogs because they've come from abusive homes themselves, or maybe they haven't, and therefore I shouldn't. Who knows?

Regardless, these dogs, yet again, like many other objects in life, are a slap in the face. They remind me of what a cruel world we live in.

My clothes are drenched; my body is cold.

Jeremy, I need your guidance. Please help me. The rain has made me very cynical.

All my love,

Jenny

9. Entering Kentucky
The Breaks, Virginia, to Hazard, Kentucky

"When we were children, we used to think that when we were grown-up
we would no longer be vulnerable. But to grow up is to accept vulnerability…
To be alive is to be vulnerable."
~Madeleine L'Engle

May 19, 2008

Jeremy,

*R*eligion has always been a subject of interest and curiosity for me. Until about the age of nine, I failed to doubt any of the words, teachings, or beliefs our parents instilled in us. There was no rationale why I should have. I trusted their words. Their teachings appeared to be consistent with that of the priests of our parish, and even if they weren't I doubt I would have noticed. I was too young.

My first recollection of doubt occurred during the third grade.

We were both students at St. Johns in Bellefonte attending Friday morning Mass with the remainder of our school. I was sitting in the front pew (on the right side) listening to the priest's sermon on Adam and Eve. You and your class were seated directly adjacent to mine (left of the aisle).

It was during this particular sermon that we were informed of Adam and Eve's fictional nature: part of a made-up, illusory story.

What?!

I never expected to hear that sermon! Nor do I think our teachers, parents, or principal expected it either.

In those few moments, during that sermon, I became apprehensive to believe in the teachings of our faith simply for the sole reason that our parents, grandparents, and teachers told me to do so.

Jen and Jeremy, altar servers

I'd been told a story of the earth's creation, the creation of man and woman, original sin, and life and death so many times that I'd practically memorized it verbatim. Then, suddenly, over the course of twenty-five minutes, I was informed by a religious figure that this story was a myth, not actual fact.

Confusion settled within me. Whom was I to believe?

That evening you and I both vivaciously questioned Mom and Dad regarding the tenets of our Catholic faith. We were searching for the truth not simply regarding the story of Adam and Eve but also in respect to religion in general. It seems young children are far wiser than adults often given them credit for.

We wanted specifics. Out of what materials was this earth created? Where did God come from? How did Adam and Eve have so many children? And, why do we all have to die?

You were in the fifth grade: older, wiser, and more outspoken than I. Therefore, your questions were grounded in logic and made far more sense than mine. Even so, from that sermon on, my premise for the existence of my world could no longer exist.

Friday morning Mass took on a new sense of fun as we each arrived with a hidden agenda. Thursday evenings we'd "innocently" ask Mom and Dad a question related to religion. Friday morning we'd compare the answer they provided us with to that of the priest's. I was typically too shy to verbally formulate the question; therefore, you'd do the questioning. None of the answers we received were ever solid. We found flaws in each theory and found there were as many theories as individuals we asked.

Soon enough the priests started to ignore our questions. "Does *anyone else* have a question?" I'm not sure they liked being interrogated by a fifth grader (you).

Eventually, I became embarrassed regarding my qualms. I wanted to please everyone including Mom, Dad, the priests, our teachers, and God, so I learned to remain quiet and avoided verbalizing my doubts. Frankly, with time, I even trained myself not to doubt anything I was taught. I remained naïve and gullible.

I never questioned religion again, at least not until the day you were murdered. My god failed me that day. I should have seen this coming.

Jeremy, instead of simply accepting what you didn't understand at the time, you sought out solid answers even way back then. You didn't give up. You were different than I: not about to settle for the round-about type of answers.

I've heard people state phrases such as: "God only takes you when you are ready." Is that why nasty, selfish, arrogant, old men live to be a hundred and incredibly amazing people like you die so young — do they require more time to learn selflessness? The god I want to believe in isn't this cruel. He doesn't randomly go about this world killing innocent souls (or evil ones for that matter). You wouldn't have believed such false teachings, for you sought out both valid and reasonable answers during your early youth.

In fact, in this moment I can picture you clearly at the age of thirteen. You just had braces placed onto your teeth in (Mom and Dad's) hopes of correcting an overbite (or was it an underbite?). Because of these metal pieces you initially talked with this difficult-to-understand lisp. You were gawky at the time and your gait was undeniably awkward. Your feet were huge. If I recall correctly, you were wearing a solid size ten. You couldn't stop talking from the minute you woke

Above: Jeremy, 10th grade, fall 1996
Left: Jeremy, Stephanie, Jennifer, and Joe,
Christmas 1994

each morning until the hour of your bedtime. You were incredibly energetic. Being that the Energizer bunny commercials were popular back then, Mom would always call you her "Energizer bunny." The only way she was going to get you to sit down was if she tied you down! Certainly, she didn't have to worry about you running up her long-distance phone bill or playing too many video games as you were not one to aimlessly lie around in your bedroom or on the couch all day long. Instead, she couldn't buy you enough coveralls to keep up with the number of pairs you destroyed cutting down firewood or laying down fencing.

Around this time, when you entered public middle school, you also began working part-time.

How you ended up with your first job makes me laugh. Mom just couldn't keep up with you anymore. She felt you had "*far* too much energy" and thought the vigor required to milk cows would slow you down. So, she called our neighbors whom she practically begged to whisk you away. They were happy for your help (who wouldn't have been?). Mom was happy to have a break from all of your questions and activity.

I can't help but put in my two cents on the matter. In the end, Mom was wrong. You were never meant to "slow down." You were Jeremy, Mom's Energizer bunny.

I wish you'd never left that job milking cows. Perhaps then you'd still be alive today...

I can still remember the smell of the iodine that you used to clean off the udders of the cows prior to milking. Your clothes were always stained with it, as were your hands. They must have been stained orange for a solid decade of your life. When Mom, or Dad and I would pick you up from the barn after your shift was completed the aroma would smother our car. Strangely enough I always liked that smell.

It's been years since you left that job but we still share "Jeremy stories" with that neighbor. You spent an incredible number of hours under the roof of their barn. You certainly earned your pay milking cows there each morning around sunrise and every evening before supper.

I can't help but recall at that time in your life your questions regarding religion once again began to surface. I believe this was because the members of this hardworking dairy-farm family were Baptist. Those days you just couldn't stop talking about both God and Darwin.

I'll never forget your Darwin phase. You bought *The Origin of Species* and studied it inside and out. Yes, at the young age of thirteen. It's hard for me to believe at such a young age you were able to develop so many questions. The truth is, you were simply that brilliant. It's a shame all of your hard work, dedication to learning, and efforts in graduate school now, superficially, appear to have been conducted for just about nothing. You died before anything could ever come of it, before you had a chance to do many wonderful things with all the knowledge you worked so hard to gain.

All of the members (and employees) of the farm family whom you were working for had a deep religious faith. You often spent your entire shift, as well as many breakfasts and dinners, discussing with them the theories of their faith and ours. You heard their concerns regarding the salvation of sinners, including Catholics. They didn't seem to believe Catholics accepted Jesus Christ as their Lord and Savior. In turn, you worried for our family, for yourself, and for the fate of all of us in eternity.

You didn't just worry for us; you visited their church, questioned their ministers, and attended their services. In fact, you were even "saved" through their church. You begged Mom and Dad to take our family along. And so they did.

By the time you graduated high school, moved into the dorms at Penn State and gave Mom her sanity back, it seems your faith won the internal war that had been playing out inside of your soul for nearly a decade. You believed in Jesus Christ, God the Father, and the Holy Spirit. You believed in heaven and, undoubtedly, you believed in hell. You feared death in the absence of salvation's promises. And so you feared for the deaths of those whom you loved. Like most of us, I suspect you hoped death would forever remain distant. But you were a realist. And so, you were willing to ask all the hard questions...

This is only me speculating, but I believe that during your short life, in your heart, you couldn't accept this world came to exist by science alone. You died a true believer. I wonder if I'll ever find the faith to do the same.

Since your death, it's been hard for me to understand how all through those years Mom and Dad could have held onto such a strong faith. Looking back, they were some of the most devout Catholics I've ever met, even after everything they'd been through: your hernia surgery and subsequent two-week long coma, the events that led up to losing their house in Waterloo, my anorexia, etc. I'll never forget how Mom and Dad went to Mass every Sunday, never failing to receive the Eucharist, reciting their prayers in harmony with the rest of the congregation. They said their prayers before dinner, knelt by their beds before nightfall, read the Bible faithfully, attended confession monthly and recognized every Holy Day set by the precepts of the Church. I can't imagine how hard it must be for them, after all that now to have lost you. Their eldest son is dead. I can't help but believe their god has failed them. He cannot make up for what he has done. You can never return.

I wonder if ever again I'll be able to find solace in religion. If you had known your outcome in life would you have believed as strongly as you did?

When you died, almost everyone around me told me to hold onto my faith. "Faith" would get me through. Possibly these people were well-versed in the fields of death, grief, and dying. Possibly they were simply speaking from their hearts. I cannot speculate. What I *do* know is that holding onto my faith was far from what *I* needed to do. For me, I needed to let go of my faith, lose my religion, and start fresh on a clean slate. What I believed in for all of those years just wasn't working for me. The theology didn't make sense. So, I have given up on my faith.

I'm starting fresh.

To this date, I haven't returned to my religion, nor have I found my faith. I recite the rosary for distraction, not out of prayer.

Don't misunderstand me; it's not that I don't yearn for a god, the prospect of an afterlife and a reunion with you. I wish for just this.

Only time will tell where my unbelief or belief will lead me.

At the time of your murder, you were frustrated with school and with life. You had worked meticulously to get to the point where you were at. But you were twenty-seven years old, unwed, in school, and without any significant financial possessions. You didn't own a house, nor did you really own the car you were driving.

A number of your friends were to the point where they were settling down, getting married, and talking about children. They held full-time jobs, some for years, and you were still stuck in graduate school.

Did you feel stuck? I hope that you didn't. You loved school. But you were becoming perturbed. The tone in your voice gave you away.

You'd just been granted the prestigious Sussman Summer Fellowship Scholarship, awarded to only the top civil and environmental engineering students in your class. The night before you died you told me about it (although I only vaguely remember the conversation because, selfishly, my thoughts were focused on the upcoming

Joe and Steph

Joe, Jen, Michelle Weaver, Steph, and Jeremy at Virginia Beach, summer 2001

Jeremy and Jennifer, Penn State, spring 2003

marathon the following day). Your professors specifically selected you, as they saw great promise in your work and potential in your research. They've told me so. You were conducting a research project on the waters of the Roanoke River. School would be paid for the remainder of the next year. Your summer research ideas would be fully funded. Living expenses would be paid in full for the same period of time.

Life should have seemed as if it were turning out swell. But because of the last phone conversation we had that night before you died I have to believe you worried significantly about your future and possibly even questioned your god.

In order to explain my reasoning, I have to provide a small amount of background information (as if you could forget). After you earned a B.S. in biochemistry and molecular biology (BMB) with a minor in chemistry, you couldn't find a job that paid much more than minimum wage. Most, if not all of the jobs you were offered (which weren't many, as the job market back then was atrocious), were situated in large cities where the cost of living was unheard of to residents of rural central Pennsylvania.

You unsuccessfully searched for a job with reasonable pay for about a year, became very frustrated with your choice of major and then finally decided to return to school to obtain a second B.S. in engineering (initially it was going to be a masters, but that is a story in and of itself). You were confident finding a job in engineering would be far more promising. More importantly, you were confident you would enjoy your work far more than had you pursued a position more relevant to biochemistry.

From the time you received your BMB degree until the time of your death anytime something would go even remotely wrong in your life you would jokingly call it a "BMB disaster." You had this sense of cynicism about you and, to you, that's what BMB turned out to be: a disaster. I can hear you repetitively saying the phrase now, with a smile on your face. Even now it makes me laugh.

I can see you, running across campus with me, training for some random race, pretending to trip while simultaneously screaming "God damn it, BMB!" I'd be humiliated. "Shhhh, people are going to think you are *absolutely* nuts!" My words would antagonize you causing you to repeat the act, only this time louder and far more obnoxiously. Thinking about this scenario, honestly my stomach pains from laughing.

You called me that night, April 15, 2007, right before you left for five o'clock Mass at St. Mary's Catholic Church in Blacksburg. I was sitting in my hotel room in Boston waiting out the rain. I wanted to walk across the street to a strip mall but didn't want to get wet. Good God, once again, I thought I might melt.

You briefly told me about your scholarship. But amongst all of your very good news, you had this sense of impending doom about you. I could hear it in your voice, and when you spoke of hoping that your graduate school experience didn't turn out to be another BMB disaster, I tried to calm your fears.

I wondered how in the world you could have even remotely thought anything could go wrong. You were excelling in your courses. You had just received this amazing scholarship. Your intro-engineering lab students loved you. Your professors thought you were brilliant. You were making friends, networking, and being introduced as a "colleague."

You were making your mark on the soils of your new school. It was your new home. Everything was going to be okay. Or so I thought.

A part of me believes you sensed something that night that none of us did. I wish we would have known. I would have bought you a plane ticket to Boston. I would have made sure you weren't there. Better yet, I would have made sure that monster was not there: that he was in jail, or an institution, or *somewhere,* anywhere other than there. All those precious lives would have been saved.

(My thoughts are not so exalted that I actually think I have such power, but I wish that I did.)

In any regard, I'm sure that during that same conversation while you were expressing your worries to me I interrupted you numerous times and complained extensively regarding how I was certain I wouldn't be able to finish the Boston Marathon because of this and that. You told me you were confident I would and after I did I would just have to take some time off of running to allow my body to heal. You told me you would pray for me. I'm embarrassed to say that I probably laughed at your kind words and responded with something like: "I'll need a hell of a lot more than prayer to complete this feat, ha ha ha."

I never did thank you for your kind words. We said our goodbyes and that was the last time I heard your voice. I'll never hear it again.

Well, what happened that day turned out to be far worse than a BMB disaster, obviously.

I can't help but analyze every aspect of your life during your last year here on this earth. I remember how plain your apartment in Virginia appeared. It was as if you knew. I can't stop myself from thinking that possibly you did know. I hope you didn't. How scared you might have been!

The only object posted on the wall of your apartment was a laminated copy of the Table of Elements. Though these "elements" were actually mixed drinks. You were given this as a Christmas gift back when you were in the prime of your college years, the first time around. Other than this, the only decorative piece in your apartment was a stack of books. Of course, you had a small sectional couch given to you by Aunt Mary and Uncle Mike, a beautiful wooden dining room table, hand-crafted, given as a gift from Mom, a retro, red-colored, padded metal kitchen table straight out of a 1950s diner, and a blue bath mat stamped with your wet footprint from the water of your daily morning shower.

I was going to get you a new one for Christmas in 2006. For some reason I didn't, and now I am sorry.

Others may laugh but you, indeed, had *three* beds in your room. One, of course, was for you. The other two were for our family's use when we visited. All were hand-me-downs.

A year prior, the same three had been in my own graduate-school apartment.

And your TV set was from the early 1990s. It was a far shot from a flat screen. Yet, you were content.

Possibly your apartment appeared this way because you weren't driven by financial incentives. I knew you well and the truth is you wanted more out of life than just money. You wanted to achieve true happiness.

For you, I believe true happiness would have come with continuing to build strong relationships with family and friends, finding true love, experiencing both international and domestic travel alike, kayaking in the spring on class-four rapids, hiking under the autumn leaves on the AT, running marathon after marathon, landing a satisfactory career where you would leave your mark training future generations of engineers to do just the same, becoming a father, a grandfather, an uncle, and a mentor.

Your desires weren't a stark contrast from most guys your age. But the truth is now you are dead and all of these questions have entered my mind. They will not leave. Is it possible you knew of your fate deep within your subconscious? I want to shut my mind and all of its concerns off but somehow I can't. I'm consumed by your death.

I have to believe if you could go back and live your life all over again, you wouldn't change a thing. For instance...

If you hadn't attended Penn State the first time around and majored in BMB, you might not have met your very best friends with whom you spent many a night with drinking "Monkey Boys" at the Saloon and listening to the "Giants of Science" play at the Crow Bar.

You might never have moved into that apartment at the "Graduate," on the corner of Atherton and Beaver Avenues, where you sorted mosquitoes and stored them in the freezer during the summer and fall. This bizarre behavior was a requirement of your part-time job with the County Extension Office, when you worked as a project assistant for the West Nile Virus Research Project.

You met so many people those humid summer months, year after year, at the Waste Water Treatment Facilities in the area and at people's homes, in their backyards, setting up traps on a hunt for West Nile. I can picture you now wading in a thriving swamp with those high rubber boots on, practically up to your waist, surrounded by who-knows-what type of little creatures indiscernibly luring beside you.

Those same rubber boots sat lifeless in your red Jeep when we found it parked in its spot outside of your apartment on Cardinal Court after your murder. Who knows what you were doing with them in Virginia. I believe it was testing stream water.

Regardless, the whole world now knows that you found the first West Nile Virus-infected mosquito in Centre County. You were very proud of this accomplishment and Dad made sure the world was told of this triumph of yours.

You might never have had the opportunity to take a year off of school; although you weren't very happy when you couldn't find a job with your infamous BMB degree. But I'm sure you'd now agree that was time spent you might not have otherwise had with Dad and Mom, your siblings, and your friends, building that suspension wall, farming, remodeling the old farm house, tailgating with friends and touring universities hoping to find your perfect fit for graduate school. I doubt you would have given up those experiences for anything — not for money, that's for sure.

We all make decisions in life we can never take back. If we choose one path, we miss out on the other. Through your death I've learned that we can't dwell on what we *didn't* do, or *could* have done, or *should* have done, because if we had chosen the opposite path, we'd still be doing the same thing: worrying we should have taken another route.

All we can do is form the best decisions we can at the time with the information we have at hand, close our eyes, jump, and hope for the best.

Today was an accomplishment for me, just as the Sussman Scholarship and that infamous first-infected West Nile Virus mosquito in Centre County were for you. I made it to Kentucky on my bicycle!

We left The Breaks hotel early this morning when the fog was still heavy and our bicycles were still damp from the rain the night before. As I biked briskly down that mountain that I'd dreadfully climbed yesterday, the wind blew strong in my face, cutting out all noise but

Joe and a new friend, Jesse
We met up with Jesse again in the Shawnee National Forest in southern Illinois (Chapter 14).

the sound of itself. I could hear your voice in the swooshing of the wind warning me of the dangers of biking on these narrow, winding roads, when the sun hadn't quite rose and the fog still was so grave. I ignored your warnings, as my desire to enter Kentucky — and leave Virginia — dominated my thoughts.

Not long after we began our ride we entered the "big" city: Elkhorn City that is. We neared in on the town around quarter to eight in the morning, just in time for the children to catch their buses to school. As I biked downhill through the hollows that led to the community's downtown, I saw children standing on the sides of the roads as I might have expected anywhere else in this country. Still, I heard far more children inside their homes rushing to finish their breakfasts and comb their hair. Moms were yelling and I could hear the hustle of both the mothers and their children. It seemed as if today no one awoke on time.

Most of the houses in these hollows were set no more than a few feet off of the road. Driveways, if even present, were gravel or grass. The structures were dilapidated. Most couldn't have been any larger than five hundred square feet. Almost all were poorly constructed out of materials not fit for even a chicken coup. They appeared like run-down bungalows. The siding was falling off. Holes were evident in the exterior walls. Windows were broken and boarded. Front doors didn't close properly. And as I glanced at the yards where I assumed kids played with their friends after school, I noticed that the grass had not been trimmed since possibly the beginning of spring. Many of these houses were located no more than ten feet from the next. The plots of land had to have been no more than a quarter of an acre of land. I could smell poverty.

As I observed the area that surrounded me, I started to become frightened for my safety. Neighbors were yelling at one another. Disputes were occurring in homes between children and their parents. Mothers were screaming like I had never heard before. Road signs were painted over with white spray paint reading "white power."

My heart broke as I thought about the futures of these young, innocent children. I assumed secondary education was a privilege most would never have the opportunity to take a chance at, just as their parents, for the cycle presented to me in that moment seemed inescapable.

Amongst all of the drama that unraveled as I rode into Elkhorn City, I was surprised to meet the people whose paths I crossed there. I say this because as the remainder of the day unfolded I met some of the happiest people I've met in my life, many in downtown Elkhorn City. Elderly men who spent their entire lives here sat together in a group, socializing over breakfast and countless rounds of coffee. The ritual occurred daily.

These men, as well as almost everyone I met today, spoke highly of their community. They weren't looking for change. They liked the way things were. They didn't want to move to a more developed area as they believed that drugs, crime, and chaos were more likely to be evident in cities. They seemed to like the quaintness of their villages.

Jen struggling up a minor climb in Appalachia, May 2008
Photograph taken by Joseph Herbstritt

I can't say I blame them. The scenery in Appalachia really is beautiful.

So, I began to wonder, if given the opportunity, would the residents of Appalachia actually leave, go to college, take a corporate job, or transplant their businesses to a suburb more financially sound?

I can't speculate. But if I had to place money on the question, my bet would be that some would leave and just as many wouldn't. Those who hypothetically chose to leave might want to return later on down the road. Something told me that money wasn't the solitary variable that made these people happy. I figured there must be something more here, whether it was family, a lifetime full of memories or quite simply the tranquility of this part of the country, I cannot be certain. But it unquestionably wasn't money as many of these people live in shacks. I doubt most have ample savings.

There were no buses or subways, no buildings taller than the tallest silo. There was no cell phone reception, so my assumption was these people still use land-lines. Internet was hard to come by and I was made aware of "what people used to do without internet and cell

Abandoned farm in Appalachia, May 2008 ~ Photograph taken by Joseph Herbstritt

phones." People used to go out and take their dog for a walk with their wife at night after work, sit on their back porch swing while staring into the sky at the sunset and engaging in conversation with a neighbor doing just the same. Gossip focused around the events of the day and the recent news of the town, not on that of the tabloids. People went to little league baseball games and county fairs not just because their children were playing or showing animals but because this was entertainment and a form of social connection.

We used to work so we could afford to live. Now, we live to work. People would attend church on Sundays, taking the remainder of the day off as Sundays were a day of rest. Shopping wasn't permitted as malls were not open, and nor was it desired, as time spent together as a family was far more vital. Work, as well, was a sin on Sundays. Nowadays, Sundays are just another opportunity to either work or shop.

Our world has changed immensely and I realize why these people, if given the opportunity, more likely than not probably wouldn't leave. Who knows, I could be wrong, but something tells me I am not. I've heard of people giving up everything they own and moving to Nevada into the middle of the desert, living on some tiny little oasis surrounded by nothing by sagebrush, using generators as their solitary form of power and electricity. I guess this could be a similar concept. Maybe all of these material possessions and white-collar jobs really aren't the answer to the pursuit of happiness.

As I continued to bicycle, I followed poorly surfaced, narrow roads, many with minimal shoulders, along the ridge of the Appalachians through the hollows and down into the valleys, each section often making up a separate community. The cycle repeated itself numerous times. Often, the roads were shaded heavily with over-grown trees pressing onto electrical lines. Tall, dense grass and foliage hit my legs as they pedaled briskly down these exotic roads. I felt as if I were in a jungle as the flora was incredibly thick.

I didn't expect Kentucky to be like this. Instead, I thought it'd be horse-and-ranch country with wealthy men gambling on horses at races, rodeos, and in casinos. I imagined champion ranches where these same horses would be housed. They'd have tall, sturdy, wooden oak fenceposts placed equidistance apart, surrounded by fields of green pasture filled with sufficient grass to feed all of the horses, cows, and sheep in the world.

This section of eastern Kentucky that we traversed through today was far from what I expected. This is a section of our country I probably wouldn't have visited if I'd planned a vacation to Kentucky. If this were the case, I would have certainly gone to Lexington or Louisville, as these are the places you hear about in travel magazines. But I wouldn't have experienced a part of America that I never truly believed to exist. That would have been shameful.

Luckily, our journey today was harmless. We did not have any major accidents; however, I did accidentally run over a black snake toward the end of our ride. I still can't help but ponder how I didn't notice his girth nearing the central yellow line. I'd been avoiding the brim of the road nearly all day as I was paranoid snakes could all too easily be camouflaged within the dense foliage evident here. Cars were rare, so my position never did prove to be problematic, until somehow

I missed this snake directly within my view. While basking in the sun, he must have been veiled in the oil stricken, black pavement beneath my tires. He was at least the width of a half dollar, three-feet long and undoubtedly quick.

Sometimes I think I worry too much about what the hour will bring. Will I know when today will be my last day? Or will it seem just like any other day? I wish you could tell me. Please help me to cease my worrying. There's no way a snake is going to jump out of the grass and bite my legs off. Do snakes even jump?

I've learned a lot during my travels today. To experience people so meek and so humble, I can only hope to one day become as dignified as they are. I wish I would have acquired this knowledge years ago. It's a shame your death had to occur in order for me to recognize so many of my flaws.

As my day came to a close I reflected on the fact that once again I found us lost at least a handful of times. I questioned why I don't give up the GPS and paper maps to an individual far more versed in paleography. I believe we all know the answer. I'm not one to easily swallow my pride.

In any case, I got us lost at least five times today. To my defense, Brad was equally to blame — we are a team. Roads were often poorly marked and quite easy to miss. In these instances, two sets of eyes never did prove to be any better than one. Each time we found ourselves lost, we'd eventually land ourselves in a small town with minimal houses situated directly off the main road and the majority hidden within the hollows. Most of these towns were nearly abandoned with only a small convenience store remaining and very few with even a post office or police station. Schools, playgrounds and grocery stores were absent.

When found in such a predicament, I would ask a local man socializing outside of a convenience store what town we had landed ourselves in and he would predictably say, "Elkhorn City, *Kentucky*," or "Big Hill, *Kentucky*" with the emphasis placed on "*Kentucky*." These people were extraordinarily proud of their state. They were from Kentucky and they would be sure you knew you were now in Kentucky and no longer Virginia. At least, this is how it seemed to me.

In Virginia, if I asked where I was at I would be told "Haysi" or "Catawba," but never "Haysi, *Virginia*." Throughout most of our ride today, I speculate not only were we still very close to Virginia but at times we were also nearing the Tennessee border. Because of this suspicion, I am confident these people were asked quite often by others passing through where they were at and what state the town was located in. The emphasis, therefore, seems to make sense.

In any case, I liked how each said "Kentucky" with that soft southern drawl and was ever so glad to have left Virginia.

It was time to leave a certain piece of me behind. I'm still not sure what piece of me that was — maybe my anger or my animosity. Possibly, it was my sense of bitterness, but it certainly was not my memory of you. Regardless, I am now in Kentucky. I've made it to Hazard, Kentucky, safe and sound on my bike.

In a few short days we'll vacation in Bowling Green, Kentucky. My thought is this area will undoubtedly be horse country. I look forward to seeing a section of the United States more familiar to me, with malls and restaurants, car dealerships, hospitals, and city parks.

For now I will enjoy the surrounding serenity of southeastern Kentucky as I prepare dinner and set up our tent at this lovely rustic campground outside of Hazard.

All my love,

Jen

Appalachian farm with mill, May 2008 ~ Photograph taken by Joseph Herbstritt

Abandoned house, Appalachia, May 2008 ~ Photograph taken by Joseph Herbstritt

Appalachia, May 2008 ~ Photograph taken by Joseph Herbstritt

10. The Dukes
Hazard to Berea, Kentucky

"Believe deep down in your heart that you're destined to do great things."
~Joe Paterno

May 20, 2008

Jeremy,

Hazard, Kentucky, was a booming metropolis compared to the other towns we've biked through over the course of the past eight days. Whereas some of these towns populated only sixty-five people, my guess is that Hazard is home to about 5,000.

A major highway leads to its city limits. Traffic seemed heavy on this highway yesterday. I suspect this was an illusion created by the lack of vehicles passing us by on earlier days. By the time I make it back to Pennsylvania, if ever I do, the Allegheny Mountains will seem like hills compared with the Rockies. This is my hope. Everything in this life is relative.

Within the town a McDonald's sat as well as numerous chain hotels, a post office and courthouse. All appeared to be of recent construction, that, or the structures were just well kept.

Immediately upon our arrival into town I knew I was in the heart of Kentucky. An aroma of fried chicken filled the air. I'd been hoping to purchase some Kentucky Bourbon ever since beginning the trip. Fortunately for me, this town provided quite the opportunity. As I entered the liquor store that presented the most enticing window display of all, I saw in front of me countless brands of this state's infamous bourbon (spoken of course with the emphasis placed on that first syllable: "Ken"). After enjoying the air conditioning for possibly fifteen minutes and engaging in an assortment of small talk with the cashier, I purchased the perfect bottle before continuing on with our tour.

Not too long thereafter I "found" myself slurping down a sublime southern sweet tea inside a McDonald's. The air couldn't have been any more humid outside and I was taking advantage of every opportunity for air conditioning I could get. Plus, I'd been craving a sweet tea ever since I awoke that morning…must have had a glucose deficiency is all I can say.

As we sat in silence watching the people of this community interact, I overheard a few of the locals discussing an imminent thunderstorm. I wasn't surprised. With this information in mind, I paid closer attention to the television set displayed to my left. Indeed, according to the local radar, a storm was fast approaching. With this in mind we quickly headed on our way to our campsite.

(Fortunately, the meteorologist's predictions ended up being just that. Thunder approached but rain was absent all night long.)

Ten miles doesn't go by all that quickly on a bike. At least yesterday it hadn't. So as I traveled farther west (in an attempt to distract my mind), I reflected on a hilly field of alfalfa a few weeks shy of harvest. This "field of dreams" provided me with the premonition that the people housed within this community were harvesting not just alfalfa and bourbon but also aspirations for their futures. At least this was my hope.

At our campsite last night a local couple offered us their already cut firewood, laundry detergent, and an hour's worth of contextual conversation. We talked about Hazard where they both were born and raised and planned to provide the same lifestyle for their nine-year-old son. I couldn't help but inquire if the town's name had anything to do with the fictional Hazzard County, Georgia, where the infamous Bo and Luke Duke raced around in their 1969 Dodge Charger. As soon as I arrived, I felt as if I'd been placed in a scene on that television hit's set.

Just thinking about that show puts a smile on my face. I can see you in the living room, relaxing, lying back in Dad's recliner, watching a re-run with Joe and Stephanie, laughing breathlessly while nearly falling backward inside of that chair. In my mind, the picture is pure bliss.

The couple boasted the same thoughts as mine. They believed a set or two had been filmed here.

I've never been to rural Georgia, but I imagine it to be something like Hazard. I thought for sure I'd see the General Lee somewhere around being chased by Boss Hogg himself, but I would have no such luck. Nor were Joe, Brad or Dad fortunate enough to get a glimpse at Daisy Duke herself in those tiny denim shorts.

I guess we aren't the only ones who were reminded of *The Dukes of Hazzard* by this busy little town as the couple informed me that each autumn there is a "Black Gold Festival" held here. What that event entails, I'm not completely certain. What I do know is that you would have loved it here. Even just the idea of that festival would have brought a smile to your face and made you laugh.

Do I ever just miss your laugh?! Funny how sometimes the smallest things in life, what we often take for granted, when taken away leave behind the biggest scars.

Jeremy, when I awoke this morning I didn't know where I would find myself in eight or twelve hours. I hadn't even the slightest clue. I can't tell you how much I love this feeling of unpredictability.

My life is now a stark contrast from just eight days ago. In Pennsylvania, I knew that when I awoke each morning I would go to work for eight or twelve tiresome hours, eat lunch in the hospital cafeteria — always a salad with Ken's Italian dressing — and go for an eight-mile run after work, always following the same route.

How lame was I?

Now, I have no clue where I'll eat lunch or if I'll even find an open restaurant. Not only do I not know this trivial detail, but I also have no clue where I'll end up sleeping for the night. I don't know who I'll meet or what obstacles I'll be faced with. It's a nice feeling to be able to simply accept situations as they arise and purely exist.

Unfortunately, I'll never be able to do this in regards to your death. I just can't accept that as it is.

My legs are becoming more and more fatigued as the days pass us by. As well, my knees are becoming increasingly sore and I didn't expect my triceps to burn as much as they do. My shoulders: well, they're bulking! According to Brad, Dad, and Joe, I do push-ups twelve hours a day on top of my bicycle. It seems I don't have the best "riding form"!

The scenery hasn't changed much since yesterday. The roads are still narrow and windy. The terrain continues to be very much mountainous. I still feel as if I am in an African jungle or rainforest as the shrubbery is overgrown and considerably dense. Snakes are now abundant on the surfaces of all of the roads. At least for today all of those I noticed had already been run over by others passing by. For me this was fortunate. Of course, I doubt the snakes would have agreed.

The traffic is picking up and I now have to be more cautious. Often the roads have blind spots in both directions due to the density of the forest; therefore, it is pertinent I pay close attention and avoid hugging the center line at all costs. I have to be realistic and acknowledge the prospect of a snake jumping out of the foliage, in an effort to attack and bite me, is highly unlikely.

The towns that we traveled through today were far from urban. Undoubtedly, just as Hazard has, they are becoming more developed but still a far stretch from Chicago, NYC, or even Bellefonte for that matter. Poverty is still a factor.

After biking nearly seventy miles this morning, without stopping for lunch, Brad and I came across Dad and Joe parked at a gas station in a small town named Big Hill. By this time we were starving. Heck, we'd been on the road since shortly after five in the morning and it was now long after one. We might have only had ten more miles until the next possible campsite, but it would have been an understatement to say we were running low on glucose.

Using our best judgment, we joined Joe and Dad for one of the largest turkey sandwiches I think I have ever seen in my life. Truth be told, it cost only $1.67. This sandwich had to have had literally three quarters of a pound of meat on it, and the woman making the sandwich put every condiment and vegetable I asked for on it for no additional charge.

The beauty of this place wasn't the food that was served. Don't get me wrong, it was delicious and dirt cheap; but the experience itself is what I will cherish.

The owner was friendly and talkative. As we sat at a large, wooden kitchen-style table placed awkwardly in the middle of the store in front of the deli section where she prepared our feast, she told us of her life and pondered ours. She wondered about our trip, where we had been to and where we planned on going. She told us stories of other bikers whom she's fed such sandwiches to throughout her days. She was confident we would finish, make it to the West Coast that is...probably more confident than we are.

After lunch I had enough energy to bike those last ten miles to Berea, a fairly large community housed in Appalachia. As we made our entrance into town we passed a number of large developments that reminded me of home. I found that Berea, like State College, is a college town, home to Berea College, founded in 1855 by John G. Fee as a one-room school house.[5] It was named a college in 1869, fostered by abolitionists with a mission aimed toward educating residents of Appalachia.[6]

It made me happy to learn that if one grows up in Appalachia, he or she can attend this school free of charge. It is a four-year university and, in my mind, a great asset to the people of Appalachia. I let out a sigh of relief now knowing that maybe the cycle, which the children outside of Elkhorn City seemed to have been so unjustly placed in, may not necessarily be so unbreakable. Opportunity for them is, after all, not far up the road.

I wonder how our lives would have turned out if we grew up in this section of the country. Would you have attended Berea, or would it have been Penn State? Would you have been a coal miner, or still an engineer?

It is unfathomable how one decision, like the decision Mom and Dad made to move to Bellefonte, Pennsylvania, became the cornerstone for so many of our experiences later on in life. I am happy with the childhood experiences we had, and I wouldn't have wanted to grow up anywhere else with anyone else as brothers, parents, or a sister. I just sometimes can't help but sit and wonder, what if?

Picking out a campsite for tonight turned into an ordeal. We found two campgrounds located almost directly across from one another. The woman from the sandwich shop had suggested one over the other. We couldn't recall her recommendation so we opted for the one closest to our route. This was our *initial* choice.

We purchased our slot and a gallon of milk, then headed to our site. The price was steep: $31, as we were charged $20 for two guests, $3.50 per additional guest, and $4 for milk.

When we saw our site we were immediately discouraged. It was small, covered in dirt and lacking water. Our "permanent" neighbor had attached his camper's hose to our solitary faucet and wasn't about to move it. Furthermore, electricity was absent and our GPS needed charged.

The woman at the sandwich shop stated her recommended campground featured a breakfast bar where one could purchase a large plate of pancakes for no more than $2 a plate. This place didn't offer such and being Dad couldn't pass up this opportunity for anything, we returned to the office with shameful faces and requested a refund. Surprisingly, the woman did give us our money back but only with a sour look on her face, the thought of which still gives me the shivers.

We proceeded across the street with high hopes that this "second chance" campground would meet our needs. If it wasn't suitable we'd be stuck with the side of the road. I could tell by the grin covering Joe's face he was praying for this exact scenario to evolve.

It turns out we made the right decision (in my mind) as this camp-ground was perfect. It was a far stretch from a KOA, but we weren't looking for a KOA. All we wanted was green grass, sanitary water and an outlet to plug our GPS into (and pancakes…for Dad). Once we get out West I have a feeling this type of camping will be considered a luxury. Surprisingly (you might think), I do look forward to that day.

By the time we finally arrived at the suitable campground Brad and I had biked eighty miles on very mountainous terrain. My legs were tired and my right hand was totally numb. As I looked at the sight of my physique in the mirror of the bathroom it seemed incred-ibly obvious biking eight hours a day was taking its toll on my body.

My body is slimming. My skin is dry and my lips are painfully cracked. Although the weather hasn't been all too warm, additionally, my skin is darkening.

I believe I am experiencing an "extreme" case of right-sided acute median and ulnar neuropathy. I am no longer able to cross my fourth and fifth digits and all of my fingers, in general, are now very weak. Stuffing my sleeping bag in the mornings into its compact stuff sack is nearly impossible. I can't stop attempting to cross my fingers. Lately, I've become obsessed with this task. Brad and Joe couldn't be any more embarrassed of me: "Look, I *just* can't do it. Err, they just won't cross!" That's me while repetitively making my best attempt!

Somehow while I'm riding my bike this problem disappears (at least for the moment). I hope this continues to be the case. Further-more, I hope there is a modification that can be performed: whether it is changing the position of my handlebars, double wrapping my handlebars with tape or purchasing a pair of more padded gloves, I hope something solves this problem. (And yes, I've put a lot of thought into this.) Otherwise, my hands will be fairly miserable for the remainder of this trip. More importantly, I'd really like to have use of my hands for the future. A lack of sensation and strength certainly make me worried about the longevity of this, albeit, tempo-rary disability.

In spite of this, I promise you that no matter what I won't quit because of this hindrance. If I have to, I'll learn to ride my bike without hands.

Good luck with that, Jen!

Since my body is slimming, from here on out I've vowed to eat ice cream every chance that I get. As if I need an excuse for the consumption of high-calorie dairy products. I'll be the only one of us who finishes this trip fatter than when she left! This isn't a joke. Seriously, I'm beginning to feel as if I have a food addiction. Every meal that we eat, Brad and I are like bears eating our first meal following a long winter of hibernation.

As I walked around town in search of tonight's ice cream parlor I noticed it is graduation weekend here at Berea College. Twenty-one-year-old students are in town with their parents, dressed in their Sunday best, walking the downtown streets, waiting in line at the finest restaurants, prepared to spend some long overdue quality time with family and friends.

I don't need to state the obvious, but I will. I am jealous of their happiness. *You* should be graduating this month. *I* should be taking *you* out for dinner. *Our* family should be celebrating *your* success.

Throughout all of the pleasure I've found in this trip thus far I can't escape the solitary reason I landed myself here. I'd give anything to turn around and give up all the wisdom I've gained since your death if only I could have you back, even just for a minute.

Under the Kentucky moon, I bow down my head and pray (to whom, I'm not sure) for the presence of a second chance at life in heaven with you by my side. How I wish tomorrow had been a guarantee for all of us back on April 15, 2007.

Jen

Our campsite, Berea, Kentucky, May 20, 2008.

Jeremy splitting firewood, Herbstritt Farm, winter break 2006

11. Bourbon and Sweet Potato Pie
Berea to Bardstown, Kentucky

*"I was brought up to believe that Scotch whisky would need a tax preference
to survive in competition with Kentucky bourbon."*
~Hugo Black

May 21, 2008

Jeremy,

As we biked away from Berea this morning, I told myself to wave goodbye not just to Berea but also to my jealousy. I realize that just because our lives didn't turn out as I had hoped, it isn't the fault of the students of Berea who are celebrating their graduation day. Still, it's hard for me to be happy for them. This will take time to achieve.

As we biked today, the scenery around me demonstrated we'd approached horse country. Here, ranchers mark their land with elaborate signposts (constructed out of fine wood) placed at the entrances to their properties, outlined by sturdy fenceposts. Their horses are elegant, graceful, and strong. Some ran alongside me as I biked today. This was exhilarating. Still, others just stood and stared at the sight of me biking by.

I almost forgot. I actually came across a few men on horseback. They were in fact trotting along down the middle of the road. And yes, they had lassos wrapped in their hands.

The scenery has changed rapidly as the miles have dissipated, so has the atmosphere. I no longer feel as if I am surrounded by poverty. Instead, an aroma of wealth is beginning to surround me. The roads seem to be well kept and the grass has been recently cut. Truly, I've exited the jungle and entered the heartland.

The dogs have still been plentiful but far sparser and much kinder. When they've approached, typically it has all been in good fun. They are playful…

By lunchtime we hadn't biked even forty miles (which tells me we were traveling at an average pace of less than ten miles per hour). I'm not sure if we were traveling this slowly because of my fatigue or my laziness. All I can tell you is that it was *me* holding us back. Brad literally was doing loops around my pitiful self. As a result, Brad and I both figured I could benefit from a calorie-filled lunch. Without much thought, we pulled our bikes (and my body) off the road at the first sight of a gas station.

I couldn't tell you the name of the town we were in. Nevertheless, it was booming with activity. Disregarding this, still we placed our bikes unlocked outside of an open window and ordered our fare. (Possibly, my subconscious hoped Bessie *would* be taken!) For me, it was a turkey and cheese sandwich with chips and a large soda (twice refilled). This has seemed to be my meal of choice lately (not too heavy so as to allow me the ability to continue on with my biking routine absent of nausea and/or diarrhea, yet not too light so as to keep my stomach and muscles content. I must say, the nearly ninety ounces of soda was a bit much).

I purchased a lottery ticket just for the heck of it as I was feeling an aura of luck about me. The ticket cost a dollar and the prize, as it turned out, was just the same. I thought about the sight of me, a young woman who had by now biked over five hundred miles, had showered possibly only twice during the same period of time, been sleeping out of a sleeping bag inside of a tent full of sweat and grime, only with clean clothes on now as I'd washed them last night, now eating lunch at a gas station, scratching off a lottery ticket while keeping an eye on my bike, my now most prized possession. I liked this vision of me. If anyone felt differently, I didn't care.

After a good hour spent in this random town, Brad and I continued on our way, this time traveling at a much faster pace. Thank goodness…at the rate we were going earlier I thought we'd never pull another century.

I've got to say, I blame my fatigue on last night's thunderstorm. I awoke to the sound of thunder around three o'clock this morning only to find myself lying in a four-inch pool of water. After shaking the men violently without response, I darted straight to the Pathfinder where I attempted to fall back asleep upright in the driver's seat (the only open space not covered in musical instruments, bike tools and canned goods). I can't tell you how Joe, Brad and Dad didn't notice their positions in a pool of freezing cold water until awakening this morning.

In any case, as we entered Bardstown only a few hours later, I felt as if we'd entered a large city although I knew we hadn't. I thought aloud to myself, "We've certainly approached *civilization*, whatever that is." Surely, my definition of this word has changed drastically over the course of the past week and a half.

I pulled off of the road to glimpse at our map, looked down at myself, and realized I didn't fit in. I appeared incredibly tattered! Salt covered my skin. And this town certainly seemed classy.

After confirming our location (this time with precise accuracy… for a change), we continued on through Bardstown in the direction of our campground. As we biked, I saw that the McDonald's here boasts free wireless internet. Of course there were numerous chain hotels in the area with this same technical attraction. Yet, I turned down the offer of an expensive yet comfortable, padded, warm bed for the sounds of nature, the smell of fresh air and a sky filled with radiant stars. Who would have thought?

We continued biking through town until we reached approximately the edge of the community. Here, we found our perfect campground: the "Old Kentucky State Park." Our campsite is not exactly primitive as our tent lies directly across from a golf course; however, if I wasn't told of this fact, I wouldn't have known. The scene is serene and I feel exceptionally secluded from all of mankind.

The grass is a perfect hue of green and our site is shaded just enough with exquisite maple trees in full leaf.

We are in the Bourbon capital of the world where fresh air has never smelled better. The entire town smells like sweet potato pie (and this time I'm definitely not hallucinating!). Although I searched high and low for this delicious treat, I quickly learned this aroma is simply the distillery. I love this distinct scent, possibly just as much as I love the smell of fresh iodine! Seriously…

A human's sense of smell is, after all, possibly the most strongly linked sense of all to our memory (or so those old wives say). The association that smell provides with happy memories, people, places and events is enchanting. I know exactly what this town reminds me of. It reminds me of Thanksgiving in November at Grandma Meier's house with you, our cousins, aunts and uncles, back yard football in the snow and warm hot chocolate afterward.

How I yearn to return.

As I exited the shower stall within the public bathroom tonight, I met a woman preparing for bed. She is on a two-week motorcycle tour of parts of the south and Midwest. She "just needed to get away." She is hoping this is her "big break." She didn't specify why and it wasn't my place to pry.

Last night at our campground in Berea I met a woman whose sister committed suicide a year ago to the date. She and her husband up and quit their jobs and are spending the entire summer camping out in the middle of Kentucky trying to "figure things out." Dad spent nearly the entire night drinking beer and socializing with these very fine folk. You should see Joe's footage of Dad, slightly intoxicated, preaching his philosophy on life!

As the miles go by I'm actually beginning to grieve. Your death was a shock; something that was unexpected and seemed far from real from the minute of its occurrence until, honestly, the day that I left on this trip. Sometimes I still can't believe you are gone. Throughout all of this, I've discovered that when the worst possible event that could have occurred in my life actually did, I was able to cope.

There were days that I wanted to jump off a bridge and escape from this world: run away from my misery. There were times when I wanted to scream, kick, and squirm and sometimes I did. Days presented when all I wanted to do was be alone, sit by myself and cry immersed in self-pity. I had my fair share of those. But throughout it all, I've found I am strong enough to continue on, just as anyone else in my shoes would be. I've been given no other choice.

Life is my only option.

Through your death a new life has been born. I can't say I like it, but I'm beginning to learn to live again through the strength you left behind and the miles I've spent on this awfully hard seat. Not just surviving, but living amidst your death, is the most superhuman aspect of this trip.

Life isn't a bed of roses. This never was promised to us. We are not entitled to an unmarred life. No one has such a thing. Even the most perfect of families on the outside have deep secrets embedded within. My jealously has been buried and I will never unleash it, never again.

Jen

Above: Mom and Dad inside Mammoth Cave, May 2008

Below: (left to right), Steph, Joe, Jen, and Brad inside Mammoth Cave, May 2008

12. Vacation
Bardstown to Bowling Green, Kentucky

"Most of the shadows of this life are caused by our standing in our own sunshine."
~Ralph Waldo Emerson

May 22, 2008

Dear Jeremy,

Well, we made it to Bowling Green. We'll be spending the next few days here, relaxing at this beautiful KOA in Bowling Green, Kentucky. And beautiful it is!

The grass blanketing the ground is perfectly green. The sky is clear, and its color strikes a vibrant shade of blue. The grounds are covered with tall, broad trees in full leaf capable of providing ample shade from any weather.

Our lot is gigantic with enough space to fit (I would guess) two large six-person tents. (By the way, we went out and bought a second tent for Mom and Steph's arrival. We couldn't be any more excited for company!) Present also are two lovely handcrafted wooden picnic tables and a circular fire pit with a stack full of already cut dry logs ready to be burnt. (This didn't stop the boys from going out and collecting wood!) Numerous log cabins surround our tent site and the air smells like the Fourth of July at Grandpa Meier's camp.

The ground's bathrooms are a story in and of themselves. Marble countertops shelve brand name, complimentary body washes, shampoos, conditioners, and hand soaps. The showers are spacious and the water is scorching (if one allows it to be). The lighting is state of the art and the flooring is tile. Every aspect of this facility is immaculate.

As we'll be staying here for possibly three nights, I hope I don't obtain the ridiculous expectation that all of our future accommodations will be this luxurious! This certainly won't be the case. And to be honest, I wouldn't want it to be. I think Joe might venture out on an adventure of his own if it were. Stephanie: she'd do the same. Regardless, we are no longer camping primitively, if ever we were. We are in Bowling Green, Kentucky. Horse country!

Today we biked from Bardstown to Sonora where we caught a ride with Dad and Joe farther south all the way down to Bowling Green. Yep, we cheated.

Well, not exactly.

We didn't bike to Bowling Green for a number of reasons. First and foremost, our legs are incredibly fatigued. To further that, Bowling Green is located a distance off of the TransAmerica Trail which, simply put, means it is off our route. We could have mapped out a separate route to get us here via bike but I think the extra mileage might have thrown both Brad and me over the edge (well, at least Brad).

If you could see us now you'd realize we are in dire need of a break from all of this biking.

And the excuses keep on rolling!

Sonora is located at a fork in the road. Here, we could have either continued traveling westward along the trail or journeyed south to this lovely town. Since Mom and Stephanie will be traveling in excess of 650 miles so that Steph can begin biking with us and Dad can go home, we chose this latter option for our meeting point solely because of its proximity to Mammoth Cave. Particularly for Mom's sake we wanted to do something special when they arrived and figured Mammoth Cave would be an exciting place to visit.

There was one kink in our plan. It is Memorial Day weekend and although I am rarely a procrastinator, I waited until the very last minute to book a campground at Mammoth Cave. Obviously, there were no sites available; hence, we are staying here in Bowling Green, located approximately twenty or so miles away. I can't say I mind as this place is incredibly relaxing.

Therefore, to make a long story short, our tentative plan is to resume biking from Sonora once Mom and Dad venture home in, tentatively, three short days.

For the remainder of the day today and all day tomorrow we will rest while awaiting the arrival of Mom and Stephanie. You'll be able to find me sitting in my Crazy Creek chair about two feet from the campfire with a marshmallow stick in my right hand and a Pepsi in my left (possibly soon enough it will be a beer).

I have a feeling this rest will be essential. You must remember Brad and I never previously rode our bikes a hundred miles in a week, let alone in one day (well, actually Brad did ride a century for a college course once, but that is beside the point). Now we have carried on in this fashion for nearly two weeks. It's no wonder our bodies appear to loathe us.

In thinking about our plans for the next few days, I can't help but be nervous about our trip to Mammoth Cave. Although I'm looking forward to it, I'd be lying if I said I wasn't anxious about the entire ordeal. These days, it's not unusual for me to panic when in public settings. In these situations, I'm incredibly hyper-vigilant: constantly looking for someone who doesn't seem to fit in, someone who might be looking to harm someone like me, you, or our family. I guess after what happened to you this behavior isn't all that abnormal. This is what I tell myself.

With this in mind, I'm sure you can imagine how scared I might be in regards to the prospect of willingly being locked underground in the largest, deepest cave in the world along with a group of total strangers. I will go through with this trip. I know that I will. I highly doubt I'll panic publically. Nevertheless, inside of my being I'm certain my heart will be racing and my teeth will be clenching throughout the entire experience.

Just the thought of being underground reminds me of death.

I should be doing what all twenty-six-year-old women do. I'm not sure what that is, but I should be doing it. Thoughts of weddings, children, career goals and sun should be my focus, not death.

More importantly, you *should* be here. Damn it: you *shouldn't* be dead. You were twenty-seven years old, healthy and full of life.

And just like that, it hit me. You actually are dead.

I hate facing the truth. I hate thinking long and hard about your death. To acknowledge you were murdered; your warm but limp body was placed on a gurney, covered in a white sheet, zipped into a black body bag and driven away via an ambulance absent of sirens to a morgue where you underwent an autopsy is undeniably the hardest task I've ever been faced with.

My mind tries to convince me you are in heaven, happy, playing cards with Grandpa, building a bridge, kayaking the swift rapids of the Red Sea and making new friends. All of your sorrows have been erased. Hate doesn't exist where you reside. Violence is eradicated. You are free from this world and all of its associated troubles. I just can't see you there, that's all. Because heaven is a place only the dead can experience.

But the truth is you're dead. Your body is being eaten by maggots. Possibly not yet as you've been laid to rest inside an oak casket as well as a cement vault. But soon enough this utterly grotesque truth will occur. And at that time, you still will be dead.

For the rest of my life, you will be dead.

The nerve of that bastard!

I hope there *is* a hell.

As I'm writing, Joe, Brad, Dad and I are driving around town touring this place. Perhaps their minds are racing with thoughts similar to mine as the silence in this car couldn't be any more profound.

Today's ride might have been lacking in mileage but it certainly wasn't lacking in difficulty. The hills undoubtedly were tough on my quads. Being we exited the Appalachian Mountains a day or more ago, I wasn't expecting the terrain to be as hilly as it was.

Throughout the day I felt as if I were on a constant roller coaster ride, just never creating enough momentum on the downhill sections to make it all the way up to the top of the next hill. Okay, so maybe that's a slight exaggeration. I'm foreshadowing the Ozarks, or will that be the Knobs?

As I sit here, now back at our campsite, taking in the scenery while feeling the warm Kentucky air brush across the skin of my face, I worry these next few days of vacation may interfere with our routine. I've finally become accustomed to riding my bike eight or more hours a day. It may have taken me two weeks to get to this point but somehow I've arrived here.

My average speed may not be anything to brag about: sixteen to twenty miles per hour depending upon the terrain (I'm definitely not Lance), but on the downhill sections I have gone as fast as forty-five miles per hour (what a rush that particular *solitary* experience provided!). On the contrary, on the uphill sections I have gone as slow as three miles per hour. (I know. I could have walked faster. Give me a break; I'm a beginner!)

The point is, my speed is improving and my legs are strengthening. I don't want to ruin such a good thing as what I've began by taking this break. Then again, I don't want to neglect necessary rest.

Rest will do us all good. My soul sure could use a rest.

Over the course of the next few days I will be certain to feed it well. Breakfasts will not be missed. Being that you are your father's son, you'd be horrified to hear that Brad and I haven't eaten an honest breakfast since that morning we left from Yorktown (and well, there was Lexington). We've simply been too tired to fix such a thing.

Dad: he's never eaten better.

We do drink about six bottles of water a day, usually refilling the two we each carry on our bikes at gas stations or convenience stores whenever possible. Most business owners are friendly enough and allow us to fill up our bottles with water and ice free of charge. In exchange, we engage in fun conversation. I tell these strangers about our trip. They tell me about their lives, their families and their community. When Joe and Dad pass us by in the SAG wagon, they almost always offer to refill our bottles as well (almost always is the key phrase here…ha ha).

We snack on granola bars throughout the morning. I think we should have purchased stock in Quaker Oats. And we always eat a decent lunch typically purchased from a local sandwich shop or gas station/convenience store as you've already learned. I like supporting the local businesses and learning about the people of the area. As you know, I'm a people watcher so sitting down, relaxing, and listening to random strangers converse is quite entertaining for me (as long as they don't notice my appearance: at that moment I turn a shameful hue of red).

But we definitely don't eat breakfast, at least not a breakfast you and Dad would consider acceptable. When Mom and Steph arrive I've scheduled for us a date to the local Shoney's breakfast buffet. Now, for that you'd be proud.

Continuing with my random thoughts, about gas stations: Just a few days ago Brad and I ate lunch at a gas station/grocery store/convenience store that doubled as a tanning salon. Indeed, in the back next to the bathrooms sat two modern aged tanning booths. Initially, I thought the sight was a bit bizarre but after I analyzed the situation in depth I decided otherwise.

This town appeared not just desolate but impecunious. If it weren't for the dusty air from coal trucks passing through I doubt I would have had a clue as to where the residents worked. This was a town absent of a gym or even a styling salon. Houses were hidden within the hollows. In retrospect, I don't think I even saw a high school.

Regardless of the quantity of standing structures, this town gave off the charm of a small Midwestern community. The woman working the register knew all of her patrons by name. As the door to the store opened and the bell chimed simultaneously, she called each by name asking if they wanted their "regular." Almost everyone was laughing, joking and gossiping together while patiently waiting for their food to be prepared.

Being that it was packed to the brim with patrons, it seemed most of the locals came to this particular outfit for lunch during their thirty-minute lunch break. Possibly they were looking to obtain only a few minutes of sanity from the constant noise of the factory or mine where I assumed the majority of them were employed. Possibly, they just liked the food. With this former thought in mind, I figured, why not? If tanning over lunch provided them with some form of peace or relaxation, good for them.

Who would have thought one could learn so much about an area by visiting gas stations? Oddly enough, these buildings may be one of my favorite places to visit.

At any rate, as the hours passed us by today, we biked past numerous farms with large fields of alfalfa-filled horse pasture. The area again left off an aroma of wealth, a stark contrast from when we came across that tanning "salon."

This aroma of wealth quickly dissipated once we reached the truck stop. Only about sixty miles from our starting point this morning, Brad and I met Dad and Joe here.

Brad and I sat in the corner of this probably five-to-ten-acre parking lot (covered in cigarette butts) eating packets of peanuts while waiting for the Pathfinder's arrival.

For some reason, I've been reminded of training for our first marathon. Possibly this is because back then you and I were novices at long-distance running. Today, I'm a novice at biking.

When we started our training regime, running more than eight consecutive miles seemed nearly impossible. The same has held true with this bike ride for me. I never would have imagined growing accustomed to riding my bike nearly one hundred miles a day.

You were the person who instilled in me an interest in running. You encouraged me to go out for high school cross country, just as you had.

That marathon: it was two days before Easter in 2005 when I decided *we* were going to run a marathon together that fall. That day I informed you of my plans for *us* to run Scranton in October of that same year. You laughed at my idea and wished me good luck.

Joe and Steph were lucky they weren't yet eighteen, otherwise they would have been in for quite a run that weekend as well.

Nevertheless, when I awoke early Easter morning at Grandma Meier's house dressed in thermal-lined spandex pants, numerous shirts, gloves and a hat, ready to take on the brisk, frigid wind of a north-western Pennsylvania winter and the slick snow covered ground of St. Marys, you were already awake, seated at the kitchen table, fueling up on toasted frozen waffles, ready to face the challenge with me.

We ran fourteen miles that morning, the most we had ever run at one time before that day.

I'll never forget the conversations we had over Easter dinner regarding our morning run. We were incredibly proud of our accomplishment, and we were eating like wolves. We told everyone how far we ran and our goal to finish a marathon in October of that year.

From that point on, we spent every single Saturday or Sunday morning —whichever worked best for both of us depending upon our schedules, the weather, and football — enduring a long run.

During the week we would meet up at night prepared to take on the "Triangle of Death," the "Walmart Loop," "Town-Loop," or another one of our infamous runs. (Only you, Joe, Stephanie, and I knew what the names meant.)

As we trained, our legs became stronger and our endurance increased. Before we knew it, running twenty miles seemed like a walk in the park (okay, so this statement might be a *slight* exaggeration).

In the end, our training paid off.

The marathon was held on a Sunday and, as luck goes, the Saturday prior ended up being the date of the Penn State–Ohio State game. Kickoff was scheduled for eight P.M. at Beaver Stadium. Our team looked solid that season, and this game was anticipated to be the deciding measure as to whether or not we'd go all the way and be named Big Ten Champs.

Jeremy after finishing his first marathon, Scranton, Pennsylvania, October 2005
Photograph taken by Stephanie Herbstritt

You couldn't have been any more disappointed regarding the idea of missing that game in person.

Kindly, you didn't back out on *my* plans for *us*.

We left for Scranton late morning that Saturday, checked into our hotel room around noon, and then attended the pre-race pasta dinner where we met fellow runners and engaged in racy conversation while consuming some of the most spectacular pasta, bread, salad, and chocolate fudge brownies I think either of us had ever tasted. (It was a wonder we were able to lift ourselves out of bed the following morning, let alone run.)

Following dinner we returned to our hotel room. It was a Howard Johnson located no more than two blocks from where we were to load onto a bus the following morning to be transported to the start some 26.2 miles away.

Soon enough, I prepared for bed.

You: for the game.

You watched that entire game, cheering loudly and becoming excited about what seemed was going to be, and did end up being, one of the biggest upsets in the history of college football (at least in our minds).

I planned on going to bed early that night but by the time half-time rolled around I gave up on this prospect. Your enthusiasm was contagious. Plus, there was no way I was falling asleep amidst the intensity of your cheers. What kind of Penn State fan was I anyway?

The people in the room adjacent to us surely didn't sleep well that night either. Those walls were thin.

We finished that race the next day just as we'd expected.

I hope they did, too.

You ate a donut and drank a beer around mile twenty-five. I sipped chicken noodle soup at the finish. (The air was incredibly cool, if you recall.) Neither of us could step off of that four-inch curbed sidewalk, which led to the road and Brad's Jeep (or was it the red Jeep?) after the race was completed due to the pain in our quadriceps. Proof of such is captured on Joe's videotape.

I got a free massage after that race. You made it to the local donut shop a half-mile down the road and purchased a dozen.

I enjoyed sitting around the house, doing nothing for the days following that race. You had no choice but to return to school. I remember your jealousy over my sitting aimlessly at home recovering with such great ease (given my state of unemployment).

Shortly after we recovered, we began training for our next marathon — your last...our last together.

I miss running with you.

I miss training with you.

I simply miss you.

It isn't fair that you're gone.

I yearn deeply for your smile and I would give anything to hear you laugh just once again, anything!

I miss you immensely.

My big brother was supposed to be the uncle of my children. He was supposed to run many, many marathons with me over the course of his lifetime. He was to exchange gifts with me on Christmas, at least until one of us died of old age. He wasn't supposed to be murdered at twenty-seven.

You *should* be here.

It's obvious that the Appalachians have certainly strengthened my legs. But no amount of mental strength could lessen the pain of your loss.

As the shock of your death unfolds, sadness arises. To compensate for this sadness, I'm holding onto a fairy tale.

When I get to heaven, if it even exists, the two of us will run together just like we used to. I bet the hills there are splendid. The grass must be long, a matchless shade of green in the spring and golden in the summers. Surely, the water is warm, but refreshing, of course. And fatigue, we'll never be faced with it.

After our first long run together, set in that incredible stage set in heaven, we'll dive into an immensely deep lake and just tread water for hours while the wildlife passes us by.

Then, after the hours have escaped us, we'll mosey along slowly down a shaded gravel road to the *Twin Kiss* and eat us some soft serve. And if somehow you forgot: it's the best ice cream shack ever on earth. You'll have either a hot fudge sundae or a banana split, possibly both. With the flavor, your memory will return. I'll have a large cone of peanut butter flavored soft serve. This flavor is so incredibly hard to find here on earth. In heaven, it will be ample, yet I'll never get sick of its taste.

From here, we'll head on home where our family will be waiting up patiently for our arrival.

We'll all be together forever. Nothing bad will ever happen, ever again.

Jeremy, I'd trade places with you in an instant if only that were possible. Honestly, I would. You deserve a second chance at life.

Then again, then you'd have to experience the same pain in which I am experiencing. That wouldn't be fair either.

These are my thoughts — thoughts consumed by grief.

I am so terribly sorry.

The events of today could be summed up as a twenty-six-year-old woman on a roller coaster ride of rolling hills in the heart of western Kentucky, covered in a blanket of long, flowing green grass not big enough to hide her emotions, which are spinning out of control. She's gaining physical strength but her mind is constrained.

I've found my Achilles' heel.

If you exist, please be my strength.

Jen

13. The Knobs of Kentucky
Bowling Green, Kentucky to Cave in Rock, Illinois

"Life is like a library owned by the author. In it are a few books which he wrote himself, but most of them were written for him."
–Harry Emerson Fosdick

May 25, 2008

Jeremy,

We spent the last few days relaxing at our campsite, sitting by a campfire at night, enjoying mountain pies and s'mores while telling tales of our trip.

While the rest of our group slept in daily, Dad woke up at the crack of dawn only to make his two-mile long walk down the road to the Waffle House for his favorite, french toast. Only our father!

Bowling Green was tremendously fun, quite relaxing I must say, but by the arrival of this morning I was ready to return to our bicycling routine. And to think, I worried I wouldn't want to return!

You may be interested in knowing why Dad came along on this journey. Yes, of course, he wanted to get away. But why didn't he and Mom go on a trip of their own?

The question is a good one. The answer to it requires a tremendous amount of background knowledge. Perhaps you already know this information. Possibly even the answer to this question you already know. Regardless, I will explain. If nothing else, writing this explanation will be therapeutic for me.

After your death, I didn't know what to expect. None of us did. Obviously, I'd never experienced the death of a loved one so close to me and so young, so abrupt, unexpected, senseless, and violent. I didn't know what would happen to Mom and Dad nor did I know what to expect in respect to my own feelings or those of our two other siblings. I didn't know if any of us would ever be able to return to work or to school, if we'd be able to enjoy minor aspects of life ever again, if one would attempt suicide, or if Mom and Dad would divorce. I couldn't fathom the next minute of my existence, let alone thirty days down the road.

Prior to your funeral, for nearly ten days our childhood house was filled with guests. They remained present even throughout the night. But when we came home following your funeral, no one was there. Our house was so silent I could have heard the drop of a pin (that is, until Mom spent the last hour of that day throwing every single solitary dish she owned up against the wall...*that* hour was loud). The phone stopped ringing, out-of-town guests returned home, and packages ceased to be delivered at our doorstep. The chaos of our daily lives slowed to a halt almost instantaneously, leaving us alone solely to ponder your death.

This setting didn't last long. On that particular day, the community felt we *needed* to be alone with one another, take a break from all of the commotion and just allow reality to settle in. The following day guests returned in multitudes.

Still, very quickly after your funeral all of our lives made a drastic turn for the worse. It's no wonder. Although we had company, truly all we had left were our thoughts and the reality of your death. Your soul had left (rather abruptly I might add), and we each felt stuck in a world filled with nothing other than violence, sorrow, uncertainty, and senselessness. None of us had yet returned to work or school so we spent each and every single solitary minute together, yet alone, in the same 1,500-square-foot box.

From the beginning, Mom and Dad were grieving in contrasting fashions. They were both struggling, as were all of us, but each was unable to lean on the other for support. Their anger was too strong, and often directed toward one another.

They honestly believed they could have prevented your death. I guess this is how parents think. All throughout our lives Mom and

Dad were accustomed to protecting us. Even though your death was out of their hands, in their minds they didn't protect you and that's why you were dead. Your death was *their* fault. Dad should have been there in Blacksburg to tell you to skip class. *He* should have been there to stop the killer *himself*. Mom should have bought you a plane ticket to Boston. *She* should have taken the batteries out of your alarm clock.

They should have known.

These statements may seem irrational to an outsider but not to those whose hearts and minds struggle to accept the unthinkable.

From the beginning, in respect to the grieving process, Mom and Dad were on different ends of the spectrum. At first, Dad was very verbal. He was often found talking about you and your death, not just to his friends and our neighbors, but also to the media, politicians, and family members of others who were killed that terrible day. We had visitors knocking at our front door constantly. Dad talked to every one of them who stopped by. The conversations held were lengthy and descriptive. He was thankful for the kindness and empathy of any soul who would listen to his heavy words.

During this phase, additionally, he was very angry. Fortunately (for us) his anger focused mainly on your killer and the administration of the university.

Throughout the first few weeks Dad held strong onto his faith. It seemed he held on because he felt this was his only means of getting to you. He believed you were in heaven, and if he were to be reunited with you one day in paradise he need not let go of his faith; so said the priests. More than anything, he didn't want to miss out on this opportunity. This was all he had left. It was all any of us had left.

He remained active during this initial phase, taking walks regularly and often going for a jog. Running made him feel close to you. His hygiene remained good. He ate well, brushed his teeth and showered regularly. I feel as if I am talking about a child, but if you take into account what came later, you'll understand why.

As I'm sure anyone experienced with grief could have predicted, this *initial* phase was short lived. Sooner than people stopped visiting our house regularly, Dad turned into a totally different human being, someone I'd never before met. We all changed, but Dad's behavior changed drastically.

When people would visit, he no longer had any desire to engage in conversation. "They can't understand. They're only looking for personal gain."

His anger escalated to the point where he started to yell at me, Mom, our siblings, his doctors, and even strangers. I worried for him and the rest of us. In my mind, this was no way to live.

He agreed. He wanted out.

We all wanted out.

Dad's experience ended up being described by professionals as more than just "typical" grief. I'd have to counter that statement with: *your death was not "typical."* People have a better chance of being struck by lightning than being murdered in a classroom.

I watched Dad closely as the events that took place in that house became my entire life. As I watched him, I realized he felt he didn't deserve the right to a break: a break from the pain, a laugh, a chuckle or even a smile. His philosophy on his new life quickly became: what *you* could no longer have, *he* no longer deserved.

He couldn't and wouldn't allow himself to enjoy life. He stopped eating. Heck, he even stopped drinking water. He lost a tremendous amount of weight. Before we knew it we were looking at a skeleton.

I didn't return to work for six weeks following your death simply because...well, I couldn't. I was that distraught. How could I have?

I didn't fail to return to work earlier because I was too lazy or because I felt entitled. I simply could not. Showering was a chore in and of itself, and carrying out the particular responsibilities of my work at that time would have been practically impossible. My mind simply could not focus.

When I did return, it was just about the time Dad became miserably depressed.

Joe and Stephanie had withdrawn from school for the semester or had asked for extensions on their work. We were all scared for anyone to return to school. When things worsened substantially, I was relieved that Joe and Steph no longer were in school. I figured, at best, they could keep their eyes on Mom and Dad while I was at work.

Surprisingly, when I did return to work I was able to function. At first, this was very difficult but eventually the task became easier. I simply put on a mask: yes, a mask.

It was as if I pretended you were away: away at school. Others would offer me their condolences and I would simply smile and say thank you. Immediately, I changed the subject. I wasn't affected.

At home, almost always I was busy "holding down the fort." I didn't have time to digest the reality of your death. I had to focus on Mom and Dad, their health and getting their lives back to normal.

Or so I thought.

I perceive this is what Mom has done since the date of your death. She keeps her mind occupied, never allowing herself sufficient time to think, or at least time to think all too intently. When she does, it is plainly too painful. She occupies her days with work, gardening, Bible study and walks with the neighbors. She will babysit the neighbor kids at the drop of a hat just to remain busy.

Mom does put on a good front to the eyes of the public but I can see her pain in her face and it's evident in her eyes. She has aged significantly since the day of your death. We all have.

I think in some regards Mom has fared better, at least on the surface, when compared with Dad because she has grown accustomed to living in a state of, not necessarily denial, but avoidance, or preoccupation with other activities.

Because all along Mom was living in this state of avoidance, she simply couldn't take the behavior that Dad displayed. Almost immediately after your death she wanted out. She wanted to forget everything. She didn't want any reminders of your absence or even your existence. It was all too painful for her. Therefore, with Dad being a constant reminder of your death she wanted him out. She filed for divorce not much more than a month after you were killed. Thankfully, the lawyer she trusted had enough common sense to encourage her to wait, possibly even a year, before filing such permanent papers.

She waited.

Still, not too long thereafter she actually moved out of the house during the middle of the night. She just needed *out*. If she wasn't married, then she didn't have her children. And if she didn't have her children, then none of them could be dead.

Her pain was (and still is) horribly immense.

She began sleepwalking shortly after your death. In doing so, I worried she would self-medicate and accidentally kill herself. At the time, she was ingesting large dosages of anti-anxiety medications. She was not weak but her burden was heavy. I worried for her safety just as much as I worried for Dad's.

We were all losing our minds. We were not professionals and none of us knew what to do in the situation we'd been placed in. We were trying our best. Mom and Dad quickly sought out help. Both saw a therapist as well as a psychiatrist.

I took our siblings to therapy hoping somehow I'd be able to erase their pain. This idea was naïve as I now know we each have to individually work through the pain death has brought to us.

Once Mom and Dad started seeing professionals, I was constantly interrupted while at work with notifications and updates as to their progress. Their physicians kept a very close eye on both of them and constantly were checking with me to make sure their stories corresponded correctly with mine. I felt triangulated.

"Yes, Mike is taking his medications."

"Yes, Mike is telling the truth."

"Yes, Peg did this."

I was like the gate-keeper, a role definitely not therapeutic for me.

Throughout all of this chaos, I went through all of the stages of grief myself. Heck, I went through each at least a dozen times.

Along the way I searched high and low for accountability, something I now realize I'll never be able to achieve. The one who committed your murder took his own life, the coward. The administration, who allowed this individual to remain a student at the university even with all of the obvious red flags, denied making any mistakes.

All I wanted was an apology. I just wanted someone to admit they did wrong, that they were negligent. It seems I'll never get this, not even through a lawsuit or settlement, for in our society there are those who think only of themselves. They want to protect only themselves and those related to them in some personal context. They don't care about you or me. Their hearts are stone.

It is hard to escape the anger. I think this stage of grief will remain with me for quite some time. Anger is the opposite of peace and tranquility. Even when and if I come across some form of peace, for now, it seems that the anger will never escape me, at least not totally.

In the end, after months of treatment, Dad was able to return to work. He is now able to function.

And Mom moved back home. She's coming to terms with the fact that you are gone. She no longer walks in her sleep, and, as well, she is now back to working full-time.

The following autumn after you passed, Joe and Stephanie returned to school. Now, we're on a trip to take back our lives, to grieve, and experience something you didn't have the opportunity to experience.

Of course, Dad didn't just come on this trip to take back his life, or to honor you. He was scared of what might happen to us. You see, he still thinks he has control over our fates. He's a parent. This is how they think.

His presence in my car for the first two weeks of this trip allowed him to gain the necessary confidence his mind required to know we'll all be okay. The last thing our parents want is to lose another child.

Thus far, this trip has given me an escape. It has been my opportunity, for once, to focus solely on me and my relationship with you.

It's been my ticket to freedom; yours too.

All along, I've worried you won't be able to rest until all of us left here on this earth are able to lay our heads down at night and experience some form of peace, whatever that is. I'm hoping this trip enables me to find this peace.

Every mile I bike is for you. I wish your legs still worked so you could pedal alongside me. I wish your heart could still beat and your eyes could still blink. But they can't, so this will continue to be my dedication to you.

It's the best I have to give.

I'm so glad Dad chose to join us. Throughout these past few days I've seen him laugh more than I've seen him laugh in the past year. He's been comical, that's for sure. As I've said before, as he ages he just gets goofier and goofier.

Last night he drank a few too many beers with our campground "neighbor." This kid reminded me too much of you. He couldn't have been much older than you were when you died. He was on his way to somewhere in the Midwest for an interview at a university I can't recall the name of. He is hoping to be hired as the head swim team coach there. On his way out he decided to spend a few days camping, alone, here in Kentucky; wanted to "clear his head."

While we all sat around the campfire, I slowly became intoxicated by the smell of the grain that everyone else was consuming.

Amongst the starry sky, we shared both humorous and serious stories of our lives. Dad and this young man did most of the talking. The rest of us primarily listened and laughed.

Dad told us all the story of how he met Mom. It was a softball game: second base. Guess she was a home run!

I'm pretty sure if Dad would have had any more to drink we all would have learned how and where each of us was each conceived.

Needless to say, this morning came early. Still, I was ready to return to my biking routine. Steph couldn't have been any more excited to begin her own journey. I've never seen her get out of bed so abruptly!

The plan for today was to make it to Illinois. Our destination was to be a small town situated west of the Ohio River called "Cave in Rock." The highlight of this village was supposed to be a large, fifty-some-foot wide and slightly deeper cave made out of rock situated along the Ohio River. Supposedly, bandits used it as a hideout back in the day. I'm sure kids today use it in just the same manner.

As I fastened the Velcro on my shoes and said my goodbyes to Mom and Dad, I wondered what events the day would bring.

The scenery our ride provided was enchanting. We passed through mainly fields of green pasture surrounded by white picket fences.

The hills certainly were rolling, and (in all honesty) quite fun to attempt. As each hill approached, I approximated the speed that would be required to arrive at the top of the next. I'd sprint down the hill as fast as I could building up my momentum; yet, only a few times being able to make it all the way to the top of the next without having to put up a fight. This game kept my mind busy and although my body was tired I was in shock when I glanced down at my watch and noticed the time. It was three o'clock in the afternoon.

Just as I was doing so I saw a road sign for Providence, Kentucky.

Somehow I thought Providence sounded like it should be situated within the Bluegrass Region of Kentucky where the hills are barely rolling and the terrain considered desirable for armies to traverse through back during the days of the Confederacy. But no, Providence is in the Knobs, a region that forms a horseshoe-shaped band on my map around the desirable Bluegrass Province.[7] The term "knobs" is a perfect description of this area as the terrain is made up of a continuation of very steep conical-shaped hills. They are physically challenging, to say the least, but fun for a few rounds. After that? Well, even while I was cursing the word knob, I knew their place in my journey would increase my strength both physically and mentally. I feel sorry for any soldiers who had to endure such brutal terrain!

When I looked down at my watch and noticed the time, I realized we were supposed to have met Joe for lunch nearly three hours prior in another town. We were all starving and figured Joe had eaten by himself a long time ago. We pulled off the road and took out our maps to analyze our exact location. Indeed, we had passed our meeting point with our brother. Once again we had found ourselves lost — I wondered if I'd ever gain a clear sense of direction.

Unquestionably, the Knobs were consuming all of my energy. My legs were starting to quiver and my head was quickly becoming a bit fuzzy. There was a gas station located across the street from where we had stopped. Quickly we walked our bikes over in search of a calorie-filled meal.

We had biked over one hundred miles in less than six hours, yet, we had somewhere between thirty and forty more to go if we were to make it to the Ohio River by nightfall.

I called Joe and requested his arrival, and encouragement.

Soon enough, he arrived catching us off guard. Mom and Dad were still by his side. This morning when we left I was under the impression they'd be heading home shortly after our departure from Bowling Green.

I was in the middle of thinking that the bite of pizza in my mouth quite possibly might be the precise definition of providence, the name of the town we were in. Its crust was thin and the grease on its surface was excessive. It was just what I needed after all that biking.

Soon enough, I learned that our parents planned on spending another night with us. Mom's anxiety was heightened at the thought of leaving us all alone "out in the wild." Dad couldn't resist.

The last ten miles of the ride that followed were simply spectacular. On my GPS I was able to see water ahead of me for all of those ten miles. The grade of the road was somewhat downhill, traversing on a slightly windy, perfectly shaded path. I watched cows to my left graze in lush meadows and saw strong men on horses trotting along the side of the road with lassos wrapped around their backs. I even saw a few deer cross the road in the distance.

The sight was really magical.

Although the arches of my feet were sore, and it felt as if I were pedaling with glass in my cleats, even though my skin was stained with grains of salt, and it seemed I'd never be able to unclench my hands from the fisted position — I felt as if I were in heaven.

I've never seen beauty like this before in my life.

Time passed by all too quickly and soon enough we arrived at the ferry.

Never before had I ridden a ferry.

We were the lone bikers present on that boat. The rest of the passengers were traveling either by car or by motorcycle. I couldn't have been happier to have been on my bike on top of that body of water in that moment in time. My body was beat.

As the ride progressed a number of tourists got out of their cars and posed for pictures just as we'd been doing.

I stood at the edge of the boat holding onto the railing staring off into the distance at the picture presented to me: a cave in a rock. It didn't appear more than fifty-some-feet wide just as the brochures I'd read stated. Simple it was: yet, it appeared to be a sight to see.

I had looked forward to going inside the cave all day long, but now my desire to do so vanished. I was swallowed by exhaustion. I decided that as soon as I exited the ferry I would go directly to my tent and fall immediately asleep. A sleeping bag had never sounded as comfortable as then. This was the longest I'd biked in one day in my entire life: 140 miles. And the terrain hadn't been easy.

To my dismay, although my body was drained, once we arrived at our campsite my mind was all too alert to sleep. Therefore, sleep didn't come easy that afternoon. Instead, I ended up spending the remainder of the day touring the cave with our family and eating like a glutton just as I had planned initially.

Providence: "divine guidance or care: God conceived as the power sustaining and guiding human destiny."[8] I wonder if it truly exists outside of this earth. I hope that it does, as this is the only explanation that keeps my tears from falling like rain.

The calm of my sleeping bag is finally ecstasy.

Love,

Jennifer

Jennifer and Brad, crossing the Ohio River, May 26, 2008

Jennifer, just as we crossed the Ohio River and entered Illinois, May 26, 2008
Photograph taken by Brad Updegrove

Steph and Jeremy, Joe's high school graduation, June 2006. Two peas in a pod!

Jen and Steph: sisters by chance, friends by choice

14. Southern Illinois
Cave in Rock to Murphysboro, Illinois

"The whole of life is but a moment of time.
It is our duty, therefore to use it, not to misuse it."
~Plutarch

May 26, 2008

Jeremy,

*T*oday *a new chapter in this bike trip began: we started our journey across southern Illinois.* When Mom and Dad left this morning, Stephanie remained; a crucial crew member necessary to rightfully complete this voyage took saddle with us.

Two weeks ago, she despised me.

Two months ago, the feeling was mutual.

Yesterday, as the two of us took our first strides together I didn't know what to expect.

Our family never was perfect. We all had our quarrels. Oftentimes as human beings we say some of the meanest and cruelest statements to the people we love because we know they will forgive us, no matter what we say. This doesn't mean the behavior is acceptable. I am embarrassed to say that I remember saying some tremendously nasty statements to you, Jeremy. I remember getting angry at you for, more likely than not, something trivial and then screaming at you uncontrollably: "I wish you never existed!" "I wish you were dead!" "I divorce you as my brother!"

You would just laugh and say "Fine."

Siblings: Stephanie, Jeremy, Jennifer, and Joe

You and I both know, we all had our fights but in the end they were nothing more than petty disputes. None of us ever stayed angry with a sibling for very long at all.

In fact, the four of us got along incredibly well. We each had our own friends but, in a sense, we were each other's best friends. Not all families are like this and we were very fortunate to be so close to one another as we were. You and I cared for Joe and Stephanie not just as siblings but almost as parental figures as well. We took care of them, looked after them, and stood up for them. Despite our age differences, if we planned a trip to Holiday Valley for a day of skiing we made sure to include one another. The same held true for dinners at Bonfatto's, weekend road trips, runs around town and weight lifting at the YMCA. Of course we did things with our own individual friends, but more often than not we did things as a family.

Because I took on the role of the "problem solver" when you died, I created unnecessary drama between Stephanie and me. At the time she had just turned eighteen. I remember being that age. The summer following my senior year of high school I moved into the dorms at Penn State and wanted nothing to do with our parents. I wanted to be an adult. I wanted to do things for myself: pay my own bills, buy my own groceries and set my own curfew. If I'm going to be completely honest here, primarily all I wanted was to set my own curfew! Like all other kids just out of high school, I wanted both freedom and responsibility. It wasn't that I didn't love our parents. I just wanted to grow up. I was done being a child.

When you died I wanted to know in my heart that Stephanie and Joe were going to be alright. The pain your death created was too intense for me to handle — I was using every ounce of energy I had available in order to simply pretend to function, and I wasn't coping very well. I put on a stoic mask for the public, including our family, but my heart knew the pain it felt.

Because I knew how difficult it was to function, I worried for our siblings' sanity. For some bizarre reason, I felt that because I was older I should be stronger, more able to cope, and more competent in my position as big sister. It became my self-appointed duty to make them well. I wanted nothing other than to take their pain away, and mine too.

I brought them to therapy. I pressured them to return to school. School would bring normalcy, or so I thought. I attempted to persuade them not to get tattoos when they wanted to put your initials on their arms. Selfishly, I worried they might contract a communicable disease during the process of having ink injected beneath their skin. I didn't want to lose another sibling. I now know I should have simply smiled and nodded when they presented the idea to me. They are very competent at making decisions on their own. They got the tattoos anyway and they love them. Now I realize that their presence has engraved a permanent piece of you in them forever.

The worst decision I made after your death was when I allowed Stephanie to move in with Brad and me. It was the end of the fall semester 2007. Christmas break was soon approaching and Dad was about to be discharged from a stay in the hospital. Stephanie (a freshman at Penn State at the time) was having a difficult time feeling comfortable in the dorms. Therefore, she didn't want to return to the dorms for the spring semester. Yet, she wasn't sure where she would live. Living with Mom and Dad was not an option, as our parents' marriage was unstable as they worked through their grief. It was not the best environment for our little sister.

Therefore, instead of encouraging Stephanie to get an apartment of her own, I didn't just allow her to move in with us, I encouraged her to do so. And when she moved in I became incredibly nurturing. On the surface this might have seemed to be exactly what she needed but the truth is it wasn't. Along with the character of nurturer came "parental Jen." And we all know where this story is heading...

I chauffeured Steph to class, made her dinner nightly, bought her groceries, scolded her when her grades were poor — and when she didn't eat enough for dinner, was out too late, was watching too much TV, etc. — and demanded she be in at specific hours of the night.

Now Steph had gone to college to obtain exactly what I had been looking for eight years prior. But what she got was a second mother.

Not only did my behavior aggravate Steph but Mom also became jealous. It was *her* job to take care of Steph, not mine. Her resentment toward me couldn't have been any more evident.

I plainly had forgotten how to be a big sister.

As I should have expected, Steph started to loathe me. And I do mean loathe. Not more than six weeks after she moved in, she abruptly moved out of our house and back home with Mom and Dad. She told me she didn't want anything to do with me, and avoided me at all costs. I had become a third parent, and she no longer could confide in me as a sister and friend.

Then, Stephanie started to struggle in school. Eventually she asked, and I consented, to her moving back in with us. I should have said no. I knew allowing her to return to my apartment would inevitably destroy our relationship. But I wanted to fix her. So I let her move back in, and eventually things once again deteriorated between the two of us.

Things were far from perfect between Stephanie and me when I left for this bike trip on May 12. I'm pretty sure she still despised me. Her reasoning was legitimate so I cannot say I blame her. Despite all of this, Steph still wanted to come along with us on this trip. She wasn't just willing to come along, she *wanted* to come along: for you, her, me, our family, and our futures. Possibly she also just wanted to feel included.

I want to get along with her. My heart tells me she feels the same. We both know better than most people in this world that life isn't predictable. Just because someone is here today doesn't mean they'll be here tomorrow.

You and I got along great. Of course I have some regrets regarding our relationship, but overall I'm happy with the bond you and I had.

It is a misconception that when a person dies the rest of the family that remains comes together. This doesn't always happen and in our family it certainly didn't. We might have been close before, but since your death we have fallen very much apart.

Yesterday, it was nice to have Stephanie along for the ride. I hope we can find peace between one another throughout this journey. Please help us to do so if you can.

Last night it poured.

There is not an ounce of our camping gear that is not drenched from one wicked thunderstorm. It consisted of some of the loudest thunder I've heard and the closest lightning I have seen in my entire life. Although the cave was lovely, I can't lie to you, the thunderstorm was the highlight of this town, so fittingly named Cave in Rock, for me! If I'd been smarter I would have slept in that cave.

The winds had to have been over fifty miles per hour, and we were camping out in an open field in the middle of it all. I slept, if you can call it that, with my Noah weather radio clenched to my side all night long. I wanted to be the first to know if a tornado warning was issued so that I could run immediately to the concrete building situated about a half mile away from our tent (uphill, I might add) where the bathrooms resided. I felt this would be the safest place to be in such an event.

It has been years, and by years I mean over a decade, since I last witnessed a storm this intense, so please do not laugh. As a child you always loved to sit out on the front porch and watch storms, as did I, but the difference between the two of us was that when a tornado warning or severe thunderstorm warning was issued I would run down to the basement and calculate over and over again in my head the probability of it hitting our house. Whereas you would continue to sit on the porch, swaying back and forth fearlessly on our wooden swing while staring intently into the sky. Throughout all of this your excitement would build. You simply couldn't wait for the storm to arrive.

Throughout our trip Joe has been our storm chaser. He can't wait to witness our very first tornado. Being around him during a storm is like watching an intense scene in the Weather Channel's hit *Storm-chasers.*

Last night's storm continued until late in the morning today. Because the rain was so heavy and the lightning appeared so close in our view we actually didn't start biking until close to noon. Instead, we ate a delicious breakfast at a diner operated by the park service which, as well, operates the campground/open field where we stayed last night. Because of our late start to the day we didn't arrive in Murphysboro until late this evening.

As we traveled today, I was astonished to find that southern Illinois's terrain remained very similar to that of western Kentucky's. I was certain once we left the Knobs of Kentucky the terrain would flatten but I was mistaken. Once again, I found myself on a roller coaster ride throughout the day.

Although the terrain was very similar to yesterday's, the scenery was very much different. Whereas yesterday we biked through horse country, today we biked through the Shawnee National Forest.

Yesterday we passed by a number of golf courses and empty fields of eloquently rolling green pasture. Today, we biked on roads surrounded by a multitude of trees, some appearing as if they could touch the heavens above.

Ranching was yesterday's prime occupation. Logging seems to be southern Illinois' industry of choice, grossly evident by the number of logging trucks that crossed our paths as we biked. Throughout the ride, I had to keep my focus placed steady on the road so as to avoid misplacing myself amongst the path of a rapidly traveling eighteen-wheeler log truck.

As we traveled through the Shawnee National Forest we unexpectedly met up with our friend Jesse. We had assumed he'd passed us by a few days ago while we were in Bowling Green, Kentucky. Because we took so much time off from biking we weren't sure we'd see him again, as his mileage seems to be comparable with ours. Luckily, our paths crossed today. In the middle of the forest he was assisting a friend who had fallen victim to a flat.

Jesse is a very outgoing and personable individual who seems to be making an effort to experience everything there is to experience throughout this long ride: from meeting other bikers to meeting the local members of each community; from eating the local cuisine to touring and experiencing the sense of community present in each small town.

I read Jesse as a genuine soul and a reminder that there is still good left in this world. He doesn't seem to care about status, class, religion, or race. He appears easy-going, good-natured, funny, empathetic, and willing to lend an extra hand at the drop of a hat. I have only met this man a few times in my life and yet am able to draw all of these details about his character. I am happy to have met such a very fine person. Dad calls him an angel. He reminds me of you.

Jesse, his friend, and our group rode our bikes together for a few miles and then parted our separate ways.

After we waved possibly our last ever farewells to one another, we continued on with our travels westward toward Murphysboro.

Most of the areas we traveled through up until our entrance into Carbondale, located only eight miles east of Murphysboro, were very rural. I saw few homes, businesses, or even people for that matter. But once we reached Carbondale a bike path arrived and people were present.

Upon entering Carbondale's city limits, I knew our ride for today was drawing to a close. We took some time to tour the town's university, Southern Illinois. Although the campus was very different from Penn State's, Carbondale reminded me of State College. I thought of Murphysboro as Bellefonte, a "suburb" of Carbondale.

As I rode my bike toward Murphysboro I was reminded of home. We are nearly a third of the way across the United States, yet somehow I am only now reminded of home. It makes me sad to think that throughout this journey I haven't seemed to miss home in even the slightest fashion. And even now I don't miss it. I've just been reminded of its existence, that's all.

Home used to be a place of comfort and joy. Happy memories were formed there. Holiday traditions were shaped there. And no matter how bad life got, I could always return knowing those I loved most would always be there...

Those last eight miles flew by rather quickly. In no time at all, we arrived in Murphysboro.

When we entered the city limits I thought about the potential this town seemed to possess. It appeared like the All-American town: a great place to raise a family, and a fun place to grow up in — one of those places where, as a child, you could ride your bike with all of your neighborhood friends down the middle of the road or set up a friendly game of inline street hockey at the end of your block and no one would disturb you. Your mom could be confident of your safety. Backyard fences were formed only to keep children of a young age in, not to keep distance from neighbors.

Murphysboro is located adjacent to the Shawnee National Forest. The road that we followed through this forest today was beautifully covered by a canopy of trees. I couldn't help but be reminded of the presence of time as I biked along these exquisite roads. The height and girth of the trees in attendance demonstrated their mature age. Time has a sense of vigor about it. It never stops; at least not time as we know it to be.

Shawnee was named a national forest back in 1931.[9] You can imagine how large the trees must appear today compared to when they were planted back then. Our grandparents were just beginning their lives in 1931. Now, they are elderly.

A retired forest ranger explained to me the importance of this forest. In 1931 the economy of southern Illinois plummeted — it was only two years following the stock market crash of 1929. In addition to the financial constraints placed on the members of this community at that time, the land in this section of Missouri was physically suffering as well. For many years, extensive timber exploitation had taken place. Soil fertility declined; a downward spiral in crop production resulted. And, to make matters worse, man-made forest fires were implemented rather frequently. As the area was struggling to survive from both financial and industrial standpoints, campaigning began for a national forest to be placed in order to conserve what was left of the moldering area. Thus, Shawnee was created.

In my mind, it's a treasure. This area is certainly a section of our country worth preserving as are so many others. I'm glad someone else agreed.

I just wish your fate could have been saved on that horrible day just as this forest's was back some eighty years ago. You would have loved it here.

Upon our arrival, Brad, Steph, and I met Joe outside of a liquor store on the outskirts of town just as the cashier was about to call the cops on him (guess he'd been sitting outside a little too long!). We decided a hotel would best suit our needs for the night. By the end of the day our gear was still drenched from last night's downpour. After a brief discussion, we agreed upon the America's Best Inn, the least expensive venue in town.

A few minutes (and a half mile) later we met up there.

After we checked in, we drove down to a local sandwich shop for dinner. It was nearing ten at night and none of us were up for cooking raviolis on the grill in the parking lot outside of our hotel. Truthfully, if I ate raviolis one more day in a row, well ...you get the picture.

As I talked to the young woman preparing my sandwich at the counter, I learned that not only does Murphysboro have scenic class but it also is truly an exceptionally family oriented community — a lot like Bellefonte. She told me of how it hosts an Apple Festival the second weekend after Labor Day each year. This festival features apple pie-eating contests, apple-peeling contests, a 5k race, an "App-L-Ympics," a parade and anything else related to apples one could imagine.

It brings to mind your childhood apple orchard on Mom and Dad's farm, and I'm beginning to find that there is absolutely *nothing* that occurs throughout my day that I can't somehow connect to you and your absence. You were supposed to pick those apples with your children, mine, and their grandpa who planted them with you. Now those days will never come.

After dinner we returned to the hotel and prepared for bed. Then, I went down to the lobby to inquire about a continental breakfast. I *need* all the free food I can get. While talking with the receptionist I learned that Murphysboro is also home to some sort of World Championship Barbeque Team. If I had known of such a team, I would have thought it'd be located in Memphis, Tennessee. Who knew?

(You loved barbeque, especially Scott's roasting stand at the Grange Fair. Damn.)

I just draped our tent over the fence that borders the perimeter of the hotel's property. Hopefully the breeze will dry it out by morning.

The floor of our room is covered in sleeping bags, pillows, wet clothes, and shoes that I've laid out in hopes they'll dry by the time morning arrives.

The air is on full blast.

Everything we own is soaking wet both inside and out from last night's shower of buckets. I'd much rather be camping, but I think this hotel room is our best chance at drying our gear.

Tomorrow we'll return to our camping routine. I can't wait. The ground of the earth is more comforting to me than any old bed. I feel closer to you when I sleep on the ground. That's where you're stuck.

All my love,

Jenny

P.S. It's long after midnight but I forgot to tell you about Brad's run-in with Dad in the bathroom last night. In between touring the cave and the arrival of last night's severe storm, each of us showered (or attempted to). The water was so hot even I couldn't manage to stand directly under the stream, and boy do I ever love a boiling shower. Turning them on for even a minute filled the entire bathroom with steam.

It seems because of the scorching temperature of the water Dad decided to take a sponge bath directly next to the open sink. We all know Brad tends toward modesty, avoiding showering in groups or anything, well, out of order. So it would only be fitting that when he walked into the bathroom to engage in a very tepid shower (as he likes his to be) he'd run in to Dad dressed only in his whitie-tighties with a leg propped up on the public sink scrubbing his feet. Oh, our father! From all accounts, Dad looked up, smiled and said, "The showers will burn you; I'm almost done here if you'd like this sink." Brad headed toward the showers with a face the shade of a tomato.

None of us could stop laughing once we heard this account.

Flooded terrain, Missouri, May 2008 ~ Photograph taken by Stephanie Herbstritt

15. Missouri
Murphysboro, Illinois, to Farmington, Missouri

"You must not lose faith in humanity. Humanity is an ocean;
if a few drops of the ocean are dirty, the ocean does not become dirty."
~Mahatma Gandhi

May 27, 2008

Jeremy,

*F*rom *Murphysboro we traveled through Ozora to Chester where we crossed the Mississippi and entered Missouri.*

As I mentioned yesterday, the scenery reminded me of home. Today, my thoughts returned to this notion. I tried to analyze precisely my previous definition of "home."

Home, to me, always means Bellefonte, Pennsylvania.

There are a number of reasons I consider that town and two-story, century-old white farmhouse with black shutters home. Yes, I spent nearly two decades of my life living in that house, one set perfectly on some of the finest soil of this earth. But it wasn't the house, the land, or even the barn that made Bellefonte home. It was the memories formed there, the time spent with family, and the experiences created, which now that you're dead only I am left to tell.

Dad and Mom bought the farm back in May of 1988. They had hoped to raise their family in that house, form memories there and one day hand over a piece of that property to one of their children so that we could raise our own families right next door to them, break bread together on weekends, and watch their grandchildren grow. The dreams Mom and Dad had for our futures (and for the farm) are the foundation for what made that property home.

We didn't move into that raggedy old house until August of 1988 as there was a lot of work which had to be done in order to make the quarters "livable."

Many years prior, the house and associated land had actually been named the county's orphanage. Then it was sold by the county to a kind family who spent their days harvesting the fruits of that land with their bare hands, raising dairy cows, milking them the old-fashioned way (by hand that is), and additionally preparing beef, chicken, and pigs for slaughter.

They resided on the farm for many, many years. The young children played in the upstairs of the summer kitchen. I remember how some of their toys remained in that space when we moved in and their names, heights, and the games they played were written on the walls. I remember how fun it was to live in their memory.

After the head of the household passed away suddenly and unexpectedly, the house was abandoned for nearly seven years. The next owner had high hopes of subdividing the land, thereby making a quick fortune. His dreams were destroyed by some sort of land preservation grant. From what I've been told, it seems he never really wanted the property, therefore, he rented it out to an individual who owned what (upon our arrival) appeared to be a herd of untamed dogs.

Go figure.

A tremendous amount of damage was done not just by those dogs but also by high school-aged delinquents whom (we were told) used the property to host innumerable parties and the like during the cold winter months.

When Mom and Dad purchased it, the house was infested with rodents and insects. It reeked of dog feces and urine. Dad couldn't count on one hand the number of high school-aged kids who showed up late at night "ready to party" while he and his friends were tearing apart the structure in an attempt to remodel it.

Mom had given birth to Joseph in September of the previous year and was less than two months pregnant with Stephanie when we finally did move into that farmhouse in August. At the time of our arrival into the neighborhood, neighbors were scarce. The closest house was nearly a mile away. The area was well wooded and, at night, very poorly lit. I remember, as a child, liking this aspect of that property particularly. It enabled us to create the most hair-raising haunted houses in the woods around Halloween. Nevertheless, Mom wasn't all too fond of living in such a spooky old house with all of us children. She only agreed upon the move to satisfy Dad's dreams of owning a farm.

Dad always wanted to be a farmer, not a gentleman farmer, but a real, get-your-hands-dirty, work-for-your-money kind of farmer.

While Mom worked the night shift at the hospital, you and I got away with a lot while under Dad's care. Weekends were even crazier. Dad was often occupied with the animals, Joe, or Stephanie so you and I could have gotten away with pretty much anything we attempted. We had free rein.

I'll never forget the time we spent with Dad by ourselves during those hours. Certainly we missed Mom, and I always worried about her catching some disease or another, but we had a ball watching football and baseball, playing catch, and being recruited to assist with projects inside the barn. It typically was you who would help Dad in the barn, while I stayed in the house and kept my eyes on Joe and Stephanie. This was when I was nine, up until I was twelve.

It wasn't long before other families started to move in to newly built houses on the main road below our farm. The area never did turn into a development; rather, it became a community, a street you never stopped referring to as "Irish Hollow." It seemed to be placed in the most ideal location, only three miles from downtown Bellefonte, a short bike ride and only a half hour's jog away.

As a child, I loved meeting up with the other neighborhood kids at the softball fields at the end of our lane for a quick game of pickup on a hot summer day. It makes me laugh thinking about how the girls and I made our numerous attempts at creating our own "Babysitters Club" by meeting at the park right next door to those fields on a biweekly basis. We sure did have a good time there being kids: pushing one another in circles on the merry-go-round, playing cops and robbers and tag in the dark.

That park was the place you and I first formed friendships outside of our house and school. All too often I wish I could return to those days. Life was so painless back then. Our biggest concerns were terribly frivolous.

How would I get that babysitter's club up and running?

Would we have enough time after school prior to dark to build up that jump (made out of snow piled three-feet deep and four-feet wide)? And would Mom and Dad catch us flying down over that jump in a line of six people each attached to one another by placing the sled's rope from that of the person in back of him around his waist?

What would Mom do to us when she found out Joe and Steph really weren't kidnapped on April Fool's Day, but simply hidden in the woods?

Would Mom let us back in the house after she discovered you and I dug up the entire front yard in an attempt to "put in a swimming pool" while she was napping?

Would I tattle for the 550th time if you called me "ASTCBdoubleT" (Adult, Sheep Talker, Cry Baby, Tattle Tale) just one more time? And if I did, would Mom actually wash your mouth out with soap?

How far could we push her and Dad?

Would one day we find ourselves lost in the cornfields only to realize Mom and Dad weren't coming out to find us?

Would they actually send you to boarding school if you so much as "pretended" an aerosol deodorant can containing chemicals, lethal if inhaled, had exploded? "Jen, I accidentally burst this [display evidence]. We'll be dead within twenty-four hours. We've got to get hold of Mom and Dad. We must save them, Joe and Steph!" Instantaneously, a flood of tears streamed from my eyes. "It's over for us, but we can still save them."

We were ridiculous.

And as we aged to our teenage years...

If you ripped off the summer kitchen from the house (with hopes of remodeling that space) would Mom actually appreciate the gesture?

Or would she require you to finance the entire project yourself? "Jeremy!!!!! It would be in your best interest to pick up some extra hours milking cows…right this minute!"

You didn't want to read *The Hobbit,* so fabricated an entire network of lies. The writing was "too small for you to read." Your vision "was poor." When brought to the optometrist, you even tricked her with your "inability" to read the Snellen eye chart. You didn't think you'd get away with your little trick so easily, now did you? Mom outsmarted you. She spent good money on a book printed in a typeface large enough for even the legally blind to read.

For my part, I just wanted to be asked to read the first reading during Mass. This was such a huge honor. Every time one of the other students in my class got asked over me, my eyes would tear.

Of course, I didn't see life as painless back then. All I wanted to do was grow up. I think I yearned to grow up from the minute of my birth. I wonder if you felt the same. Do you ever want to go back in time? Replay a conversation or even an entire day? Do you even still recall these memories? I hope that you do.

We were normal kids back then. We played games like most; but that house was our home. Now, though, there is something very different about it. The vibe it gives off is almost eerie. Yet, I don't want to remove it from my memory. Because you loved that place. You loved that rickety old barn and those calming yet noisy animals. We all did.

Dad loved his lambs sometimes more than life itself. He'd bring the sick ones and the runts into the house in the winter, place them on the heat vents, use Mom's hair dryer to keep them warm if the heat of the wood burner wasn't sufficient and accidentally use Joe and Stephanie's baby bottles rather than those intended for the lambs, many a time to feed them if the mother couldn't provide enough milk herself (or if for some reason she rejected her offspring).

The lambs loved Dad just as much as he loved them. He certainly was their shepherd. When they heard his "bah," they'd run directly over to him as if he was their mother. They'd latch onto the bottles

he offered them without fear and with what seemed like a smile in their eyes.

I learned a lot about life in that barn and probably just as much about death. Oftentimes, the lambs wouldn't survive through the cold winter months. It wasn't uncommon for a ewe to have difficultly giving birth and for Dad (and later in life you, me, Joe, or Stephanie) to have to play obstetrician. The lambs weren't always born alive or at term. In these scenarios the lambs didn't have a chance at life. Sometimes, we would tube-feed premature lambs and accidentally place the milk into the lungs rather than into the stomach.

Farming is not an exact science. As humans we do make mistakes. We did our best, but there were times when lambs did not survive. And the ewes eventually aged or became ill for a reason that we often didn't understand.

I learned that the death of our animals was permanent and inevitable. This was one of the hardest lessons I learned growing up. In a sense, my experiences on that farm prepared me for your death.

As much work as that house, barn, and farm in Bellefonte were, I loved that place with all of my heart and it is the one and only place I will ever refer to as my childhood home. It was *our* home.

Bellefonte is where our family transformed from two parents with three children to two parents with four. We grew up in that home; our heights are written on the walls. Traditions were formed there and it is where memories were engrained deep within our beings. That farm is where we learned of life, death, love, and hate.

I can't imagine you don't miss Bellefonte with all of your heart. It was your home, mostly because it was a place without disappointment, full of love, life and happiness, where you spent most of your years surrounded by the love of a family I'm sure you still hold dear to your heart.

I only now am beginning to understand why the simple thought of home is so painful to endure.

When I begin to picture heaven, I think of it as another dimension of earth. I hope you are able to visit us here and see, not necessarily our sorrow, but perhaps our happiness. I hope you are able to remember our home, experience it and enjoy it with we who are still left here within its loving arms.

We stopped for lunch today in a town called Chester. I wished Dad was still with us when we made our way through. Why, you might ask? Possibly it was because I missed hearing the nicknames he created for us. But that story is for later. The more likely reason is that Chester is home to Popeye and Popeye was Dad's childhood idol. He would have enjoyed the experience. When I was sixteen, he gave me his Popeye doll, a gift Grandma gave him when he was four. I still hold dear this keepsake displayed in my bedroom at the farmhouse.

Because of Chester's history, today's lesson was on Popeye and his creator. An ingenious storyteller, Elzie Segar was born in Chester in 1894.[10] Rumor has it Segar based his comic characters on some of the authentic residents of Chester during his lifetime.[11]

One particular building present in Chester sticks out in my mind. Located in the center of town, it was covered in paintings of all of the characters of this cartoon. We passed it by as we biked toward a statue of Popeye present in a park located on the east side of the Mississippi River.

Chester certainly is a town with a theme.

After zipping by this monument situated at the bottom of a brief downhill grade, I waved goodbye to Chester and crossed the Mississippi on my bike.

This aspect of the ride was thrilling simply because of the fact that I was riding my bike across the Mississippi, a river I, like almost any other kid in America, learned so much about during my elementary school years. I can still hear my class reciting the spelling of that word harmoniously in rhyme. Better yet, I can see me, a young, innocent and content eight-year-old little girl dressed in overalls and brown pigtails counting aloud while standing in a dark corner in the barn surrounded by hay bales, eyes shut, while you and the rest of our friends hid yourselves ever so cleverly within that space. "One Mississippi, two Mississippi…"

The next famous bridge I'll cross over will be the Golden Gate Bridge. I can't stop smiling just thinking about it.

The instant we entered Missouri territory (after leaving Chester and crossing over this renowned river), I convinced myself a tornado would plow right through our paths. The sky was ominous. The storm was drawing nearer, the clouds had turned to black and the thunder was drastically intensifying in volume.

The ground in front of me was flat as a board. At the time, I wish I'd had a level to confirm how flat this area of our country really is. I was in the midst of a floodplain, but it looked more like a swamp.

I sympathized with the farmers and worried for their crops. What appeared to be an excess of rain so far this year could either be fruitful for their harvest, or if they had just planted their crops, very detrimental.

My heightened anxiety made crossing the Mississippi River all the more exhilarating.

Within ten more miles of biking, this dark sky passed and we all made it to our destination, Farmington, just as dry as we had left this morning.

Unfortunately our gear is still as wet as it was when we left this morning so it looks like we'll be staying, against all our desires, in (yet another) hotel tonight. We're watching our costs as best as we can so the room that we bartered for has only one bed. Looks like I'll be taking the floor inside of a musky damp bag. I wished for the ground last night: seems my wish has been granted only a day late. Oh, to imagine how I will smell tomorrow morning!

But I won't be alone in my position. Since Joe (by constantly tending to our every need) gets shafted quite often, tonight he'll be treated like royalty with a full bed made solely for him. Brad and Steph will accompany me on the floor surrounded by the warmth of a few thin sheets that Joe so kindly has offered to us.

Truth is, Joe doesn't want to be caught dead sleeping in the same bed as either of his sisters, or Brad for that matter.

I should mention, at the start of this trip I expected the people of Missouri to be your stereotypical, friendly, midwestern folk. When we left Virginia, I couldn't wait to arrive in Missouri and then Kansas where I expected I'd meet some of the nicest people present on earth. To my dismay, the gas station attendants, waitresses, and drivers whom we came in contact with today were the exact opposite of this very description.

Log truck drivers seemed to make a game out of pushing us off the road. Women driving station wagons with babies in the back seats seemed to do just the same while adding a long, obnoxious loud horn to the equation. Waitresses would sigh rudely when I couldn't make up my mind and attendants laughed at the fact we'd driven our car (albeit Joe) this far west despite the price of gas. "It serves you right gas is as pricey as it is."

In fact, $3.99 per gallon to be exact. Maybe these individual's attitudes have nothing to do with me and what flavor of milkshake I can't decide I want. I could leave it at that.

But the truth is some people are just plain jerks. They don't care about anyone other than themselves. Of course, some people are rude because of the anger and/or sadness they are suppressing but others are just assholes who will provide nothing to this society in the grand scheme of things.

Please forgive me but my anger has been building for months now.

Take for instance the "cell phone company" bitch. Not more than eight weeks following your MURDER we received a letter (addressed to you) stating that your cell phone service was going to be deactivated (because of your death). I still have to wonder if you murder wasn't made so public if the company would have learned as quickly as it did of your death (and subsequently acted so promptly) being that we continued to pay your bill in such a timely manner.

And why in the world would they have sent a letter to a dead person anyway?

In any case, your cell phone recording was all we had left of your voice (other than the message you left on Mom and Dad's machine the Friday prior to your death). We couldn't bear to close your account.

Upon my inquiry regarding this matter, the particular woman with whom I spoke insisted on closing your account: "You have ten days and that will be that. It's company policy."

Ten days left to listen to my beloved brother's voice one last time!

Upon overhearing this conversation and the emotion present in my voice, Kristi (from work) took the phone and gave that woman a piece of her mind. "That cell phone recording is all Jennifer has left of her dead brother's existence. Once that account is closed, there won't be anything left of his remaining here on this earth. His Social Security number is obsolete. His apartment has been cleaned out. His bank accounts are closed. And his clothes are now shoved into boxes that may possibly never be reopened again. Need I say anymore?! For God's sake, just give her this!"

The end result: I pay ten dollars extra each month to keep your account activated. It's worth the money to hear your voice. I'd pay anything for that.

So, again, some people are just jerks.

The bastard who killed you sure was. No, he was an egotistical, self-seeking, worthless, poor excuse of human flesh. It disgusts me how every few days I hear of another person just as selfish as him, willing to cowardly "sacrifice" his own life for the sole purpose of fulfilling his lifelong, pathetic dream of robbing hundreds, if not thousands, from a life time full of happiness, joy, friendship, companionship, desires, and dreams. How will we ever be able to stop people like him from engaging in such vile acts of violence, when the possibility of losing his own life along the way, in the process of fulfilling such a heinous dream, isn't enough to deter such a sick individual?

We co-exist with incredibly evil people. People who could care less about you and me, how their actions may adversely affect another, or what the ramifications of killing another might be.

And don't get me started on Virginia Tech. I realize one sociopath pulled the trigger to the gun, encased with the bullet that ultimately killed you, but at least a dozen people could have acted in a multitude of varying fashions that might have resulted in the prevention of thirty-two deaths, including yours.

I wonder how they would feel if placed in my shoes? How would they feel if their brother, son, daughter, sister, spouse, or parent were the one murdered? Would the tables be turned?

After all we've been through, I honestly thought your killer's private instructor would have *personally* apologized to all of us for not doing more.

I would have thought the reciting of a poem entitled "We Will Prevail" could have been postponed past two days following your murder. How could anyone have even considered "prevailing" at such a terrible time!?

I would have thought we could have been allowed to hold onto you tight as you lay still on that certainly cold metal table positioned inside the cement walls of that poisonous morgue the minute we arrived on the premise, not seven days later.

I would have thought the policy group members who made the decision to delay notification of the first two student's murders to your student body for approximately two hours thereafter would have sobbed with us, apologized relentlessly for their inactions and done everything in their power to ease our pain.

I wouldn't have thought your killer's medical records would have mysteriously disappeared from the university counseling center. Nor would I have expected to find myself frozen in some sort of settlement meeting with senior university officials only to notice one policy group member was wearing a bullet proof vest while another volunteered she'd informed her very own family members of the first two shootings prior to sending out official notification to the entire campus.

And never would I have expected the majority of the policy group members to stare blankly at me while with tears flooding my eyes, through a cracked voice, I kindly requested a simple apology.

That bullet proof vest cloaked all of their souls.

How could anyone fail to understand my rage!

The senior officials of that university purposively withheld information from the student body that they felt was crucial enough that their own loved ones needed to know. Couldn't any one of them have mouthed the simple words: "I am sorry. I failed you. No, I failed your loved ones. I am *sincerely* sorry."

A simple apology was too much to ask for.

In the weeks following your death, there was one man who stayed on the phone with me on multiple occasions totaling hours on end. He explained every single, solitary detail I needed to know about that terrible day: where were you lying and how; did he suspect you suffered; did you appear to be lying in a defensive position; what were the results of your autopsy, etc. He knew I *needed* this information. Otherwise, I'd haunt myself with such questions for the remainder of my time left on this earth. Some people need details. I was (and still am) one of them.

He even returned to our family all belongings found on your body that day. He knew we *needed* these. He jeopardized his job so as to provide us with the materials essential for healing to begin. This man knew compassion. He was a genuine soul.

I want my heaven to be filled with people like him, people who think first of others. I can want, can't I?

Anger consumes me. Please help me sleep.

All my love,

Jenny

Missouri, May 2008 ~ Photograph by Stephanie Herbstritt

16. The Ozarks
Farmington to Alley Spring, Missouri

"Every artist was first an amateur."
~Ralph Waldo Emerson

May 28, 2008

Dearest Jeremy,

*T*hose trail names. You can call me Crotch Rocket from here on out. As Joe tells me, he doesn't want to hear another word about my — well, you get the point. Saddle sores, yeast infections, uncomfortable, diaper-like shorts, well, none of these variables are helping my situation.

As for Joe, we like to call him Red Stripe. As he's been growing out his beard for months now, we've noticed he has a stripe of red hair present in that beard. I think he likes the name.

Steph, she's known as One Ring-a-Dingy, Two Ring-a-Dingy. Every opportunity she gets, she's on the phone talking to that boyfriend of hers.

Dad named himself Nimbo Cumulus. He claims this means Gray Cloud.

And for Brad, dear Brad! He was a bit cranky and somehow got the name Stick Up Ass. Dad claims Brad appeared to be walking as if he had a — well, again, you get the point. Brad *is* having some problems walking due to a knee injury but we're all pretty sure he got this name because he's been acting a bit miserable due to his knee pain, foot pain, hard bike seat and, therefore, bum pain, back pain, etc. As you can imagine, being called Stick Up Ass isn't helping matters much at all. Nevertheless, we can't stop talking and laughing about it.

We all love Brad.

Oh, and I must not forget Mom. Somehow, she is Moon Flower. Don't ask because I have no clue where that name came from. Our father is a nut.

I think I saw a half dozen moving trucks throughout the day. Between them and the logging trucks, I'm surprised I was able to finish the ride out alive. Still, what a beautiful bike ride the day provided.

A moving truck is supposed to take a person and his belongings to a new place. That place may be innovative and unknown, but it's supposed to be exciting and full of the opportunity for a new and better life.

The moving truck that brought your belongings back to Mom and Dad's house following your death didn't fulfill the expectations I had set for it. Sure, it brought with it a new life, but that life wasn't something any of us wanted to experience. Its arrival wasn't exciting. And the pain its presence brought was utterly gut-wrenching.

Your belongings returned to Bellefonte without you, without your permission, your signature, or even your knowledge. When they arrived, I sat for hours swallowed in your clothes just taking in your scent.

This would be the closest I'd ever get to experiencing you alive again. I could smell you. Your scent was alive. Yet, you were dead.

I saved your toothbrush and razor. Just in case years from now scientists are able to bring back the dead using skin cells, strands of hair, or something of the like. I wanted to have that opportunity. Call me crazy, but I want you back that bad. I'd do anything if it were possible.

Today we approached the Ozarks. This mountain range covers the vast majority of the southern half of Missouri and extends just barely into southeast Kansas. These mountains in actuality are tall, deeply dissected plateaus. Once you reach the top, you're on a plateau but all the way up and all the way down it's like a roller coaster ride of gradually rolling inclines and declines that increase in length as you go up and decrease in length as you go down. This is the most extensive mountain range present between the Appalachians and the Rocky Mountains, which means soon enough our riding conditions will become incredibly flat. I am not sure if this will necessarily be in my best interest as sometimes the challenge of a climb can be rather distracting to my mind. Biking in a straight line for miles at a time with minimal change in scenery might be a bore. I'll let you know in just a few days.

Our ride through the Ozarks took us through Centerville, Ellington, and Eminence before we reached our destination of Alley Spring where I am sitting by a mill right now writing this to you.

The mountains were heavily forested. Even so, I felt as if the climate was more suggestive of summer rather than spring. It seems the sun has returned just in time for May to draw to a close. It's a little late for Memorial Day weekend as that was but a few days ago. Still, I'm grateful for its arrival, even if slightly late. Yesterday was too cold for me. Whine, whine!

The Ozarks turned out to be much steeper than I'd ever expected. They felt more like a roller coaster ride than the Knobs of Kentucky. Most of the time, I did not gain enough momentum to make it to the top of the next hill. Nevertheless, a rare occasion did present itself when I would sprint down a hill gaining enough momentum to go up the next, down the next, up the next, and so on for a good three or four rounds, until Bessie finally slowed down to the point where I had no other choice but to pedal her up the final climb. Until that point, I was absolutely thrilled.

Momentum is a good thing.

Sticking with the subject of rolling hills, I fell off of my bike for the *second* time today. The first time was back in Virginia. It was Lexington. I had just finished talking with that fellow PSU alumnus over breakfast when I walked outside to get started on my ride. It was there that I fell, right in front of the large glass window where I sat just moments before watching the fog lift while eating my breakfast

Another view of Missouri, May 2008 ~ Photograph by Stephanie Herbstritt

and conversing with this man. I clipped my right foot into its pedal and proceeded to take my very first stride of the morning but before I could clip my left foot into its place I lost my balance and fell flat on my right side with my right cleat still stuck in the pedal. I'm sure the alumnus got quite a laugh out of this. He probably thought to himself, "Good God, help this girl. She will never make it across the country at this rate."

So, I'm sure you are curious about *today's* fall. Looking back, the scenario was hilarious but at the time I was petrified as the events played out in the center of logging country. This means that the roads here were narrow with minimal shoulders and the loggers drove by at very high speeds. They hugged what was present of the shoulder through quick curves that oftentimes boasted blind spots in both directions.

I was on one of those downhill sections that didn't provide me with enough momentum to get me to the top of the next steep incline. I downshifted rather abruptly and (as even a novice could predict) my chain slipped and derailed immediately. I was pedaling uphill with my chain off, obviously going nowhere, with my cleats still clipped into my pedals, a recipe for disaster. And then it happened. It was all too quick. I fell over onto my left side, this time directly *into* the line of traffic. My cleats did not disconnect upon my painful landing. Therefore, I was lying on the ground, mind you in the middle of the road in a blind spot, stuck to my bicycle unable to get out or up.

Oh, good God!

Thank goodness Steph heard me yell for help as not more than a few seconds later she hurried on back and set me free. Luckily, traffic stopped entirely during this period of time and I was able to safely resume biking with injuries no more significant than a few abrasions to the left arm.

Like I said, looking back the ordeal was rather amusing but at the time it sure stirred up quite some fright.

This was not the only excitement we encountered today. In fact, today was relatively eventful. We stopped in a town called Eminence just five miles east of Alley Spring. We were eating lunch at the Ice Cream Shack when we came across one of the most fascinating, appealing people I have ever met in my life. This man is riding a penny farthing around the world. You read that correctly: *around the world!* This is one of those bikes you might have seen in an old English movie. Invented in 1871, today's version has three speeds. The front wheel is very large (ranging from thirty-eight to fifty-two inches in diameter) and the back wheel much smaller (about the size of the front wheel of a child's tricycle). According to Joe, the bike got its name from British coins used at the time it was invented, a penny and a farthing, with the penny being much larger than the farthing (the front wheel is much larger than the back). Who would have thought!

This fellow was riding his penny farthing through the Ozarks of Missouri. Now, I could barely make it up some of the climbs presented to me on my featherweight Trek Madone, a.k.a. Bessie. Yet, wearing an old English helmet, this man was riding a giant three-speed bike harkening back to the nineteenth century.

"Joff," a man we briefly met at the Ice Cream Shack in Eminence, Missouri who is riding a penny-farthing around the world, May 2008 ~ Photograph taken by Joseph Herbstritt

Eminence was nestled in the heart of the Missouri Ozark Mountains and populated by approximately six hundred people. It seemed to sit within a valley. Its downtown section consisted of one main street where the Ice Cream Shack sat. Though there were very few businesses present, all seemed dynamic with customers.

Eminence is a fairly "touristy" town. I can see why. According to the locals, it is considered the "Canoe Capital of the World." The Jack's Fork River flows through the center. This river parallels the town's main road and, I'm told, eventually feeds into the Current River nearby.

Today, the water of the Jack's Fork appeared to be a perfect hue of turquoise. Its current was swift. I am sure you would have loved to try your hand at kayaking here or possibly fly fishing.

From a few miles outside of Eminence, all the way to Alley Spring, traffic was heavy. Hectic tourist traffic combined with heavy logging traffic made the roads very dangerous to bike on. Personally, I felt the scenery was well worth the risk. Nevertheless, you'd be happy to know I did bike with extra caution.

We arrived in Alley Spring around five P.M. after enduring a very steep, approximately three-mile climb out of the valley. This climb would have been considered short had I been driving, but by the end of a very long day of biking it seemed nearly impossible. The sad truth is, after a quarter-pound hamburger, fries and a soft-serve ice cream cone, I think my body needed this climb.

Alley Spring lies six miles west of Eminence and, to me, it doesn't appear anyone actually lives within Alley Spring as there are absolutely no houses in sight. The only structures I've seen are the shower houses located on the property of our campground and a small bait-and-tackle shop situated adjacent to our campground on the opposite side of the road. Both lie on a quick curve in the road.

I learned this town (named Alley after a prominent farming family who resided here long before either of our times[12]) actually houses a grist mill built in the late 1800s and no longer in operation. Alley Spring was first built in 1868 and "later reconstructed during 1893–1894 by George Washington McCaskill as a merchant mill."[13] The mill was the focus of the town a century ago as the farmers in the area brought their grain there. Today, the National Park Service operates a store in the mill, and there are exhibits too. Natural springs, as you might have guessed, are the main attractions for tourists in this area. From Rocky Falls, to Big Spring, Blue Spring, and Round Spring, as well as to scenic Route 106, this area of the Ozarks has so much natural beauty to offer.

This mill is a hidden treasure that I doubt I would have visited had I not gone on this trip. The mill's presence at Alley Spring reminds me that, while the subject never did fascinate me in school, I now know the importance of history.

If we don't pass along stories and facts like these to our children, they'll plainly disappear like a stream during a drought. The same holds true for your name and the names of all other souls who have passed from this earth. If your name is not said aloud and your story never told, then future generations will be disadvantaged, for you had so much to offer this world.

I feel it is our duty to honor your legacy. We must honor all those who have gone before us. This is why I take the time to read as many names as I can aloud whenever I pass by a cemetery. These people must never be forgotten, not now and not five hundred years from now!

Missouri takes me back to my days as a high school girl reading the 1961 novel *Where the White Fern Grows* by Wilson Rawls. I am reminded of better days, days where school shootings didn't affect my family and certainly didn't occur in my community.

I am enjoying this trip thoroughly and Missouri truly is majestic, even amidst the few rude people I crossed paths with yesterday. The oak-hickory forests that surround the narrow winding roads of these roller coaster hills that lead to massive plateaus are breathtaking, something I've never before seen. However, I can't help but wish my life had never brought me here.

Jenny

17. Brutal Terrain
Alley Spring to Marshfield, Missouri

"And in the end, it's not the years in your life that count.
It's the life in your years."
~Abraham Lincoln

May 29, 2008

Jeremy,

*T*oday, we continued through Missouri from Alley Spring to Marshfield. We ventured through small towns with names like Hartville, Summerville, and Houston.

The terrain was brutal. In fact, I didn't see a section of flat land measuring greater than one hundred feet in length all day long, except of course for the plateaus, but *I* wouldn't call them flat (just my opinion).

Don't get me wrong, I like mountainous terrain. It makes the miles fly by. Each ascent provides the mind with a unique distraction. But I expected by the end of today I'd see flat land.

My legs are becoming increasingly fatigued and my mind is weary. *And* my recollection of Missouri's geography told me western Missouri would give rise to flat land right before entering the Kansas border. *Yet, we're still in central Missouri.*

Oh well.

The scenery here really is exceptional. And I'm finally beginning to feel as if I've entered the Midwest. The people here are extraordinarily friendly.

People passing by wave and say hello — *both*. They are eager to give directions when we find ourselves lost, as happens often (of course, as a result of me leading us in the wrong direction). They welcome us into their places of business for water, ice, a simple conversation, or for shelter from the rain, and they don't even expect a penny.

This section of our country is a whole different world to me; one I'm incredibly anxious to explore. As you know, I'm looking for good in this world. Possibly, this will be right where I'll find it.

An event occurred today that demonstrated this type of genuine kindness. Midmorning, for a reason unbeknownst to me, the dogs decided to return to the hunt. They'd been absent for days. In retrospect, I think I might have forgotten they ever existed. But today, I wished I'd purchased pepper spray for this, their red-carpet entrance.

You see, the one item I asked Mom to bring to Bowling Green, Kentucky, was pepper spray. For what might you ask? Well, as cruel as this may seem: the dogs. Our mother stopped in at PetCo and asked if they had any pepper spray for her "kids to squirt dogs with." As you might have expected, the cashier didn't have any to sell her. Honesty, I'm shocked Mom didn't get carted off to jail!

I'd been forced to sprint up a number of steep grades because of these dogs by the time this particular ordeal decided to play out. My legs were fatigued. The remaining miles for the day were decreasing quickly in quantity as was my energy level.

Just as I was getting caught up in the midst of a day dream and my speed slowed to the same pace as that of the turtles that love crossing the roads here, out of nowhere three dogs arrived.

The scenario wasn't anything I wasn't used to. The first began to chase after my back tire, a second presented himself no more than two inches from my left foot and the third decided to go after my front tire. I was pedaling as fast as I possibly could but this, clearly, was not fast enough. The dogs were on me like hawks hunt their prey.

Brad was behind me screaming obscenities at them. Steph was doing the same, as was I while simultaneously attempting to avoid being pushed off the shoulder of the road.

They continued to follow me for probably a full five minutes. It seemed like thirty.

I became frantic and actually started to cry. My whole body was quivering.

Then, the dogs pushed me off of the pavement and into the gravel, making up an extension of the road's shoulder. At this point in time I thought for sure it was over, "it" being my life. If these dogs got a hold of me I didn't think I'd make it out alive. They were snipping and snapping and their hair was standing up straight on their backs.

Somehow, by the grace of God, I did not lose my balance and fall over. Instead, I got myself out and continued to bike vigorously with the dogs still on my back. I didn't know how much longer I could keep this violent chase up when *it* happened. I began to cry harder and louder and *then*, out of nowhere, after I hadn't seen a car in hours, a lovely woman in a pink VW convertible pulled up beside me and threatened the dogs. She nearly ran them over while simultaneously honking her horn repetitively and carefully avoiding my frame.

Finally, the dogs left. They ran right back into the woods, right where they came from, probably waiting for the next group of bikers to pass by.

This woman then kindly escorted me for nearly another mile so as to ensure those dogs were definitely gone and not just waiting for her to leave so that they could return for round two.

I waved goodbye to her while wiping copious tears from my eyes, the type that just don't stop running. I was both horrified by the experience but grateful for this woman's arrival and incredibly kind gesture.

In that moment, I liked the Midwest. This type of kindness could make anyone smile. I hope to stay here for quite some time.

We arrived here in Marshfield a little after five P.M. Our campsite tonight is a little peculiar. Situated on the county fairgrounds, under a vacant barn's roof, we placed our tent. The Pathfinder's under that roof as well.

Surrounding this barn are two others that look just the same. And no more than a few feet away are public restrooms with flushable toilets. I assume we'll be the only ones using them tonight. (I'm in heaven.)

Outside the fairgrounds, no more than a hundred feet away, are apartment buildings surrounded by houses placed on streets that wind around this town like a maze in a cornfield. The only dilemma with this description is that this town is incredibly hilly. We're still in the Ozarks.

The traffic around me is unexpectedly busy. People are cutting through the fairgrounds so as to avoid what must be a much busier road elsewhere.

Work definitely just let out.

If I were to take a left out of the parking lot, in less than a half mile (uphill) I'd find myself at the town square. This square is truly shaped like a square, unlike many other town "squares" I've seen in my life. It has a pharmacy, courthouse, grocery store and the like all on the outskirts with the center of the square being an open field of grass filled with historical references.

Across the road from me is a playground with ball courts and all your typical park playground equipment. Children are busy at play here. I assume they must live close by as their parents are nowhere to be found.

This park reminds me of our childhood park where you and I would ride our bikes to during our youth. When we were nine and eleven years of age respectively, Mom and Dad, too, felt secure enough in their environments so as to allow us to make that half-mile long journey up the road totally unsupervised.

I look at the kids here playing on the swings, sliding down the slides, climbing the octopus and riding on the seesaws. Sometimes I'd like to go back to those days and just for a moment freeze time. I hope for these kids that they grow up slowly, savor each moment and not be forced into adulthood by some act of deceit, cruelty or unfairness.

To the left of me is a high school track and behind me is a bonfire ring. It seems this must be a popular place to camp or hang out as I've just now laid my eyes on a makeshift fireplace made out of limestone and brick with newly formed ashes and a few logs propped to the side.

Marshfield is busy, yet quaint. I learned it is the county seat for Webster County, the birthplace of Edwin P. Hubble, and the "Top of the Ozarks."[14] I guess this town's little nick-name explains the terrain.

Marshfield to me is the definition of a Midwestern town, a place I would expect to have abundant corn mazes present in autumn, tractor pulls at county fairs, cherry blossom festivals and little league baseball all summer long. On weekdays, I'd have to bet all the downtown stores close at seven. On Saturdays, closing time is probably five o'clock. And I'd have to believe everything here is closed on Sundays.

Family has got to be important to these people. My money says they work to live, not vice versa. These folks define, for me, the Midwest.

Let me return to the fairgrounds.

According to our maps, in most of the Midwestern communities it is permitted for one to sleep at a town's city park free of cost as long as he or she clears this with the sheriff. Tonight was our first "city park" experience.

When we arrived in town, Steph phoned the sheriff's office, explained our situation, and inquired if it would be possible for us to spend the night here, at this, Marshfield's city park. The woman Steph spoke with was very polite. With a gentle voice she said our presence wouldn't be problematic at all.

Welcome to Marshfield.

Stephanie was given directions, informed of where we could find water for drinking as well as for showering, and voila, we had a free place to stay. Free is important. Especially, after all those hotels!

I remember thinking to myself, "Finally, I'm beginning to feel as if I am roughing it. I'm sleeping at a city park!" Wow, *I'm sleeping at a city park!* And to me, it feels like home. It's funny how a campsite or even a park and a small, green four-person tent turns into "home" after only a few weeks on the road.

I like this feeling.

We set our tent up under this barn roof hoping to keep it and our other belongings dry. The skies here look dreary and the wind is starting to pick up. Logic tells me this barn roof may be the key that protects us from any anticipated heavy winds and/or hail.

Suddenly, I'm reminded the temperature might have been extremely warm today but humidity was practically obsolete. Possibly

Our campsite, Marshfield, Missouri, May 30, 2008
Photograph taken by Stephanie Herbstritt

a storm isn't so likely. Oh well. If nothing else, I'll remember Marshfield for this barn and our tent placed ever so curiously underneath.

We used your portable propane stove to prepare dinner tonight. We use it practically every night. You bought it only a few years ago to use during your weekend kayak adventures. Don't worry, we're careful with it. We always make sure to clean it up even if we're tired, and it has its own special spot in the Thule.

Tonight's dinner was raviolis — from a can. Yes, again. On the dirt floor of this barn we ate our meal. All of us were quickly covered in dust and looked like we'd been roughing it far worse than we were. The raviolis were good, repetitive, but good, yet not very filling.

Before we had a chance to run out for ice cream, a middle-aged local man and his teenage son approached us from inside their rustic, navy blue, Buick sedan. As he wound down his window he placed his elbow on the car door, smiled and introduced himself and his son. The two made this stop to visit us out of the kindness of their hearts simply to verify the bathroom doors were unlocked for our use. They figured we were due for a refreshingly warm shower after our ride today.

Word sure does travel fast around this town. I wondered how they knew we were staying here. They said they'd "just heard."

We learned that during the summer months this park is a popular resting place for bikers passing through. In fact, two young women in their mid-twenties were just here a few nights ago. These two men figured we'd run into them in just a few days. Supposedly, they are traveling at a pace much slower than ours. How would they know? These men were very familiar with the roads we traveled on east of their town and, in turn, congratulated us on our accomplishments.

It is midnight and a trucker just parked his eighteen-wheeler next to the building we've placed our tent beneath. This is slightly frightening. Possibly, he has the same idea as we do: a free place to stay for the night in what appears to be a safe, charming, Midwestern community.

Still, Blacksburg appeared to be safe. And we all know the outcome of that dreaded place.

He probably just finished a twelve-hour shift of driving. He's exhausted. His children and wife are sound asleep at home anticipating his arrival back tomorrow night.

He's a serial killer.

Guilty, I am — of stereotyping that is. Truckers always seem to get such a bad reputation due to their presence in a number of old-school horror films.

Jen, go to bed. You're being ridiculous.

Nearly five hours have passed just that quickly. Somehow I, yes I, fell asleep right next to some random stranger/truck driver.

I just awoke, as did that trucker. He seems to be preparing his truck for his drive today. I'll wave good morning. *What am I doing?*

It's not quite light out but I can't return to bed. I'm simply too anxious for our ride today.

We are biking to Kansas, a place I've only heard of within the context of the *Wizard of Oz*.

Goodness, it seems I have yet another unwelcomed guest. This guy is dirty!

You guessed it: I'm in Missouri, so it would only be fitting that there would be an armadillo feasting on our leftovers outside of our tent. I'm stuck. Wish me luck as I begin to unzip this tent.

Good thing I'm clumsy. He heard me stumbling around and quickly waddled off in the direction of what I assume is his hole. He's away from our tent. That's all that matters.

I can still see him. Now, he's making his best attempt at fitting himself into what appears to be a fairly small hole. Good god.

Before this trip I never once saw an armadillo before. These are the most peculiar of creatures. They look like a mix between some form of shelled animal (such as a turtle) and an opossum. They are large, bigger than the biggest cat I have ever seen and they smell. Do they ever smell! Of course, they have a large shell on their back and their tails appear to be shelled as well. The end is quite pointed and I suspect quite sharp. I wouldn't want to touch it in order to find out. I sense they are dirty, sneaky little animals. They seem to like trash, and ever since we entered Missouri I've seen at least five a day dead on the side of the road so I can't imagine they are all-too-fast on their feet. I certainly don't like being close enough to know, as right now he's not all too far from the tent. If I move too quickly and startle him, my suspicion is I could probably find out rather quickly. I'll save this task for another day. This morning I am not up for such a misadventure. I'll leave this one to Joe.

The thought of the Hubble telescope can't seem to escape my mind. (In case you're wondering where that random thought came from…recall, I'm in the birthplace of Edwin P. Hubble.)

The stage was our front lawn in Bellefonte about 1989. The sky was black. The air was warm and the breeze was calm. You couldn't have been more than ten years of age.

For months you'd been intently studying the stars, memorizing the names of the constellations and their precise locations within our galaxy.

Before bed each night that summer, we'd all go outside together (Mom, Dad, you and me; Joe and Steph were already asleep at that point in time), admire the sky, catch a few lightening bugs and close with a prayer: "First star I see tonight, I wish I may, I wish I might, have the wish I wish tonight."

Then, Dad would take me in to bed while you and Mom stared into the clear night sky.

You'd point and Mom would reassure you, "Yes, Jeremy, that's the Big Dipper."

You desperately begged her for a telescope every solitary night up until that one special night Mom was saving up for. "You know, Mom, the stars would appear so much closer, so much clearer—"

"If only we had a telescope!"

While she saved up her money, every few weeks she and Dad would take both of us to Penn State's astronomy lab where we would peer through the lens of an incredible telescope on the roof of that building in awe of the sight.

"If only we had this in our back yard… Please Mom!" But Mom and Dad couldn't afford it; not yet.

The thought of our family's sight in that lab brings tears to my eyes. The memory is bittersweet.

In any event, on that particular night, Mom was busy doing something with (baby) Joseph. Or so you thought. You were outdoors awaiting her arrival. You needed her confirmation as to whether or not what you were pointing at was, indeed, the Big Dipper and not, rather, the Little Dipper. She knew far more about the stars than did Dad.

It was then that she walked out to our front lawn with that telescope wrapped in her arms. You were gleaming with joy. Mom must have been pleased with the outcome her surprise fashioned. She didn't need to hear your words to see the delight in your eyes.

A kid with such a future! A kid with so many dreams!

When I relive childhood memories such as this, I begin to appreciate why losing a child is often described as the worst loss of all. First and foremost it is plainly unnatural for a child to die before a parent. It is not how we expect life to turn out. Second, in a parent's eyes, even when their child is all grown up and has kids of his own, he will always be that nine-year-old little boy holding that bat ever so awkwardly or that five-year-old girl who proudly walks around the house in her mother's high-heeled shoes.

When I think about all of the things our parents wanted for us to get from this life, wanted us to accomplish, gave up so that we could have a better life than they had, I start to see their pain. To think all of that was taken away, all those dreams and desires, right before their very own eyes, so brutally, senselessly, and tragically, it is no wonder their pain is so profound.

I doubt it will ever lessen.

For now, I must move my thoughts to the morning: to the low plains of Kansas I'm heading. Wish me your best!

Jen

Joe skateboarding, May 2008 ~ Photograph taken by Stephanie Herbstritt

Following his confirmation, Jeremy between Grandma and Grandpa Meier, circa 1997, Bellefonte, Pennsylvania

18. The Plains
Marshfield, Missouri, to Pittsburg, Kansas

"Sorrow was like the wind. It came in gusts."
~Marjorie Kinnan Rawlings

May 30, 2008

Jeremy,

Today will be remembered for numerous trivial details: primarily the wind, heat, and humidity.

The wind truly was dire.

We biked directly into a thirty-to-forty mile per hour head wind all day long. I have to believe I expended three times as much energy as I usually do. By the end of the day it was difficult for me to unclench my hands from the fisted position as I had been holding on to my handlebars relentlessly all day long, steadying my bike in an attempt to avoid getting pushed over by the erratically recurring strong gusts.

The wind just wouldn't give up today, not for a second.

I thought for sure the roads would flatten, at least by the time we crossed the state line. I was wrong on this account.

Extreme eastern Kansas is hilly and I'm becoming both cynical and tired. I expected today's ride would be pleasant: physically effortless and scenic. This was a fantasy. In all actuality, the scenery was lovely but with the wind and the heat (did I mention the heat?) this day was miserable. And I think I've transformed into a lobster. My skin is burnt to a crisp. Yes, I wore SPF 70 but it wasn't enough.

Possibly I'm just an idiot. Yep, I wore a tank top today (out of all days) and (being that I'm riding a bicycle) my entire back was exposed to direct sunlight all day long.

Tomorrow, I doubt I'll be able to move. My risk of developing skin cancer just suddenly doubled. I'm not showering today. Or tomorrow for that matter.

For now, all I can think about is this burn. Ironic, isn't it that I, myself, became "golden" on my way to Golden City, Missouri.

Enough already with the complaining, Jen.

Through Ash Grove, Fair Grove, Walnut Grove, (Missouri sure does have a lot of Groves) Golden City, and now Pittsburg, we are traveling across America and it finally seems real!

We met some of the nicest people in the world today including our waitress at Cookie's (in Golden City), and a gas station attendant (in Ash Grove) who claimed Bonnie met Clyde right there at that gas station. Truth be told, she met Clyde for the first time in West Dallas, Texas (so another local filling up on gas at that same gas station claimed). According to him, the two merely passed through Ash Grove during a crime-run (go figure). Regardless of the facts behind either of these stories, it was fun to hear the arguments this topic erupted.

Starving, we arrived at Cookies a little after two P.M. Cookie's is a diner located in Golden City, population roughly nine hundred.

Golden City has an average temperature of 90 degrees Fahrenheit with humidity about the same this time of year. If Cookie's had air conditioning I doubt it was working up to par today as it felt like an oven inside. Still, we chose to eat there.

The man at the gas station some thirty miles back recommended the food, particularly the pie; said he traveled there regularly just for the pie: "You'd be stupid not to stop." He was convinced we wouldn't find pie that tasted like this anywhere else *on earth*.

Immediately upon our entering, the owner realized we were bikers. Who wouldn't? I don't typically walk around town with padded spandex shorts on!

She brought us each two large glasses of water with a pitcher to refill. Then, we were handed menus and at the same time a book. This book was a diary filled with entries written by bikers traveling across. I read through a number of these and then wrote in there myself. It was funny to read of other's escapades: from running over dogs in Kentucky with recommendations for purchasing pepper spray for those traveling east to stories from the heart of why one decided to leave everything he/she had known and enter the trail: stories of lost loved ones, divorce, depression, and poverty.

We reviewed the menu, ordered our food and devoured it like animals as soon as it arrived.

We couldn't have even been done with our meal for more than a second when our waitress returned to inquire what type of pie we desired. We weren't given a choice as to whether or not we *wanted* pie. We were just asked what type.

From a selection of at least thirty freshly baked pies, I chose peanut butter. Joe ordered lemon meringue, Steph strawberry, and Brad apple. It was delectable, so good that I ordered a second; we all did.

Cookie's was probably the most charming diner I've ever eaten in. Old-fashioned, it made me feel as if I'd been transplanted back in time to the sixties, although I've never been to that decade before.

Our food was prepared directly next to our booth on a wide open grill and as we ate the waitresses put together pies, rolled out dough, talked with patrons, amongst themselves and with us. The environment was incredible.

If I lived in this town I'd probably stop in at least once a week until I was retired. Then, I'd increase the frequency of my visits to once a day.

Most of the patrons appeared in their late sixties, early seventies, and my guess is they spend nearly two hours a day here catching up on the town's gossip.

As we finished our meal, none of us wanted to exit that diner and enter the "sauna." We sat back, kicked our feet up, and relaxed while simply listening to the conversations of those surrounding us for probably a good half hour. Any rest we can get, these days we'll take. We're all running on empty.

Soon enough, we decided it was time for us to get moving. As we stepped out of Cookie's, I realized there must have been air conditioning running inside as it felt far warmer outside than I'd remembered. And humid — very humid.

From Golden City, we *drove* to Pittsburg. Tomorrow we'll make up the mileage. Today, my burn is too painful to continue sitting on that seat, my mind too confused from the time already spent in the heat, and I'm still far too bitter in respect to the wind.

Getting a ride from Joe was a hard decision to make. The word "failure" is a perfect description of how I felt. In Golden City, I wanted to quit. I desperately wanted to return home.

Riding a bike directly into a headwind, day in and day out, can become rather draining. Sometimes I can't even begin to remember why I'm doing this. In these moments I try to step back, realize there are aspects of life much harder than this journey, and bike on.

Today, I couldn't bike any farther. Tomorrow, tack on twenty.

So far, Kansas reminds me of the *Wizard of Oz*.

Do you remember how we put on that show back in elementary school? Our parts weren't all that significant. We were just extras hanging out along that yellow brick road. Still, while watching our performances our parents must have aspired for us to achieve great things in this life. The thought makes me terribly sad for them and for you.

At a Pittsburg bike shop we ran into a few local bikers. They congratulated us on our "accomplishments" thus far. As they did, it sunk in: *I've ridden my bike to Kansas* (twenty miles shy of it, to be exact).

From sorrow to bliss; it happens so quickly.

Following our visit at the bike shop, we showered at the YMCA. Brad, Joe, and Steph literally forced me into the water. Still, the only part of my body I washed was my hair: the only part shielded from the sun's UV rays. I couldn't bear to willingly drench the remainder of my burnt body in *any* temperature of water. The thought itself was too painful.

The familiarity of that YMCA made me feel as if I were back in high school all over again. Just for a minute I dreamt of returning to those days: finishing up a two-hour long, strenuous swim team practice and relaxing in the warmth of a cleansing shower before returning home to "hit the books" in preparation for an AP chemistry exam scheduled for the following morning. "Swamms" was our teacher. You and I both somehow landed in the same section of that course. When problems couldn't be solved, we'd all turn to you for assistance. Those were the days.

And so, even through the physical pain of this burn and the mental anguish of your loss, I am learning to find comfort if only in some of the simplest memories that remain.

Then again, I hate myself for the way I treated you during our high school years. I was a brat, wanted to be cool and hanging out with you, my "dorky" big brother, didn't help my cause much. At the time, I was being a typically teenager. Typical people's brothers don't get murdered at twenty-seven. Most people have the opportunity to spend more than twenty-five years total on this earth with their brother by their side.

So, in this moment, I hate life.

For the second night in a row, we are sleeping in the middle of a city park.

I was sitting beneath one of the park's gazebos when I heard our Noah weather radio announce a tornado warning in effect, at which time I panicked. I ran directly over to a local police officer sitting in his parked cruiser watching the events of a little league ball game play out. A grin covered his face.

I hated to interrupt his thoughts but my mind was racing. Clearly, if I were rational at the time I would have realized he didn't seem alarmed in even the slightest fashion; nor were the kids playing ball. Still, the sky was *black*.

After introducing myself and explaining my worries he kindly proceeded to educate me on tornados. Interestingly enough, he actually is some sort of storm chaser, incredibly knowledgeable on the subject of tornados. Just as Mom once did when teaching you about constellations, he pointed into the sky at a particular cell he felt could potentially turn worrisome. He told me what to look out for and drew me a map of the town highlighting the location of the police station where I should run straight to if the tornado sirens should sound.

What a kind guy; didn't make me feel stupid in even the slightest fashion.

As we talked, we were surrounded by the largest city park I think I've seen in my life.

Tonight, it's my home.

For a small, quaint town like Pittsburg, it's a massive park, clearly the town's focal point (at least during the summer months). The YMCA is located directly next door, as is the community pool. A children's train is currently making laps around the right side of the park, which includes at least three gazebos, one of which our tent is set up underneath. There are volleyball courts, charcoal grills, swing sets and sliding boards dispersed on what seems to be at least ten acres of land.

There were at least seven or eight children's ball games going on up until a few minutes ago. At this time it was nearing ten P.M. The activity was energetic despite the eminent storm.

But then, without even the slightest warming, it started to pour. Lightning struck so close to us it seemed as if it was no more than five feet away.

As the bolt flickered, everyone (except us) charged off to their homes, surrounding the park in the classic Midwestern grid. I thanked the officer and ran rapidly to our tent where Brad, Joe and Steph already were. Lucky them!

Pittsburg is Kansas, Kansas at its best. I like this place. I think you would too.

I'm sleeping under a gazebo in the middle of Kansas. A tornado warning is in effect.

Be with me,

Jenny

19. Girard
Pittsburg to Toronto Lake State Park, Kansas

*"I like living. I have sometimes been wildly, despairingly,
acutely miserable, racked with sorrow, but through it all I still know
quite certainly that just to be alive is a grand thing."*
~Agatha Christie

May 31, 2008

Jeremy,

*T*oday we embarked on our ride during the wee hours of the morning.
Getting dressed was miserably painful, a lengthy ordeal, but
eventually I was *suited* up. When it was all put together I
looked like a jockey. And if you think that's funny: Stephanie looked
just the same.

You better believe it; we purchased this gear last night at the
Walmart located in Pittsburg.

We covered every square inch of skin present on our bodies with
a very attractive layering of full length, gray, cotton leggings (placed
on top of padded, spandex bike shorts of course) and matching short-
sleeved gray t-shirts with complimentary gray arm warmers.

Sunblock failed us yesterday. Today, we resorted to plan B: cover
every square inch of the body in cotton. Still, our sight was atrocious.
Brad and Joe couldn't stop laughing.

Walmart didn't offer white-colored "cool-fit" spandex so gray
cotton leggings and t-shirts will have to suffice.

Looks like today's going to be a hot one!

Speaking of the weather, in contrast to yesterday, the weather
today (*initially*) was beautiful. There was minimal humidity present

Jen partially "suited up" — minus a few items due to the heat — Kansas,
May 2008 ~ Photography by Stephanie Herbstritt

Even wooden telephone poles aren't able to maintain an upright position here
due to the wind's force and consistent northern direction, early June 2008.
Photograph taken by Stephanie Herbstritt

and the temperature of the air actually felt cool. And (believe it or not) there may have been a tailwind present while we were riding.

With the strength of the wind present yesterday, I thought for sure we'd never make it through Kansas. This morning, I was assured that we will. Brad: he still had his doubts!

Unfortunately, I now know that these favorable conditions were the calm before the storm. (That Brad: he's a wise man.)

About five miles outside of Girard, I saw the largest flash of lightning I've seen in my life twenty feet in front of me — larger than last night's. The sky abruptly darkened. Since we were only a few miles from Girard we decided to attempt to get there via bike rather than call Joe for help (yet again).

Due to a detour in our route, those five miles turned into ten. I couldn't have been any more frantic.

When we arrived in Girard the sky's color suggested we'd arrived during the middle of the night, yet it was roughly eight o'clock in the morning. We quickly ran into the first gas station we saw just as the rain started to fall and begged kindly to sit there until the storm passed us by. The two women who were working the register smiled at one another and said that'd be just fine. I'm sure they were thinking: "Easterners!" We took a seat in the eating area and unloaded our gear. My subconscious must have known we'd be there for awhile.

Within minutes, local farmers filed in, first filling Styrofoam cups to the brim with coffee, then, proceeding to the checkout area to pay for this, their breakfast, and their countless gallons of diesel. They advised us as to their predictions regarding the storm and its path. Together we watched the local radar on television displaying only red and purple hues in all areas we intended on biking through, at least until noon. Our route was to take us directly into the storm's path. It seemed Pittsburg was just about to be hit.

With this knowledge in mind, we immediately called Joe, woke him out of a cold sleep and strongly "encouraged" him to pack up camp as soon as possible and meet us at the gas station.

As we waited for his arrival I contemplated what I'd do in this quiet little town all day long. Biking had become such a routine I didn't know what else to do.

None of the local businesses were open quite yet (except for the gas station I was currently sitting at) as it was just shortly after eight on a Saturday morning. I needed to print off a few documents (contained in an email) pertaining to your estate. Then, I had to have them notarized. I figured now was as good a time as any to complete this dreadful task. I must have been talking to myself aloud, inquiring where I could find a computer with internet access, printer and notary, preferably all in the same place.

Within a few minutes, a man who had been sitting at the table adjacent to ours, reading the newspaper and drinking coffee, walked over to our table and initiated conversation. He introduced himself, asked where we were biking to, where we had come from, and if he could take a look at our maps. He was incredibly curious of our adventures. Soon enough, I understood why. He was a retired truck driver who had been all over this country himself time and again. He'd traveled Interstate 80 from the east coast to the west, and vice versa more times than he could remember. He'd taken the scenic routes as well. He knew this country inside and out.

As he studied our maps he made notes for us as to where he felt we should visit, where we should take some extra time, go out of our way and see something special: the Royal Gorge in Colorado outside of Pueblo, Garden of the Gods, Lake Tahoe, the northern rim of the Grand Canyon, etc.

Joe joined our conversation once he arrived (rather quickly after we called him and forewarned him of the "imminent tornado" I might add).

All four of us talked with this man for hours. As we did, we sipped on scolding hot chocolate and the ladies at the register offered all of us left-over breakfast sandwiches free of cost.

Soon enough, a local elderly couple arrived seeking a secure shelter. They were definitely "regulars." Said they lived in a run-down trailer situated on the outskirts of town and didn't feel safe in it during storms of this nature so they would come down here and spend the day completing crossword puzzles in the company of good friends.

The retired truck driver eventually mentioned he overheard me talking about a notary. His wife worked as one in Pittsburg. He wasn't sure she'd have her equipment with her today (as it was Saturday) but he would check. He left only for a brief instant in time, as he lived directly across the street. Unfortunately, his wife didn't have her equipment with her but he knew of another notary just down the road. He directed me there but first showed me to the library where he was certain I could print off the documents.

I was permitted to use the library for free. I didn't need identification or a library card, just some small change for the copies. I headed to the notary and, truth be told, I wasn't charged a thing for this service. The woman said that this was just "one of the perks" of living in a small community like Girard. I insisted I should pay something as I was just passing through but she said the service was her "privilege."

Kansas *is* America. These people have hearts of gold. I wish this were true for all of mankind.

Now drenched, I returned to the gas station where Joe, Brad, and Steph still were intently engaging in conversation with our new-found friend.

We stayed for a few more hours.

After about five hours spent there, as the weather improved we decided to risk it and bike toward the next town some twenty miles away. We didn't make it more than five miles when the lightning started to strike far too close by, particularly for my comfort. The thunder sounded loud enough to awake even a hibernating bear, and so we agreed to return to Girard.

We arrived back in town just in time for a late lunch at the local Pizza Hut. I highly doubt I need to explain my obsession with "all-you-can-eat buffets" to you! As we ate, rain dumped from the sky, the winds picked up and thunder and lightning put on quite a show. As quick as these storm savvy elements arrived, they disappeared. Just in time for our lunch to be finished the skies cleared and we were off to our next destination: Eureka!

Well, we didn't make it to Eureka. There simply wasn't enough time left in the day. Instead, we stopped at Toronto Lake State Park.

As for being "off schedule," it is far more difficult to bike through Kansas than I'd expected. Surely it is flat (compared to Pennsylvania that is), but when traveling from east to west the elevation increases approximately 2,500 feet over the length of the state. I didn't expect this incline to be noticeable whatsoever, but it certainly is. The wind is extraordinarily strong here and there is absolutely nothing to break it as the fields here are wide open, empty and "relatively" flat. Crossing Kansas will be a challenge. Our friend the retired truck driver told us so!

Wheat seems to be the crop of choice here this time of the year. The fields have been golden for miles. The sky here is massive. I never expected it would appear so colossal. When I look around, I can see for miles and miles in the distance without a single object obstructing my field of view. Of course, there are windmills, barns, and livestock present in abundance but skyscrapers, large buildings, strip malls, and parking garages are nowhere in sight.

The farms here span for thousands of acres. I can bike for five miles straight, paralleling a solitary farmer's land. With the price of diesel these days, I expect (and know from speaking with these men this morning) that the farmers here spend nearly $1,000 a day farming their fields and sowing their crops. This is unfathomable to me.

Toronto Lake State Park is hidden in the valley of the Verdigris River. It is beautiful here. The grass is actually green. The grounds are secluded: perfectly placed in the middle of Kansas's Chautauqua Hills where currently only the sounds and smells of nature fill the air.

Although it's lovely here, it *is* copperhead country. Trust me: I am careful with my gait; no need to worry about me (a.k.a., Nervous Nelly)!

Although, I *did* almost have a conniption earlier in the day when I nearly stepped on a turtle. Just as an aside, these little guys blanket the ground here (and that's no exaggeration!). Many attempt to cross the road during the hottest hours of the day. Most don't make it across alive. I've thought about rescuing a few of them, but feared their bite.

To live anxiety free!

Our Noah weather radio has issued another tornado warning. As well, the camp host arrived to inform us of what to do if and when (in the middle of the night) we hear his voice instructing us to seek shelter: we are to dart to the cement bathhouse about a half mile down the road and *pray*.

This makes me even more nervous.

Once again, I'm the only person here who seems so anxious. People are playing catch and cards, eating dinner, laughing, and enjoying their time here at this unruffled park. Brad is oiling his chain. Joe's playing the guitar while playing with fire and Steph, she's on the phone.

On that note, I'm currently telling myself that the lightning here looks like a fireworks display set in the sky only without all the booms and the bangs. I should enjoy this natural beauty with which I have been blessed.

We devoured dinner rather rapidly tonight. Then, Joe brought out his guitar. We all sat around the campfire, listening to his music and the crackle of the fire while eating s'mores and falling into a trance set by the flicker of the fire.

The stage we created was bittersweet. It took me back... As a family, we'd surround the fire-pit in Mom and Dad's backyard, all propped on lawn chairs, encircled by cotton throws. We'd laugh and joke, bat at one another, and tell stories.

Do you remember the time Jeremy was re-enacting that automobile accident for his EMT class at Penn State when he actually wrecked his brand new Blazer into a large tree while his good friend Scott filmed the escapade? We'd all look at you and laugh. You'd be hurled over practically on the ground absorbed in your own laughter as we all talked about you in jest.

How about the time Great Aunt Sister Helen gave Dad that horse laxative? It was a given, one of us would then stand up and imitate Dad jumping out of his truck and running awkwardly into the house on a mission aimed toward the bathroom.

Or when Steph pulled the fish tank over on top of Joe? "I just wanted to feed them! He always got to do it. I just wanted my turn."

Wait, wait! Remember when you and Dad kayaked down the Spring Creek right after it flooded? "That water was so high, every time we went underneath a bridge all we could do was duck down and hope for the best. The water literally was touching the base of the bridges." The stories you guys had about that trip were hysterical! And to watch Mom's facial expressions as you told them; that was the best part of all.

Those days will never be again, not in this lifetime. I'm trying to savor the time I've been given here with those I have left, drink up the moment. It's just so hard to do, knowing you can't.

Jeremy, we've ridden our bikes nearly 1,500 miles. We've made it to the Midwest where our lives were just beginning roughly two and a half decades ago.

I am certain we'll complete the task set in front of us, no matter what. The odds have been against us since day one but they're getting better. We'll finish this mission for you.

On this stormy night, I'm laying my head down with the hopes of falling into a deep sleep filled with dreams full of only fond memories.

Love,

Jen

Waiting out a thunderstorm inside the Pathfinder on our way to Toronto Lake State Park, Kansas, May 31, 2008 ~ Photograph taken by Stephanie Herbstritt

Brad and Jen biking in Kansas (This time Brad's in the lead — Jen's losing her battle with the headwind.) ~ Photograph taken by Stephanie Herbstritt

Left to right: Jen, Brad, and Joe in front of "Grandfather's Horse," sculpted by John Kearney, 1973, using car bumpers, Wichita State University, Wichita, Kansas, May 2008
Photograph taken by Stephanie Herbstritt

20. Wichita
Toronto Lake State Park to Wichita, Kansas

"Be open to your dreams, people. Embrace that distant shore.
Because our mortal journey is over all too soon."
~David Assael

June 1, 2008

Jeremy,

*L*ast night as I sat by our campfire listening to Joe's performance I thought about whether or not ten years from now I'd remember the events of "that night at Toronto Lake." In doing so, I was reminded of the worth of memories. The human mind recalls many details, some, obviously, more clearly than others.

Some memories of mine have faded to the point where now they appear as nothing more than pieces to a puzzle. Oftentimes, with the right clues, these pieces can be placed back together in just the right order.

Or so I think…

I remember a lot about how our lives began and how yours ended. I can recite most of the conversations we had during the last two weeks of your life, practically verbatim. Most of the contents dispersed in between those times have turned to gray. Each individual memory seems to have complied with a multitude of other memories, transforming into a hazy picture I no longer can decipher. Particularly, memories of my late middle school and early high school years packed with all sorts of activity, from participating in sports to spending time bonding and fighting with friends and family, have blurred into one massive, incredibly disorganized and multicolored portrait.

What I do remember of those years and the many years of my life before and after this period surprises me to no end. This simple discovery serves as a reminder that what is important to the mind will *never* fade. I presume the events of last night and the events of this trip, generally speaking, will be engraved in my mind forever, just like a name scripted on a tombstone will never wane.

I'll never forget you. Your silhouette will forever be engrained within my mind. When I close my eyes, I'll always be able to see you. You'll never be more than a memory but you'll always be there.

And, just in case I develop dementia years down the road, I'll have these letters for my grandchildren to read to me.

The human brain is amazing. It is an aspect of this universe so complex I doubt even the most renowned scientists will ever be able to replicate it to perfection.

What is fascinating about the mind is that it remembers not just the good, but the bad and the ugly. Often we attempt to disguise negative attributes of ourselves or others, particularly after they have died, because we don't want to jeopardize another's name or that of our own. But the mind won't forget the truth.

I recognize I've lived a far from perfect life. Both of us were human. Each member of this human race makes mistakes and we've all participated in silly spectacles. For example, I attended fraternity parties as an undergraduate. I drank alcohol before I was twenty-one years of age. I lied to our parents and I lied to myself.

I can't speak for you but I do remember vividly the events of our early college days. Even though you, I and our very best friends acted irresponsibly during those days, I'll never erase those memories because they are just as important to me as the "kid-friendly" ones. For instance…

Prank calling Mom in the middle of the night, drunk, pretending you were in jail, arrested for DUI — this is one of my favorites. Although you scared the shit out of her and brought tears to her eyes, I'm sure she'll never forget that conversation either. Although it was a total invention of our imagination and simply an immature and cruel prank, I can't think of a person who knew you who wouldn't give anything to trade April 16 in for a real scenario like the one we played at years ago.

We left Toronto Lake early this morning and traveled to Wichita, the largest city in Kansas with 354,865 residents (as of a 2005 count). The TransAmerica Trail does not traverse through this city but we modified its course with this tiny detour.

Lynn and Tim (our second cousins) recently moved here and we were hoping to surprise them with our arrival. Unfortunately, they are out of town and won't be returning for two weeks. Darn.

Wichita is filled with shopping malls, byways with heavy traffic, chain restaurants, car dealerships, major medical and trauma centers, universities and people. As much as I've been enjoying rural America, it is nice to be inside a booming metropolis.

From what I have seen of Kansas thus far it appears its industry of choice is agriculture. To see a city in the middle of farmland is slightly bizarre. Nevertheless, I like its place.

After lunch, we visited Wichita State, Newman, and Friends universities. No matter how many universities I visit, I will always bleed blue and white. I know you felt the same.

As I walked the streets laid out in a far more complex grid than some of the other downtowns we've visited here in the Midwest, I realized how much I love being a tourist. I'm not sure what it is about walking around in a foreign place with a camera in hand, taking pictures of everything under the sun from signs that read "man who eats jelly beans farts in techno color," to recording the most bizarre of activities on video. Whatever it is, it makes me smile. And, we all know, these days it wouldn't hurt me to smile a little more.

Activity downtown was nominal today, just as we'd expected: it's Sunday afternoon. Finding a parking spot was easy. And we were able to walk for blocks without seeing another solitary human being.

Midwestern motivational roadside sign, June 2008
Photograph taken by Stephanie Herbstritt

I love the Midwest. The people are friendly. The food is good. Traffic is minimal. The sky appears close. The stars are bright. The air is clear. And everyone seems content. I could live with the storms.

As we walked in silence, my mind raced with endless thoughts most of which focused on you and what you meant to me. When you died, I was petrified of forgetting your voice. We only had the two recordings of it, at least in your older years. The first was your cell phone answering recording: "Hello, this is Jeremy. Leave a message and I'll get back to you as soon as possible."

The second: a message you left to us on the house machine Friday night prior to the marathon. "Hey, what's up? This is Jeremy…" You were just curious how everyone was doing with the flu. Joe had been sick. You mentioned you had only twenty-one days remaining in the semester, I believe you called it doing "geek-work" and then you'd be home. You were ecstatic. The year was just about over. You were proud, had something to tell us and that was the good news regarding your scholarship. Thank goodness for cell phones as you caught us on these while we were in Boston.

You were probably pacing casually around your apartment while you left that message on Mom and Dad's machine. The entire apartment complex below you could probably hear your call as you talked louder than usual while on your cell phone (as most people do). And the sounds of your size-thirteen feet pounding the ground never were quiet.

It makes me laugh just picturing you in that moment. As you paced around your apartment, you would have passed by piles of homework all over the place, laid out in an order only you could decipher.

I wish I could just sit in and listen to you engage in a conversation even just for a minute. To see you so full of life, just once again, would make me so happy. But I can't and I now know I don't need those recordings to remember you or your voice. I don't have to hear you speak in the moment to remember you and your unique quirks. Even if I tried to forget you, I wouldn't be able. You're a permanent piece of my life.

Still, it saddens me to know that your time here is over. I don't think there is such a thing as time allotted here on this earth. I think sometimes things just happen, and by no means is it always fair. For no reason whatsoever, you got shafted in this life. So did thirty-one others that day. This world should be lost without you.

My life will forever be empty without you in it. I will always have a void where you should be. Children, new memories, nor time will fill this void. Never again will I be able to run with you, kayak, hike the Appalachian Trail or talk over a beer. My children will never know you. They certainly will know of you, but unfortunately for them they will never be able to have a conversation with you or introduce their friends to their Uncle Jeremy. The next generation of engineers will never have the opportunity to learn from you, and a firm somewhere out there will be missing something forever because they won't have the ability to hire you. Generations to come are lost without you for countless reasons. They won't ever know, but you and I will. We had a connection that can never be replaced.

Left to right:
Tussey mOUnTaiNBACK
"B-Unit" teammates
Jeremy Ford, Jeremy
Herbstritt, Joe, and Jen,
fall 2003

So what are you to me?

You're my big brother and you always will be. You're Jeremy Michael Herbstritt, son of Michael and Margaret, brother of Joseph Paul, Stephanie Marie, and Jennifer Therese. You're the splitting image of your grandfather, the sparkle in Steph's eyes, the hope for our futures, the soft summer breeze, the eagle above me and the warmth of the sand that will be beneath my feet when I reach the West Coast. You're the center of my universe, the pit in my stomach, and the void in my heart. You're the reason I go on. You're my big brother, Jeremy Michael.

I would give anything in this world if I could have you back if just for a second. *Anything.* I don't care. I just want you back.

As the shock starts to fade, reality is setting in. I will never see you again. At least, not in this life.

With this said, it is time for me to lay down my head. We're at a KOA outside of Wichita. Tomorrow will be a mental challenge as we'll be bicycling on the same stretch of road, exactly as the crow flies, for one hundred repetitive miles.

I better get some rest. Tomorrow will take mental stamina.

With all my love,

Jenny

21. The Higher Plains
Wichita to Larned, Kansas

"Seek the wisdom of the ages, but look at the world through the eyes of a child."
–Ron Wild

June 2, 2008

Jeremy,

Today we traveled from Wichita to Larned, so named after Fort Larned, now a National Historic Site that previously served as a military base along the Santa Fe Trail and Arkansas River during the mid 1800s.[15] The town itself is situated in Pawnee County and has a population of approximately 4,000.

More importantly (if you ask me), Larned has the nicest outdoor swimming pool of our trip thus far. The teenagers here may stay out the latest of any teenagers I've ever met, and the ducks are the absolute most dreadful, loudest creatures I've come in contact with in my life, but I'd put up these flaws, just for the pool.

We're not in the high plains of Kansas just yet (as far as I know), but we certainly are, slowly but surely, rising in elevation. Today's plains were definitely "higher" than yesterday's. And the higher plains of Kansas undeniably are beautiful, just as I expected. We're still biking through fields of gold laid out in a grid.

I just can't get enough of this wide open space, fresh air, and colossal sky. Whoever said Kansas would be flat and lame must never have spent the time to appreciate this place like I am right now.

The farmers here are talkative. They remind me of you. Inevitably a few are present at each gas station we stop at, filling up on diesel and searching for good conversation.

And the *Wizard of Oz* was almost right when describing the bricks laid here in Kansas. Red bricks (not yellow) surface almost every town's centrally placed roads. When I bike over these surfaces, I actually feel like I have been taken out of a scene from that memorable film. It must be because of these brick roads that I've spent the day mulling over which specific roles each of us has mimicked throughout this journey. For you, this shouldn't be any surprise:

I've taken on the role of the Cowardly Lion: afraid of everything. I certainly could use some courage.

I'd have to name Joe the Tin Man (by process of elimination) although he already has a heart of gold.

Stephanie: I'd name her the Scarecrow, not because she is stupid but because she is just the opposite. Just like you, she is brilliant.

Brad: Well, all that is left is Dorothy, the Wicked Witch of the West, and the Good Witch of the North, Glinda. I best leave him out of this naming game.

But you — you'd be the Wizard. You'd provide us with courage, intelligence, and heart. Now you know all of the answers for which we are searching. You've made it to heaven, if it actually exists.

Today's sleeping arrangements mark city park #3. When we called the local police station to request our one night's stay here, we were kindly also offered a warm shower across the street at the town's community pool. When we got there, we were also offered a free dip absent of a time limit. Now do you understand why I love this place?

After our free dip, we barbequed at the park. Earlier, we picked up a few pounds of hamburger at the local grocery store, as well as a can of baked beans and a few cobs of freshly picked sweet corn. Our meal was delicious; a nice change from canned ravioli.

After we finished our meal, we proceeded to set up our tent underneath (you guessed it) another gazebo. It's for rain and/or wind protection purposes — cut me a break. Then, using the same public outdoor faucet, we cleaned out our cooler (wow, did that ever smell foul!), refilled our water bottles, brushed our teeth, and washed our dishes. In the midst of this now typical nightly routine, I realized we were being watched by a group of children playing ball in the park. Their game froze in time as we went about our business. It looked as if they'd all been captured in the context of a very good movie. Under their gaze, I became slightly embarrassed. All I could do was chuckle at the thoughts I figured were going through each of these youngster's minds.

I like living on the road. Possibly one day these children will understand.

As the night drew to a close, I attempted to sleep. Unfortunately, I don't think sleep will come all that easy tonight. A group of high school-aged teenagers is congregating outside the pool, directly across the street, engaging in very loud conversation and giggling. Possibly we're the topic of conversation.

I'm praying for a prank-free night. Looks like I'm in luck. A local police officer just kicked them out. I can hear him telling these youngsters they're in violation of the community's curfew. He'd given them "ample opportunities" to finish up their business by simply cruising by a good four times prior to interrupting their party. It's "time to go home."

Well, the kids might be gone, but the ducks won't stop quacking. Obviously, we weren't thinking when we set up our tent directly next to a group of ducks (and geese) caged in together no more than ten feet away. I'm not sure what is worse: the teenagers or these ducks. Either ducks are nocturnal or they simply don't require much sleep: all I hear is constant, obnoxious quacking in abundance.

Excellent, the ducks have stopped quacking, possibly just for a second. I am going to make my fifteenth attempt at falling asleep. As Mom used to say about us when we were little, I guess I'm "overtired."

From Oz, good night! (If only I had ruby slippers.)

Jen

Dilapidated silo, June 2008 ~ Photograph by Joseph Herbstritt

22. Scott City
Larned to Scott City, Kansas

"Courage is the art of being the only one who knows you're scared to death."
~Harold Wilson

June 3, 2008

Jeremy,

Today we biked over 120 miles from Larned through Alexander, Ness City, and Dighton to Scott City, Kansas, population roughly 3,800.

Sorry to bore you with all the population figures; it's just that they're marked on all the city limit signs; that or the "Welcome to _____" sign.

Lately, I've read a lot of signs. Bet you didn't know signs existed that warned of armadillos crossing?

Anyway, Scott City, the county seat for Scott County, is situated in the high plains of Kansas with an elevation of nearly 3,000 feet. You guessed it: the elevations are marked on these signs as well.

To put all this elevation mumbo jumbo into perspective, when we entered Kansas territory our elevation in Pittsburg, Kansas, was below 1,000 feet, just shy of the same elevation we lived at in Bellefonte, Pennsylvania. Over the course of the past few days, on what has topographically appeared as flat land, we have increased in elevation over 2,000 feet and still have some climbing to do before reaching the Colorado border, which, mind you, is only sixty miles away. Both literally and figuratively speaking, my life is a constant climb.

Scott City is vertically situated equal distances from Oklahoma and Nebraska, dead center of both. Its appearance is similar to that

Joe filming wide open spaces, western Kansas, June 2008
Photograph taken by Stephanie Herbstritt

of the other towns we've passed through in Kansas, but intuitively I know I am nearing Colorado: a place I am very anxious to experience.

Outside of town, the wheat was still golden. Where wheat wasn't growing, the ground appeared covered in a fine film of dust. It appears we're approaching the desert.

As I rode my bike past these fields of gold on roads that were absent of even the slightest twist in their path, I could see what appeared to be exactly the same picture ahead of me for miles on end. No longer is Kansas hilly. The road we were on was the only one I saw. Farmers were operating large pieces of machinery, harvesting their crops while cattle waited in herds to be taken to slaughter, fenced in compactly alongside the edge of the road. As I passed by these hundreds if not thousands of animals, the aroma resembled that of a field recently fertilized (with organic materials).

Telephone poles paralleling the road pointed north. Due to the wind's strength and direction, they all obtained the same forty-five-degree angle. As only makes sense, windmills were present in mass quantity here as well, lining the roads.

Snakes inhabited the roads, beaching in the sun during the warmest hours of the day.

The air felt incredibly dry but the sun's rays were scorching. I felt like I was biking through an oven being preheated to bake a batch of fudge brownies. Water stops have become scarce as communities are now becoming much farther spread out. Thank God for Joe and his "water mobile."

Oh, and I saw what appeared to be the Pacific Ocean! A mirage of sunlight reflecting on the black, oily pavement ahead of me, but still… An optical illusion combined with mild dehydration must have made the perfect recipe for this not-so-amusing joke.

Directly outside of Scott City an aroma of Mexican cuisine filled the air. Possibly this was a hallucination as well; regardless, the smell seemed fitting. This section of Kansas resembled Mexico as I knew it to exist in the movies: desolate and dusty with a sense of mystery about it.

Not much farther down the road activity flourished as we entered the city's limits. Scott City appeared emblematic of a Midwestern community with friendly people, red brick roads, tornado sirens, and streets laid out in a grid. It's incredible how abrupt and drastic the scenery often changes when traveling from town to town.

If I had to change one thing about this community, I'd be lost to do so. It's perfect the way it is.

On that note, tonight marks city park #4. The process of setting our tent up here was particularly comical (when is it not?). We arrived fairly early in the evening, early enough that the park was still relatively busy. Although people were rampant, this park couldn't have sat on more than a few acres of land. As well, the playground equipment was dispersed rather vastly within the space. Therefore, in finding the perfect place for our tent, seclusion was nearly impossible to find.

As happened yesterday, as we pieced the pieces of our tent together the children all stopped doing whatever it was they were doing and glued their eyes on us. After a few minutes of this silence, they started pointing their fingers in our direction while simultaneously chuckling.

Then, a few high school-aged adolescents requested to go inside our tent, "tour it," and "see its size."

What?

I told them that would be fine, but they should be aware in advance none of us has showered in weeks. The smell inside might be fatal to an outsider (possibly a white lie). With this said, they were content just watching from a safe distance. Sleeping in a city park is classified as bizarre behavior. I know this.

Soon enough, two siblings (a boy and a girl) spotted us out effortlessly inside the crowd. Running toward the swings, they insisted we accompany them and be their strength, "Push us high, please!" They must have been only three and five years of age, respectively. In their attendance were two babysitters, clearly preoccupied with the events of their own lives. Engrossed in conversation, they didn't even notice the location of the children, now on the opposite end of the park engaging in conversation with us, four very filthy strangers. I pushed the children on the swings "higher and higher."

After some begging and the arrival of their caregivers, I agreed to give them an "underdog" and then another and another. You know how it goes with little kids and swings. They never want to get off once they get started. While I continued to push the children, their babysitters and I carried on a conversation regarding boys.

The night drew late and soon enough it was time for the children to return home and prepare for bed. We said our goodbyes and each drew to his home. My home is a tent. Theirs, a more permanent structure. At this time in my life, I don't particularly trust the permanence of any aspect of this world. My tent is ideal.

It was time for dinner: spaghetti with butter bread. Sadly, I wasn't able to savor my butter bread. As soon as I took my last bite of spaghetti and prepared to clean my plate with that bread, the sky turned an ominous shade of black. In an instant, the clouds released buckets of rain. As we all darted across the street to seek shelter in a seasonal ice-cream shack, our plates were cleaned by the force of the rain.

Fast approaching Kansas thunderstorm, June 2008
Photograph taken by Stephanie Herbstritt

As soon as I finished my cone, the storm passed. It was this quick. Unfortunately, it was long enough to drench our tent. The raindrops here come in mammoth sizes. Just like the thunder, lightning, and the sky, all aspects of nature here seem to come in a package much larger than I remembered to be true back in Bellefonte.

Around ten o'clock, I tried to unwind. As traffic was absent, under the light of the moon, Joe and I kicked around a soccer ball in the middle of the road. No words were exchanged, but my mind raced. The utter silence of this town enabled me to get lost in my thoughts. I suspect Joe was doing the same.

As we bounced that ball back and forth, I was brought back to our youth and the memory of evenings spent at Penn State's Recreation Hall playing racquetball as a family. Bouncing the ball off the wall in that large, hollow, rectangular room created an echo similar to that which a deep valley creates. The bouncing of our soccer ball created the same type of echo. In that moment, I just wanted to scream, listen for the echo, and pretend it was you calling back to me. But I didn't. Instead, I went to bed.

Sleep is the only escape I can get. Sadly, often sleep itself can't provide me with a total escape. My dreams these days are stranger than I remember them ever to be. They seem to be finely crafted, displaying all of my fears and unconscious thoughts. Each morning when I awake, my subconscious provides my conscious self with a detailed snapshot of the previous night's dreamed events. Then, I spend the remainder of my day trying to figure out what it was I was obsessing about that created such a complex series of happenings within my mind. I often worry these violent dreams will come true.

Two weeks before you died, I had one of the most peculiar dreams I've ever had in my life. In it, you died. Of course, you already know about that dream because I detailed it to everyone I came in contact with, including you, hoping someone would be able to calm my anxieties. People died before in my dreams, but never you. No one could explain to me what that dream might have meant. Possibly I was hurt you'd moved to Blacksburg. You were making new friends, engaging in new activities, and moving on with your life. It was true that I was afraid of losing you.

In the dream, our family was on vacation, somewhere in the Caribbean. Everyone was there, except for Joe. Mom, Dad, and I were attending a funeral. It was yours. But it wasn't *only* yours. Three bodies were carried up a narrow aisle, formed by no more than five rows of folding chairs placed on both sides, to an altar. The altar was a long plastic folding table, very simple. The bodies were placed on long bamboo sheets (pulled taut) and carried above the heads of numerous shirtless islanders. The first body carried was that of an island native. Then, a woman I believe represented Steph was carried up and laid directly on top of him. Finally, you were carried up on that sheet of bamboo and placed on top of the others. I knew it was you because of the complexion of your skin, your hands, and your hair. Your head was full of dark hair. Steph — I wasn't so sure it was her. But you, I was certain of your position.

That island was beautiful. The sand was perfect. The air was warm and the breeze was calm. We were seated under a white, pop-up tent with wide open sides. Still, I was horrified. You were dead. And so possibly was Steph. I still wasn't sure that body was hers, but I had no clue where she was at if she, indeed, was alive. My anxiety escalated. You were dead and I didn't know how I'd continue on.

Then, the dream transitioned.

Vacation continued on and I met up with Cousin Katie. She and I climbed up a very steep wall, covered from top to bottom with t-shirts and sweaters. Once we got to the top, we each grabbed onto a shirt and slid all the way down the wall. We did this over and over again. As we did so, we discussed how I would get through. "With time, you'll figure this out."

The dream transitioned again.

Now, I was at Brad's brother's wedding. (In real life he was actually getting married but in this dream he wasn't marrying the woman he was scheduled to marry in real life. Instead, he was marrying one of the girls from our church.) It was the most bizarre wedding I've ever attended. Children were the bridesmaids and groomsmen and a morbidly obese woman was outrageously dancing on very thin high-heeled shoes during the service. I worried her girth might break those heels. The service had an energy about it similar to that of Pentecostal or Charismatic services where members "speak in tongues" and are "slain by the Holy Spirit."

After the wedding we sat around in Brad's brother's new home watching him and his bride open gifts. One of the gifts was a couch cushion intended to be used so as to prevent air from drafting in underneath a door. Attached to the end of that cushion was a bear that just couldn't stop roaring. This bear struck me as odd, being that it roared just as you used to do while joking with me out in the woods when we were hiking or running. You'd kid that possibly we'd be "lucky" enough to run into a wild black bear: "Rrrrrrroar!"

Never before has a dream of mine come true.

Two weeks after I experienced this dream, you were murdered.

Also, as far as the hill of t-shirts: after the events of April 16, the Penn State community sold copious numbers of maroon and orange t-shirts. Almost all of the students who attended the blue/white game that year wore the shirts in support of our family and all of the other people affected by that horrific, senseless act of violence.

And what about the girl from our church who, in my dream, married Brad's brother? Well, less than a month after my dream you were buried in a plot adjacent to the plot containing that girl's mother…It was the only lot left in the cemetery.

Now, every time someone I know dies in one of my dreams, I can't help but panic. Who will be next? Will this dream come true?

Our minds are impressive. Mine knows my biggest fears. It knows I can't possibly go through another death. It knows all I want is to make you return. So it comes up with scenarios webbed in a dream. My dreams focus on loss, whether they're as simple as the loss of a tooth or as complex as the murder of yet another one of my loved ones. They focus on what I can't let go of, on what consumes my every waking minute: your death, who will be next, uncertainty, unfairness, and violence.

Hopefully tonight my sleep will be peaceful. The beauty of this place sure is lovely. I just need a break from what I am coming to realize as true.

Sleep, I *need* sleep.

Goodnight, Jeremy. From Kansas: goodnight.

Tomorrow I'm off to Colorado! This will be as far west as I've ever ventured!

Love,
Jennifer

23. Colorado
Scott City, Kansas, to Ordway, Colorado

*"Man cannot discover new oceans unless he has
the courage to lose sight of the shore."*
~André Gide

June 4, 2008

Jeremy,

*T*oday we biked *171 miles from Scott City, Kansas, to Ordway,
Colorado.*
    One hundred seventy-one miles. Holy cow! And I'm still a
rookie!

Sixty miles into the ride we crossed the state line and entered
Colorado.

From day one I've been looking forward to Colorado. I've eagerly
anticipated the experience of a characteristic Colorado ski town
nestled in the middle of the quaint Rocky Mountains. Now, I've actually made it here: the first state I've been in actually considered a part
of the *western* United States. I'm in awe.

Kansas was farmland on *relatively* flat terrain. Towns were pleasantly small and dispersed miles apart. In between, there was nothing
other than flat to mildly rolling fields of gold, wide open space, and
gigantic sky.

Naively, I pictured Colorado to abruptly present mountainous
terrain. Instead of experiencing this misconception, I was faced with
even flatter terrain. No matter what direction I look in, I can see for
miles and miles in the distance without anything obstructing my view.
It is that flat.

Entering Colorado, June 4, 2008

Joe, yet again, filming wide open spaces and gigantic sky, eastern Colorado, June 2008
Photograph taken by Stephanie Herbstritt

Eastern Colorado is a very dry desert filled with nothing other than brown sand, dusty air, tumbleweed, and mesas in the distance. The stage set in front of me reminds me of an old western movie.

Large ranches are present here, but not the type of ranches I'd envisioned. Cows graze freely, rarely being surrounded by fence. Over-sized, immaculate houses and barns are nowhere to be found. Driveways (or entrances of any sort) leading to these properties are completely absent. Intuitively I know someone owns the land and cattle here. Logic tells me he or she is a rancher. This only makes sense. But if it weren't for this logic, I couldn't be certain.

Periodically, we did pass through terribly small, practically deserted towns, each with a post office, solitary gas station, and one or two farmers fueling up on diesel, set on no more than a half-mile stretch of road. If it weren't for these diminutive signs of existence, (again) I may have thought this section of our country was completely abandoned.

Other than for the cattle, the fields here appear absolutely unin-habited. And the ground is terribly dry. All day long I wondered how animals could possibly survive out in these fields of dirt. Water is nowhere. How can farmers possibly produce a harvest?

Snakes (on the other hand) are very prominent, as are lizards. The air is sweltering. Humidity is absent.

All around me is silence. The only noise I can hear is the sound of the wind (the strength of which came to a climax around the end of the day today). Here, there is nothing surrounding the road to block the wind and its force. All I can do is "truck through." When I bike, nature is all that I hear — that and the rhythm of my cadence mixed with an occasional crank from the bike's chain.

Even the railroad appeared deserted. I haven't seen a train run on its tracks yet, and I followed its distance all day long.

Yet, in the middle of this flat, hot and dry desert, I saw two jack rabbits — evidence wildlife can survive in these harsh conditions. Also two antelopes came along within ten feet of our group.

The first merely stared at us as we pedaled by. He was standing on the railroad tracks, which parallel the road all the way through

Kansas and into eastern Colorado. His head followed us from the point we laid eyes on him until we were out of his sight.

The second ran alongside us in between the railroad tracks and the road for nearly two miles. I must admit, initially I was petrified he would attack. But after I realized that running beside us was simply a fun game for him, I grew comfortable in his presence and enjoyed his company. I was disappointed when he decided to leave us behind. He must have noticed his prey somewhere off in the distant sandy desert.

I know this sounds silly, but I pretended he was you, a sign from above that you are okay, still with us, protecting us, providing us with advice and divine intervention.

I wish this could be so.

I wish a lot of things could be so.

In any case, you might be interested in learning how it is we came to ride our bikes a whopping 171 miles. The truth is, when I awoke this morning, I never would have predicted I'd ride my bike that far. I hoped we'd make it to Eads, a Colorado town located fairly close to the Kansas border about a hundred miles west of Scott City.

I'm not exactly sure what it was about Eads that persuaded us to bike an additional seventy-one miles. Possibly, it was the food. You see, in Eads we stopped for lunch at a fabulous Mexican diner where we consumed the most authentic Mexican cuisine I've tasted in my life. The daily special consisted of beef tacos with refried beans, chicken enchiladas, corn, an all-you-can-eat salad bar, dessert, and iced tea — all for only five bucks! We couldn't resist it.

From Eads, I initially hoped to make it to Sugar City. But once we arrived in Sugar City, I wasn't ready to stop. So we continued on toward Ordway. (Sometimes Brad and Steph get so delusional they just do what I say!)

As we neared the two hundred-mile mark, a huge part of me wanted to continue on all the way to Pueblo. In that moment, I wanted nothing more than to complete a double century. Unfortunately, Brad and Steph put an end to my nonsense. (To be honest, ever since we got here Brad hasn't been able to stop talking about how he wishes we rode a full two hundred. According to him we're going to do just that by the end of this trip!)

Pueblo is located fifty miles west of Ordway and we didn't arrive in Ordway until nearly eight o'clock. Although my thoughts in this moment are still quite euphoric, the realist in me is saying "I highly doubt you would have been able to bike an additional fifty miles." Brad and Steph were correct. Upon our arrival into Ordway, I didn't have even an ounce of energy left to spare. Not only was this so, but the hours of daylight remaining were decreasing in quantity rather quickly.

Still, I wanted terribly to complete a double century. Before today, I never had the desire to do anything like this, but today I was disappointed when I hadn't. We all were…particularly Brad.

At the "Welcome to Colorado" marquee we met another biker. He was taking photos of the sign just as we were about to pass by. I'm a firm believer that vacation photos of signs are meaningless without a person set in front of them (Joe and Steph would strongly disagree). Therefore, in seeing this man, I pulled off of the road, introduced myself, and offered to take a photograph of him posing in front of this sign. Steph (being that she hates how my pictures turn out) insisted she'd take it.

After this spectacle, he repaid the gesture. "Say cheese!"

Discovering our common interest, an alliance was formed. He's traveling west, just as we are, but plans on following Route 50 all the way across Utah, through Nevada, and into California in hopes of arriving in San Francisco within the next two weeks. A college student with only a year remaining in his educational plan, he's dreamed of this feat since the days of his youth spent many a night around a dinner table listening to his dad tell tales of his own adventure "across." Turns out he's staying at the same hostel we are.

Tonight we came across three options for housing: the city park (watered nightly by sprinklers), a field of dusty sand located adjacent to a lively truck stop, or the town hostel. Steph and I voted for the hostel, Joe for the truck stop, and Brad for the city park (out of jest he claimed the sprinklers could double as showers). Of course, Steph and I won.

Slightly out of place, the hostel seems to tower over Ordway. It reminds me of some of the spacious, elegantly designed Victorian homes of downtown Bellefonte. Inside, we walked through an open lobby with vaulted ceilings where a dining table, masqueraded by reading materials, sat in front of a fireplace and mantle. The owner, a local middle-aged man, was reclining within a darkly stained wooden rocker. As we swung open the front door, with a grin covering his face, he hopped out of his chair and swiftly crossed the room while reaching his hands out to shake ours. "Welcome! Where'd you bike from today?"

Before we had a chance to inquire about the price of a room, he showed us upstairs to two long hallways outlined in available rooms. "Take a look around." The bathrooms were shared amongst guests, as was a small workspace and desktop computer. But clean towels, coffee, good company and air-conditioning all were provided for a nominal charge. Goose-feathered pillows, a plush mattress and sheets (it's been awhile since I've slept on a sheet!) won me over. Free internet stole Brad's soul, and talk of vitamin C tablets was all Steph needed to seal the deal (we've all been fighting a bit of a cold).

With our minds made up, we lugged our gear up into our rooms, obtained dinner suggestions and a bag full of vitamin C tablets from the owner, then proceeded to walk across town to a locally owned diner. In doing so, I couldn't help but notice an element of silence. The streets were vacant.

But activity was flourishing inside the diner. For dinner we treated ourselves to burgers and fries. The food was superb, cheap, and the portions were filling. As we ate, our waitress told us about Pueblo, tomorrow's destination located only fifty miles down the road. She said she loves venturing to the city for dinner, a movie, or a show. We must visit Papa José's, she said, a privately owned diner that features "the best and most authentic Mexican cuisine in the city."

As dinner concluded, I glanced up at the clock on the wall. With hands pointing to nine and twelve, I realized the restaurant had stayed open an hour past closing time. I apologized to the waitress for keeping her past her shift.

As we walked out the restaurant doors, I wasn't quite ready for the day to draw to a close. A decision was made to return to the truck stop for soft serve. Who would have thought!

As we entered this excessively long, ranch-style building set beneath the black sky, I was comforted by the thought of falling asleep with my head nestled softly on the overstuffed goose feathered pillows of the town's hostel and not rather here. The dark sky on top of the brown sand beneath, mixed with the absence of noise and activity, made the presence of tarantulas here seem all the more promising. I was sure they were lurking nearby just waiting for me to fall asleep! Once I was told the price of a cone, however, (less than a dollar), I forgot all of my worries.

As we ate our ice cream in silence, about thirty truck drivers congregated outside the doors while tumbleweed blew swiftly across the sandy ground in front of them.

I remembered the tone in the hostel owner's voice as he informed us of how Ordway just recently had fallen victim to a devastating fire. The cause was deemed accidental but this didn't change the fact that practically everything surrounding the town burnt to the ground. Thankfully, the town itself (where most of the residents reside) was spared. Still, at least one person died in that fire.

The ashen ground makes the essence of this town feel all the more eerie.

I wonder if the individual responsible for starting that fire now lives with regret. "If only…" As the hostel owner insisted the fire was a freak accident, I hope this isn't the case. I know how painful it is to live with regret. And regret will solve nothing.

In looking back on my life, I spent a considerable amount of time consumed with thoughts of food (calorie counting, exercising, and striving to reach the perfect weight). Anorexia stole a huge chunk of time away from me. If only I would have spent that time hanging out with you. Looking back, I wasted nearly five years on that all-consuming disease.

And then there was high school where I spent quite a few of those days pretending we weren't related…

"How's it going, Jen?"

"And who are you?" (Tilt head away from brother and snarl.)

No other word suits the person I was at that time: bitch! My behavior was cruel. It was asinine. You were my big brother, and I should have been proud to be your sister. During that year, we could have formed mutual friendships and bonded. I screwed up. I was selfish back then, self-centered and arrogant. Truly, for this I am sorry.

Sadly, my apologies are meaningless. I might have only been acting "like teenagers do" but the reality is, now I can't go back.

You'd be annoyed with me for dwelling on these ridiculous moments, I know that you would. I just can't help but do so. Learning from a mistake doesn't make the pain it elicits go away.

The last few years of our lives spent together were great, but I can't help but be angry with myself for not being a better sister to you every solitary day of those short twenty-five years.

I should have given you a better gift for Christmas your final year here. I should have visited you more often. Ran the Marine Corps Marathon instead of Scranton. Paid for your dinner. Listened more intently. Asked more questions. Not been so selfish. Bought you a plane ticket to Boston. And actually went to your gravesite with you, so that you didn't have to suffer through being dropped into the ground all alone.

I am sincerely sorry.

I can't take any of it back. I can't even tell you how remorseful I am for all that I've done and failed to do; you're no longer here.

God damn it. You shouldn't be dead.

It has to be nearing midnight, and I'm writing on a napkin. I can sense Joe, Steph, and Brad are sick of waiting for me to finish this note. They've wanted to go "home" to bed for practically an hour now.

Please help me let go of the regrets.

Those 171 miles: they were all for you. Each mile representing one of the many, many reasons I'm proud to have had you in my life for those twenty-five years.

From Ordway: Goodnight!

Jennifer

24. A "Thunderstorm" Warning
Ordway to Pueblo, Colorado

"The man who is swimming against the stream knows the strength of it."
~Woodrow Wilson

June 5, 2008

Jeremy,

*T*oday, what was intended to be an easy day, turned out to be rather eventful.

We anticipated biking a measly fifty miles from Ordway to Pueblo. Then, our second "vacation" was scheduled to begin.

We planned on spending the remainder of the day today and all day tomorrow touring the city, eating at Papa José's, walking across the Royal Gorge and enjoying the Garden of the Gods, just as our new friend (the retired truck driver from Girard, Kansas) had recommended.

All our plans panned out just fine — with the exception of our ride being labeled as *easy.* The use of the term "easy" never ends well.

Those fifty miles should have taken us no more than three hours to complete. The terrain was flatter than a board, and we had a tailwind…well, initially. Clipping away at twenty miles per hour should have been a breeze. So what went wrong?

When we left the hostel early this morning, we knew a thunderstorm warning was in effect. What we didn't know was that this thunderstorm warning was actually a *tornado* warning. And we were traveling directly into its path.

That kind hostel owner failed to inform us of this detail. According to what Joe later told me, the man *"didn't want to scare us."*

Brad, Pueblo, Colorado, June 2008 ~ Photograph taken by Stephanie Herbstritt

As we biked toward Crowley, ten miles west of Ordway, I heard thunder in the distance. "Heat" lightning flashed all around me. Initially, I wasn't all too concerned. According to the hostel owner, we were traveling away from the storm and as we progressed farther west these storm-savvy variables "would soon disappear."

Although I was surrounded by lightning and thunder, initially the ride was rather enjoyable. I didn't have to exert much energy: the wind did most of the work by pushing me along.

The air was cool and the sky was dreary. I was in the middle of eastern Colorado's barren "desert" and I liked the conditions. They reminded me of myself: sad, alone, depressed and hopeless.

Misery loves company.

As the thunder grew stronger and my anxiety heightened, I counted the seconds between each sound. They were soon close enough together that I knew the lightning striking in front of me was not simply an optical illusion; it was striking down less than a half mile away. (Or so I predicted.)

At this time, we decided it'd be in our best interest to seek out shelter immediately. For God's sake, our feet were strapped into metal cleats and we all know there was nothing around us that the lightning would rather have struck down except for those flat fields of tan sand.

My panicked thoughts quickly switched gears. *Would the town of Crowley have anything (or anyone) in it?*

As anticipated, it appeared like a ghost town: barren. Most businesses were closed permanently. Windows were boarded shut and the remaining structures appeared severely dilapidated. The scene was ominous.

Literally within seconds we biked through the town, made a U-turn and looked with fright for some form of life. To our luck, the owner of what I believe may have been the only restaurant/bar in working order in this town was cleaning up her business from the previous night. She literally darted outside while waving us in saying, "I don't think you want to be out in this type of weather, not on those bicycles…you *do* know a tornado warning is in effect!"

Obviously we didn't.

We spent the remainder of the morning watching the Weather Channel in this atypical western bar.

The bar section was segregated from the eating area, laid out like a typical diner. I presume this was advantageous for me being that an enlarged photograph boasting something like three-hundred rattlers killed by two men (in a time span of four hours) within the perimeter of Crowley some thirty years ago hung on the wall.

Oh, did my mind ever race after seeing that picture! Brad, Joe, and Steph couldn't have been any more excited!

"Hey Brad, how about some *snake* for dinner tonight?"

The bar looked more like the basement of one's house (possibly a fraternity). It wasn't fully renovated. The floor was concrete and the walls were plaster. In the back sat the bar, fully furnished with a tap and a refrigerator filled to the brim with bottles of beer and malt beverages. Positioned side to side in an L-shaped fashion, were two tattered leather couches facing a brand new flat-screen TV. This is where we spent most of the morning.

Once the storm passed by Crowley we offered great thanks to this incredibly kind woman and continued on our way. Before we had a chance to leave, we learned a tornado had touched down less than a few miles away (just around the precise time we entered Crowley).

Now that's luck.

Nature has so many faces…

Not long after we resumed biking with our goals yet again set on Pueblo another storm fast approached. Five miles outside of Crowley the sky blackened, the force of the wind strengthened and hail started to fall violently from the sky. Lightning surrounded us in every direction. We continued riding in these conditions for possibly ten minutes, closely accompanied by Joe driving the Pathfinder. At this time we decided it was too dangerous to continue on. Sitting inside the vehicle parked on the side of the road, we waited out the storm for nearly an hour. As all four of us pointed with angst to what appeared to be a tornado touching down in a field to our left we hastily decided to continue on to the city by car.

The mileage will have to be made up another day.

As we finally neared in on Pueblo we got our first glimpse of the Rocky Mountains. In the distance, just faintly, I could see their silhouette.

This mountain range is huge with some passes rising above 13,000 feet in elevation. We are probably seventy-five miles away from the first pass, but as I look out of our second floor hotel window they appear within miles. These mountains must be gigantic.

Obviously, I can't wait to arrive at the base of our very first pass. I wonder what the grades will be like: eight, ten, fourteen percent? I ponder how abruptly the scenery will change.

I've never seen mountains that span just great distances, nor reach such great heights. The Appalachians might have been steep, but these mountains are enormous.

Crazier yet, I've never been as high in elevation as I am now. I can't begin to imagine what it will feel like to cross over Monarch Pass in just a few days. Pueblo sits at nearly 5,000 feet. This will be 6,000-feet higher in elevation than where I am standing right now in this moment.

This world certainly is filled with natural wonders.

For the next two nights we will be staying at a Days Inn. The price is steep (in comparison to that of a campground), $50 per night, but not bad (we figure) for a city like Pueblo.

At the continental breakfast buffet tomorrow morning we will consume as many donuts as we possibly can for no reason whatsoever other than because we can! At least *I'll* be guilty of gluttony this "vacation," but for today I am okay with this fact. I've rode my bike to Pueblo, Colorado. From Yorktown, Virginia, I rode my bike to Pueblo (well, just about)! Unbelievable!

As I write this letter to you, I am relaxing on an incredibly soft, queen-size bed, layered with ample pillows suited for a king. I'm watching the rain fall heavily to the ground out the large glass window to my left while simultaneously attempting to locate Papa José's on my complimentary city map.

Somehow I feel as if I am in Mexico, rather than the States. As we all know, I'm no architect, but I'd describe the architecture here as "old-world pueblo" (whatever that is). I don't see any grass in sight. On the contrary, previously dusty sand (it's now drenched) is plentiful, and mesas encompass this hotel in every direction.

Of course, Mexican restaurants are everywhere; hence, my trouble in locating Papa José's on this map.

The economy (outside of the city) appears to rely heavily on agriculture. Even though the ground yesterday appeared terribly dry, I know the geography of this city, as I've rode my bike through it. I suspect Pueblo's location at the confluence of the Arkansas River and Fountain Creek, ensures that the surrounding farmers prosper.

The wonders of modern day irrigation: given your experience in hydrology, you'd know about this.

The Arkansas River (or as those from Kansas like to call it: the "Ark-Kansas") runs directly through Pueblo above a section of the city called the "River walk." It flooded in 1921 during what is now known as the "Great Flood of 1921."[16] I presume this flood caused horrific devastation and sheer chaos.

As I stood earlier staring at the contained rapids of this river, I absolutely could not begin to fathom the fear that recklessly overflowing, frigid water must have brought along with its current.

Bad things happen everywhere.

Misfortune and evil certainly don't discriminate.

As a result of the murders at Virginia Tech, universities now have early notification systems. I'd have to bet as a result of this flood, Pueblo now has a flood plan. If so, some might say these people did not die in vain. I wonder if their families would find this any consolation.

All I can do is pray for their souls.

I assume practically all immediate family members of the flood victims are now dead themselves. I hope they've been reunited with their loved ones in a place far better than this tragic earth.

I wonder if they've forgotten the horror they went through. I wonder if they've forgiven their god.

I wonder if one hundred years from now, our family will all be reunited. All I can do is hope. Yet, even this doesn't come easy.

I've found it: Papa José's. Possibly a divine Mexican meal will take my sorrows away (at least temporarily).

All my love,
Jennifer

Above: Colorado cacti, June 2008 ~ Photograph taken by Joseph Herbstritt

Below: Friendly deer we came across causally roaming through the Garden of the Gods, Colorado, June 2008

Rocky Mountains, June 2008

Jen (l) and Steph (r) approaching a climb! Colorado, June 2008
Photograph by Joseph Herbstritt

25. The Rockies
Pueblo to Salida, Colorado

"Finish every day and be done with it. You have done what you could. Some blunders and absurdities no doubt have crept in; forget them as soon as you can. Tomorrow is a new day; begin it well and serenely and with too high a spirit to be cumbered with your old nonsense. This day is all that is good and fair. It is too dear, with its hopes and invitations, to waste a moment on yesterdays."
~Ralph Waldo Emerson

June 7, 2008

Jeremy,

Our trip to Pueblo was unforgettable.

You better believe it: after the rain passed, we crossed over the Royal Gorge. Due to my almost always obnoxious fear of heights, it may have taken me a half hour to walk across this 1,053-foot high,[17] quarter-mile long[18] bridge, but I made it. The canyon beneath tightly hugged the Ark-Kansas as its contents tried to escape. (I love saying "Ark-Kansas.")

As I walked across this questionably sturdy wooden bridge with boards fitted not quite perfectly together, I could see you jogging in front of me with a smile across your face. There was a jump in your step. That'd be you; "just checking out the construction."

From here we visited Garden of the Gods, a park filled with giant, naturally formed, red rock formations. Each had a name of his own: "Kissing Camels," "Balanced Rock." Each stuck out in the distance like a sore thumb.

As I stood motionless in front of each of these inconceivable creations, I thought to myself, *Possibly this is the proof I've been looking for all along. Someone supernatural had to have had his hand in this.*

Red rock formations, Colorado, June 2008

Just as hastily and sporadically as that thought entered my brain, it dissipated. I couldn't help but be saddened by your short life. All I could think about while we were in Pueblo was the fact that you are not here. A common phrase I've heard from countless people since the day of your death is, "They have three living children." Well, I also have three living siblings, two living parents, and a school of living friends, but even I can't focus on them or the fact that they are alive. I'm consumed by your absence. I'm harried by your death and I'm agitated by your murder. I'm angry, livid, filled with a simmering rage that sits below the surface whenever I think of your murder. Life was so unfair to you, even before April 16, 2007. Your life never was easy. You never had a fair shot.

After the coma you suffered as a child, initially, you just weren't the same. (I suspect after painstakingly watching you spend two weeks unconscious following what was supposed to be a minor surgery, none of us were the same.) While other kids were learning to form friendships and figuring out how to conform, you were starting all over again, learning even the simplest of tasks.

"Jeremy, what is this object?"

Display object.

"Sound it out slowly."

As you progressed through your early elementary school years, you stopped stuttering, your fine-motor skills returned and physically you appeared like any other typical kid. Still, you missed out on a lot due to that coma. It only makes sense that when Mom and Dad transferred you out of Catholic school, the adjustment didn't come easy. You were a pre-adolescent boy. Your stance was like all other boy's your age (awkward), you didn't fit into your body, and your voice was beginning to deepen. Having missed out on all of those early childhood experiences when everyone else was trying to figure out exactly how one is to fit in with the "cool kid's crowd" put you at a slight disadvantage in regard to the social scene.

I remember hearing about your first day of middle school vividly. (Of course, I wasn't there. I was still in elementary school. But I think you told the story a hundred times.)

This is how I saw it play out.

It was the first day of school: sixth grade. You were wearing a new pair of shoes purchased from Value City, Gee Bee's or a store of the like.

As you stepped off of the bus, excitement filled your mind. You were now in middle school, no longer a little kid. That day, you would make new friends, be assigned more homework, shower following gym class, and definitely not have recess. That was for children.

You were slowly transitioning toward adulthood. Granted your teeth were recently covered in braces, your voice was only beginning to deepen, and body hair hadn't yet shown up, but you were on your way.

A smile was hiding your face. Sadly, this quickly turned into a blank stare.

One coward ruined that day for you. Just like one coward stole your life in the end.

The class bully presented himself, pointed to your shoes and called out that dire name: "Scruff." Of course, you'd never heard it before. Nor had I, until you came home that night. We didn't use names like that in Catholic school for fear of punishment.

What was the problem?

You liked the shoes. They fit just fine. So they weren't designer! What's "designer" mean anyway?

With the one word that bully spoke, your innocence was taken away. Shame, hurt, and humiliation sunk in. All you wanted was an opportunity to start fresh, make new friends, laugh a little and learn. No one wants to be made fun of.

You came home that night livid that Mom and Dad sent you to school dressed as you were. Couldn't they buy you the best? Didn't they know what would happen? Weren't they once your age? You knew these feelings were unwarranted, but you were hurt and spoke out of turn.

You didn't say a word back to that kid. He didn't deserve a response. But Mom and Dad, they sure got a mouth full.

That night they went out and bought you *another* new pair. This time, they were brand name. Even so, you were still mad. You didn't want yet another pair of new shoes. You simply wanted to fit in.

I remember a few days later you apologized for your outburst. "Shoes are just that. They are shoes."

You were right. They keep our feet clean, warm and dry, and provide proper support for our backs. One is not smart, cool, or successful because of his shoes. There is more to a person than what covers his flesh.

Looking back on the events that played out that day, I sense it was then and there (during that exact confrontation) that you realized you didn't want to turn out like that materialistic kid. You knew he didn't become who he was simply because of society, his parents, or his friends. He had a brain with synapses that connected perfectly fine. He could form opinions for himself. He didn't require others to do so for him. He knew his words were spiteful, discourteous, and offensive. He wasn't a robot and you were ashamed for his thoughts. You didn't want to be like him. You wanted to make something of yourself, not because of your shoes, but because of your actions.

You might never have been president, CEO, or a department head, but you gave life your all. Still, it doesn't seem right. That wretched kid will probably live to be ninety years old. You were murdered by a sissy at twenty-seven.

The ride to Salida was unbelievable. The first fifty miles or so were fairly flat, inching us toward our first pass through the Rockies.

We supposedly had an "easy" first pass, as the summit just barely hit 9,000 feet. You should know we started this climb at approximately 5,000 feet. That's a 4,000-foot ascent. I'm not sure I'd agree climbing 4,000 feet sounds all that easy.

Surprisingly, it wasn't as bad as I thought it would be. I expected climbing for three, four, five, or more hours continuously would be nearly impossible. It turns out when we reached the top I wasn't nearly as exhausted as I'd anticipated. I didn't even notice shortness of breath or lightheadedness as I'd predicted might occur with such a "drastic" change in elevation. Nor were the grades as steep as I thought. Six to eight percent really isn't that bad.

Within minutes, as the climb began, we traveled out of the Wild West (where tumbleweed crossed our paths and mesas encompassed us) into a forest of tall pines set on a mountainous stage.

The view from the summit was nothing like I've ever seen before. I could see Pueblo and other smaller communities in the distance. The structures within these communities reminded me of a tiny Christmas village similar to the one I used to love placing beneath our family's tree.

Literally, I felt as if I were on top of the world.

All my worries suddenly disappeared. Just for a second. I wished I could have remained in that moment (worry free) for the remainder of eternity.

It seems ironic that all the way up that mountain I was looking forward to going down, but as I started to descend, the wind grew strong.

I was forced to grip the handlebars of my bike with all my strength in order to prevent it from blowing over. Between my hands tiring and my body shivering from the cold (somehow I failed to consider the difference in temperature at 9,000 feet of elevation compared with 5,000) I had to periodically pull over to the side of the road, rest and unclench my hands, place them in between my legs, and aggressively rub them back and forth in an attempt to keep warm. Additionally, I did jumping jacks on the side of the road. What a site I must have been for those passing by.

"Come on Jen, this house feels like an oven. Do a few pushups!"

I almost fell over just now thinking about you scorching in our house in Bellefonte even while you were sitting directly next to an open window...in the winter. Meanwhile, I sat frozen, encircled in a blanket atop the baseboard furnace vent!

We traveled through a number of (what seemed to be) classic western towns between Pueblo and Salida including Wetmore, Westcliffe, Cotopaxi and Howard. Out of Pueblo we took U.S. 50 toward Canon City. Prior to arriving there we exited this busy byway and entered the road less traveled.

Seems our lives are all about taking the road less traveled.

We won't see U.S. 50 again until we reach Nevada where it's labeled "The Loneliest Highway in America."

We'll see about that.

There was a small climb into Salida but nothing impossible. I shouldn't have been surprised by this, so Steph says. Being our language expert with four years of Spanish in high school, she claims Salida's Spanish translation is "exit." Who knows if this statement is true or not? Regardless, it is fitting being that we climbed out of the valley and into Salida.

Then again, possibly this literal translation doesn't make all that much sense. After all, tomorrow's ride starts with a climb. Salida definitely sits on the side of a mountain.

Who would have thought? We're in the Rockies!

The wind was heavy as we made this final ascent. I wasn't sure my knees would be able to continue on to our campsite. They sure are taking a beating. Between the combination of strong winds and the repetition of cycling nearly all day long, day in and day out, somehow I wonder if they'll ever feel normal ever again.

Guess they'll blend in well with the rest of my being.

About a mile from our campsite we ran into the same man we met at the Colorado sign. He arrived in Salida yesterday and spent today visiting with a friend who plans on riding over Monarch Pass with him tomorrow. It was nice to see a familiar face.

From our conversation, I learned Monarch Pass was impassable today due to a snowstorm. A snowstorm in the middle of June!

Tomorrow the roads "should be open." Well, I've got high hopes.

As crazy as it sounds, I couldn't be more ecstatic to climb to 11,000 feet. The view from this height has to be out of this world.

After our visit, Steph and I made a trip to Walmart, located directly across the street from our campsite. I haven't seen a Walmart in days (okay, so the last one was in Wichita, but still). I didn't even see one in Pueblo, although I'm sure one was present. We bought supplies for mountain pies, which we feasted upon for dinner.

You're right: tonight, we ate well!

As I savored my pie, I imagined walking down the streets of an American town in the Southwest sometime in the early 1900s. You know, the type featured in western films. Soon enough, I saw myself in the midst of a bar fight overflowing onto the streets. Abruptly, the villain barged through the swinging doors of this building, angered, grasping a pistol in his right hand.

Dominos collided.

As he shot his gun blankly into the air, arguments emerged with men on horseback. Two horses facing one another, both standing on their hind legs, were neighing with their heads held high. Each was ridden by a man fit with stirrups and boots, tight jeans and a button-down plaid shirt, kerchiefs tied at their necks.

Just as my mind was about to create a major warzone, reality set in and I looked at where I really was.

My daydream might have been a scene out of Salida a hundred years ago, but today Salida is a quiet Rocky Mountain town. If it ever were known for gambling, prostitution, or salooning, surely those days are now long gone.

This is a railroad town through which the Ark-Kansas (boy do I ever love that pronunciation) travels (right in the middle of our campground, I might add). In order to arrive at the bathrooms, I must cross this eloquent, yet strong river. (I hope I don't miss the bridge in the middle of the night.)

Soon enough we'll be traveling to Telluride. Like Salida, I'm certain it has history. For now, all I know is that it had a reputation for prostitution back in the day. Telluride, as in "to hell you ride," actually came about due to the prominence of brothels within the community. I can't wait to get there. For now, I've got today.

Next to us, about thirty teenagers are camping out as part of a church youth group. They plan on hiking to the top of Monarch Pass tomorrow. Tonight, they'll be sleeping in five of those musky, old fashioned, teal-colored tents set up in a circle: the type held up by aluminum poles pieced together, similar to what the Boy Scouts used to use. They take a good hour to put up and almost always have a piece or two missing.

I hope these kids have a good time at their camp. I hope they bring back to their homes many memories and stories to tell for years to come. I hope they learn lots about themselves: how to get along with others and how to live life on their own. I hope they are able to accomplish their goal of climbing to above 11,000 feet. I pray for their safety. I pray they never experience anything like our family has.

It looks like a storm is coming in. I better help the gang out before it's too late.

Goodnight from Salida. This will be my last goodbye I send to you from this side of the continental divide (at least until the trip home).

There's a twinkle in my eyes.

Jenny

Jen, Steph and Brad coasting with ease, Colorado, June 2008
Photograph taken by Joseph Herbstritt

Snow-capped Rocky Mountains seen while biking up Monarch Pass, Colorado, June 2008

View from atop Monarch Pass, Colorado, June 2008

Above: November 6, 2005

*Left: Jeremy and Jen at PSU
graduation, 2003*

Jen and Jeremy following completion of the Scranton (Steamtown) marathon, October 2005

Small red barn covered in crawling flora and surrounded by overgrown grass, Southern Illinois

Random purple bus permanently parked in a field of green grass found in the Ozarks
Photographs taken by Joseph Herbstritt

Moving Appalachian trees. Wow, were we ever biking fast while I snapped this shot! Okay, so possibly that's a white lie. Photograph taken by Stephanie Herbstritt.

Eastern Kentucky

Jen, Rockies, Garden of the Gods

Vicinity of Riverwalk, Pueblo, Colorado ~ Photographs taken by Stephanie Herbstritt

Royal Gorge, Colorado

Gaping Rocky Mountains

Jen riding in the gondola, Colorado

Mesa Verde

Steph, Bryce Canyon

Pinnacles of red rock encased in ponderosa pines present at Bryce Canyon National Park
Photograph taken by Stephanie Herbstritt

Bryce Canyon National Park, Utah
Photograph taken by Stephanie Herbstritt

Tunnel view of blue skies created by two of Utah's many towering red rock formations

Endless red rock, Utah

From left to right, Steph, Brad and Jen posing in front of Utah's vast red rock formations
Photograph taken by Joseph Herbstritt

Brad biking in Utah

Window view of the northern rim of the Grand Canyon

Northern rim of the Grand Canyon National Park, Arizona

The San Franciscan mountain range seen in the horizon under peerless conditions from atop the northern rim of the Grand Canyon, Arizona

Joseph Herbstritt at the Grand Canyon

Colorful wildflowers found at the Grand Canyon National Park
Photographs taken by Joseph Herbstritt

Reaching the Pacific Time Zone was an important milestone on our journey.
(Left to right) Joseph, Stephanie, and Jennifer
Photograph taken by Brad Updegrove

*One of a handful of trees seen throughout Nevada, this "shoe tree" was found
on the outskirts of Middlegate.*

Deserted terrain under bright blue skies . . .
Basin located on the outskirts of Fallon, Nevada ~ Photograph taken by Stephanie Herbstritt

Impeccable Nevada just as the sun is about to set

Sand Mountain, Nevada
Photograph taken by Joseph Herbstritt

...And then there was nothing but sand colored white.
The sky here couldn't have appeared larger, Nevada.

Mountain lake filled with crystal clear water bordered by ponderosa pines, Sierra Nevadas

Golden fields in the Golden State, California

Sunflowers in California

Orange trees located outside the Governor's mansion, Sacramento, California

Jennifer and Stephanie celebrate completion of their journey

Golden Gate Bridge, San Francisco, California
Photographs taken by Joseph Herbstritt

Playing in the sand at a beach found in the vicinity of the Golden Gate
National Recreation Area, San Francisco, California
Photographs taken by Stephanie Herbstritt

Scenic stream enveloped by ponderosa pines, Yosemite National Park

Sequoia National Forest, California

Pacific Ocean seen en route to Big Sur along California Highway One

Glacier point, Yosemite National Park

Dad (Mike Herbstritt) standing atop another peak looking out toward Glacier point

Jen resting alongside the road, Yosemite National Park

Replica of how the Crazy Horse monument is expected to appear when complete

Yellowstone lake bursting with a variety of active fish, Yellowstone National Park, Wyoming

Charming view of teal-hued stream lined by ponderosa pines, Yellowstone National Park

The Grand Tetons with peaks reaching 13,770 feet, Grand Teton National Park, Wyoming

Old Faithful

Colorful volcanic hot spring found in Yellowstone National Park

We came across this supposed popular scuba diving site in northern Utah just east of Salt Lake City.

Buffalo grazing through Yellowstone National Park

Mike Herbstritt in an open field of green peering at a mammoth mountain of solid rock, Yosemite National Park

Mountain lake surrounded by pristine peaks, Colorado

On the outskirts of the Badlands we found these horses grazing freely outside their assumed-to-be intended fence.

Hay bale near Badlands

Horse ranch from where we rode on horseback into the Rockies, Jackson Hole, Wyoming

*Picturesque Wyoming farm surrounded by an incredible view of the
Rocky Mountains in the horizon*

26. Winter
Salida to Gunnison, Colorado

"In the middle of the journey of our life I came to myself
within a dark wood where the straight way was lost."
~Dante Alighieri

June 8, 2008

Jeremy,

*T*oday brought us to Gunnison.

I love leaving one town in the morning and not knowing where I will end up at night. It is the greatest feeling in the world to just be free. I have no commitments. I no longer have a job. I don't have a house that needs to be cleaned, laundry that needs to be done or bills that need to be paid...well, maybe I have laundry. But my point is: my only true obligation is to ride my bike and that (in and of itself) is only an obligation I've chosen.

I wake up each morning and ride my bike to a destination I know nothing about. I don't know if it will have showers, electricity, cell phone reception, or if the town will even be in operation.

In a sense, the overall theme of this trip is similar to that of our earthly journey. No matter where I am at or what I am doing, whether it is riding my bike across the country or going to work, when I wake up each morning, I don't know what the day will bring. Every minute has the potential for spontaneity and impulsivity. Just the same, every single event that plays out both directs and affects my future in some regard.

Each day when I awake, I know death is a possibility. Previously, I woke up denying death. I kept so busy — planning for my future, getting caught up in work and the drama of everyday life — that I almost failed to recognize death as something that affects every one of us. But I now know no one gets left out of the game that death directs.

Now, I have no choice but to face your death straight-faced, eye-to-eye. Every solitary morning (until I die) I will be faced with the truth of our own human mortality. After all, we are *all* human. We are *all* mortal. Each one of us will one day die.

So many people talk about "choices" in life. You have the choice to remain abstinent, abort your baby, get married, have children, buy a new car, purchase a gun, etc. The list of our life long options or choices is practically endless. But life itself is one consequential aspect of our existence we never were really given a choice at. I have no choice but to wake up each morning, live and engage in life amidst all this horror. Of course some people choose to end their lives, but for me this has never been an option.

Excluding the reality of your death, the worst part about waking up each morning is knowing one day I may not. One day I, like you already have, will die.

Death is the only aspect of life which is certain.

This scares the shit out of me.

I often wonder what death will be like: if it will be painful or scary, if I'll sense its coming, and what will happen after I die. Will I go on to another world? Will that world have suffering and sorrow? Will you greet me with open arms?

I worry incessantly about your specific experience with death. I play out scenarios repetitively in my mind. If you were shot here first, then x could have happened. If you were shot there first, then y could have happened. You definitely would have suffered in scenario *1*. In scenario *twenty-two*, you were panicking, watching your life pass before you in front of your very own eyes. In scenario *fifty*, there is no way you could have possibly known what was going on until it was over. And when you're dead, you don't suffer.

Your death was horrific. I can't say whether or not you suffered. That's why I've created all of these scenarios. So many variables were present. All I can do is hope that you didn't.

Photograph taken by Stephanie Herbstritt

I hope you are still in existence, in a place where you are now able to totally forget all of what happened. I yearn for you to live and enjoy life in all forms; to experience its simplicity and perfection for all of eternity.

If I knew this were so, possibly I'd be able to cope. If I knew without a doubt in fifty or seventy-five years we'd see each other again, I could be patient. For now, all I can do is ride my bike and write to you.

I hope that there is a "next world," one where I will hopefully end up, a place called heaven where you are right now, a place where we will all be reunited once again and will "live happily ever after" forever, together. It sounds like a fairy tale, doesn't it?

For now, I will focus on the events of today.

We left Salida around 5:40 A.M., traveled to Poncha Springs, up over Monarch Pass and into Gunnison. I got my second flat tire ten miles outside of Gunnison. I wasn't so pleased. I will explain.

Initially, the day seemed superb. The weather and riding conditions couldn't have been better. The presence of the wind was minimal and the temperature of the air was just right for biking.

The scenery kept my mind busy. Although I was biking up grades sometimes exceeding six to eight percent, I wasn't affected in even the slightest fashion as I was biking through a forest, up a mountain much larger than I have ever witnessed before in my life.

My adrenaline was rushing.

Even when we reached the top of Monarch Pass, some 11,000-plus feet in the sky, I didn't notice the temperature. It might have been 28°F and a considerable amount of snow may have been present on the ground, but my body was warm.

Joe and Stephanie built a small snowman.

Like a child, I walked repetitively back and forth from one side of the continental divide to the other.

As my heart rate started to slow and my mind started to calm, I looked for a bathroom. I needed to go. Due to yesterday's storm, the gift shop was closed. The water pipes froze resulting in a lack of water.

I believe it was in that moment when I finally realized the temperature. I was no longer in Pueblo. Nor was I in Salida. I was on top of Monarch Pass and it was 28°F.

In June!

Suddenly, I felt chilled.

Altitude sickness; did I have it?

My thoughts raced.

No Jen, it's the weather. You will be fine.

As we started the descent, I couldn't stop shivering. The wind became heavy, as did my burden.

When things are going well, I can be fine. But when even the smallest obstacle gets in my way, my world falls apart.

I imagined for nearly a month riding briskly down my first pass through the Rockies: a cool breeze was to blow softly on my face and the sun was to shine warm on my back. The intended picture was bliss. The actual picture was painful.

Tears filled my eyes as I debated whether or not my fingers would soon fall off. Could it be possible to develop frostbite in the middle of June?

Top photo: Steph (l) and Jen (r) resting while Brad snaps a shot, Colorado, June 2008

Left to right: Steph, Jen, Brad, and Joe atop Monarch Pass
Here, snow falls practically all year round. ~ Colorado, June 8, 2008

Jen (with blue, chattering lips) and Brad atop Monarch Pass, Colorado, June 8, 2008

Photograph taken by Joseph Herbstritt

I'd much rather ascend with a struggle than "effortlessly" travel downhill.

The amount of energy I had to exert in order to make it to the bottom of that mountain was certainly far more than was required to get me up to that summit. Between the painful fingers and toes and burning triceps (from using the brakes) I wanted to scream.

When we finally made it down, the terrain transitioned to rolling hills that remained all the way into Gunnison. I was happy for this but distraught because of the wind. It wouldn't let up. From the time we got to the summit until we arrived in Gunnison, my mind couldn't stop thinking about that damn wind. I just wanted it to cease.

It was so intense I couldn't move myself and my bike at a pace faster than eight miles per hour. The wind and I were at war.

Typically I bike an average of sixteen to twenty miles per hour throughout the course of a day. This certainly is not the speed at which I climb, but when I average the flat, downhill and uphill sections together I can easily end the day at around eighteen mph.

Today's terrain was mainly rolling, except for the climb and descent over Monarch Pass. Still, I couldn't exceed an average of eight mph.

Eight!

Want to hear something even more pathetic? I climbed up Monarch Pass at a speed of about ten mph. I was climbing faster than my overall average! Considering a twenty-or-so-mile downhill section was present following the ascent to Monarch Pass, one would think this would increase one's overall average speed! Not mine!

Add to my slow descent this next deviant variable and I think you may understand why my day seemed so horrible. (I know: it could have been worse!)

I was ten miles outside of Gunnison traveling downhill, yet, I felt as if I wasn't moving at all. My anger was intensifying. The wind was my arch-enemy.

Just as I was about to scream some sort of obscenity into the valley, all of a sudden I felt as if the road surface became incredibly uneven.

You better believe it: a flat tire. Same tire as before — same drill. I actually screamed in frustration.

I suspect I ran over a miniscule broken piece of glass or sharp piece of debris littered on the side of the road. Possibly I ran over a tumble-weed type of briar. Who knows?

While mumbling obscenities, I placed my bike upside down on the side of the road balancing it on its handlebars. Brad insisted he'd do the job. He might have been even angrier than I was. The wind was getting to both of us.

Steph is much calmer.

As Brad made his first attempt at changing the tube, within seconds, my bike blew over by the strength of the wind. My greasy chain landed smack on his clean white shirt.

This happened three additional times.

I thought Brad was going to throw that bike right into traffic. I was about to do so myself. Bessie, she was begging for mercy!

Finally the tube was changed.

We did make it to Gunnison: slightly more insane than when we left this morning. I'm now at war with the wind, the cold, and poor old Bessie. I want to finish this trip but my mind is struggling.

Dig deep!

I wanted to make it sixty miles farther than Gunnison today. Unfortunately, there was no way that was happening…not today!

When we entered town we immediately went to McDonald's, the first place we saw to get some food.

I ate a hot fudge sundae with my helmet still strapped onto my head, my bike shoes still on my feet. I didn't notice my appearance until I was about to exit the premise.

I was disgusted with life, and unfortunately the ice cream didn't make my problems go away. Thoughts of the wind just wouldn't leave my mind!

From McDonald's we marched ourselves down to a very nice KOA on the far west side of town (actually we didn't march: we drove; I couldn't bike another foot in that wind).

Gunnison is definitely one of the typical "ski towns nestled in the middle of the Rocky Mountains" that I have been so eager to experience. Possibly ending up here as a result of this wicked wind was a blessing in disguise. (That's Mom speaking!)

Located at the bottom of several valleys, Gunnison is home to Western State University. It is also, I now believe, one of the coldest places on earth. Seriously, I was told by a local member of the community that during the winter months Gunnison is one of the coldest places to be within the United States. Well, it is bitter cold here tonight, anyway. Though the average high in July is around eighty-one, right now the marquee reads: "52°F ~ 4:30 P.M. ~ June 9, 2008."

I'm not prepared for this type of weather. I sent most of my winter clothes home with Dad and Mom after Memorial Day. My sleeping bag is only a thirty-degree bag. The low tonight is scheduled to be in the low twenties. What was I thinking?

We're going to need a fire. Possibly, I'll sleep on top of it!

The owner of this KOA was a riot. As a reward for our "hard work and determination" he gave us all goodie bags. Mine was filled to the brim with razors, toothpaste, floss, lotion, tea, Vitamin C drinks, gum and everything else you could possibly think any of us could potentially need for the remainder of this trip.

Brad, Steph, and Joe sure created one hell of a fire. Currently, I'm sitting no more than one foot away from the flames.

My hope for tomorrow is that the temperature will rise!

Is this really too much to ask for?

Am I *ever* full of complaints?!

I know, in twenty-four hours the climate will change. Soon enough I'll be traveling through the desert complaining about the heat!

Forgive me. It's been a long day.

Good night!

Jennifer

Snow-capped Rocky Mountains amongst deserted terrain, June 2008

Steph and Joe resting above Black Canyon, Colorado, June 2008

27. To Hell We Ride
Gunnison to Telluride, Colorado

"A true friend knows your weaknesses but shows you your strengths;
feels your fears but fortifies your faith; sees your anxieties but frees your spirit;
recognizes your disabilities but emphasizes your possibilities."
~William Arthur Ward

June 9, 2008

Jeremy,

Well, my wish wasn't granted. At approximately 8:45 this morning, I found myself back at the McDonald's experiencing déjà vu.

I awoke three hours earlier to frost on the ground and the sight of my breath present in the air in front of me each time I exhaled.

Am I in Antarctica?

We left for our ride a little after six. Although it was cold, I was excited to be riding in the direction of Montrose. But to my dismay, no more than two miles into the ride we reluctantly decided to turn around. It was entirely too frigid to continue on. Even Brad was confident his fingers would develop frostbite if we biked any farther in that arctic morning air.

We were all wearing long-fingered gloves, but this wasn't sufficient. We needed something more resistant to the wind, being that one's fingers are the first body part to break the wind while sitting on a bicycle.

We returned to our campsite where Joe (fortunately) was still asleep. I must say he didn't appear entirely too comfortable, being his sleeping bag is also a thirty-degree bag.

We looked at a thermometer posted on a marquee just outside of the KOA and, truth be told, it read "28°F." This is the same temperature it was at 11,000-some odd feet yesterday.

The decision was made to bike to the ACE hardware store and purchase PVC-coated gloves to not only keep our hands warm, but also to protect them from the deplorable wind. I am not sure how many more mornings we will experience like this one, but I'm hoping the number is very few. If there are more, alas we will have these gloves, costing us only $3 a pair. I hope they work.

Next stop was McDonald's, clearly for breakfast. So much for avoiding chain restaurants! Two trips to McDonald's in less than twenty-four hours, you've got to be kidding me! Naively, we were waiting out the cold.

"The temperature will rise."

"Today's ride will be better than yesterday's."

"It has to be so."

As I sat there enjoying a calorie-filled Bacon, Egg and Cheese McGriddle while sipping on hot tea, my mind traveled to some of my most treasured memories.

I recalled a visit Joe, Stephanie and I had made to Blacksburg. It was early autumn 2006. The leaves were changing colors in Appalachia; just beginning to fall off the trees. The temperature was perfect: not too cool but not too hot, with tolerable humidity.

Our drive down was miserable and rainy, but once we arrived the skies cleared and the remainder of the visit couldn't have been staged in any better of an environment.

You and I had just finished a seventeen-mile long run incorporating sections of the Huckleberry Trail. (We always wished for a trail like that to connect Bellefonte and State College.)

In any event, my appetite was immense — like usual. I insisted you drive me to the closest McDonald's for a Bacon, Egg and Cheese McGriddle, a favorite of mine from the minute my taste buds were first exposed.

It was 10:50 A.M. and the breakfast menu at McDonald's expired at eleven. Realizing your apartment was located approximately ten minutes away from the nearest McDonald's my craving intensified.

"I really want a McGriddle! We ran really hard this morning! Please!"

Due to my persistence you drove me there as fast as you could (what a good host!) as I wouldn't have been able to find my way there alone without getting lost. We arrived in the nick of time.

Courteous and hospitable, you failed to vocalize a single sly word regarding my craving throughout the entire fiasco. And I savored every bite of that very divine sandwich.

After breakfast you gave the three of us a tour of your office on campus. You were proud of that space. It wasn't anything fancy. It didn't house black leather couches or have a large glass window with a view of the Appalachian Mountains, but it was yours. That was satisfactory enough.

You spent many hours in that space: studying, preparing for exams with fellow graduate students, working through homework problems, conducting research, organizing and preparing lesson plans, and (of course) joking around.

On your desk you had a picture of our family, numerous books and copious pencils: the type you used to purchase in mass quantity from Office Depot.

Mom and Dad have a photograph they took of you sitting in that space. With hands resting behind your head, your elbows were wide. Your legs were spread apart as you leaned back in your chair, sitting almost in a reclined position. Relaxed, a smile — suitable for a recently awarded lottery card winner — spanned your face.

To this day, that picture sits above the telephone in Mom and Dad's house. When you were living, each time you called, not only would they hear your voice but your face stood out proud posted on the cabinet above as they answered the phone. For the remainder of their lives, and mine too, we will all await that call where we will once again be able to congruently hear you speak and look into your living eyes.

Because of that sandwich you kindly bought for me, I had the energy to spend the remainder of the day hiking the Cascades with you, Joe, and Steph. We hiked all the way to the top, anticipating the immense waterfall you said was present there with every step that we

Jeremy working from his desk at home in Bellefonte, circa 2005

took. On a path made of mulch intermittently featuring man-made stairs, we walked, talked, and admired the scenery, the water and the rapids present to our right. The entire hike took us maybe three hours to complete. It wasn't long, but I will treasure the memory of it for all of my life.

You and Stephanie went swimming in front of that massive waterfall we all desired to see. I was too cold, go figure!

Go ahead; blame it on the anemia, Jen!

Joe stood by my side. Ask him, it was *very* cold!

The Cascades were beautiful: a collection of waterfalls surrounded by hiking trails and wildlife. The name explains it all. In retrospect, I must have recognized why you loved Virginia so much the minute I set my eyes on that place. It was a nature lover's paradise.

That night, we ate dinner at your favorite pizza parlor in town. You said your advisor took you there a few times before. We had both Greek pizza and a Buffalo Chicken pie. I can picture you there, in that moment, picking those black olives I chose not to eat off of my plate with your fork, enjoying them, piece after piece. To this date, your closest friends still talk about you eating bowls of black olives, late at night in the bars of State College. Almost everyone under the sun, other than you, would have vomited at the very thought of such a feat. You sure loved black olives, just like you loved wings, cookie dough, and Chinese buffets.

I miss you.

I'm amazed by the details that I remember. I can tell you exactly what you wore that very day we hiked the Cascades: those khaki cargo shorts and a white short-sleeved t-shirt sporting the Tussey mOUn-TaiNBACK fifty-mile relay's motto: *Just for the hill of it.* Your hair was short, as it almost always was, but not freshly trimmed. I can picture you in my mind: your clothing, your smile, your personality, and your face, just as if I last saw you yesterday.

I like seeing your face in my head, as it is a reminder that our minds are smart and they will not forget what is truly important to us in this life. Organic chemistry from my early college years, as well as physics and statics — those memories are gone, but your face will never be erased from my mind.

The thought of that race brings tears to my eyes. Fifty miles run through the forests and hills of central Pennsylvania in the prime of autumn accompanied by family and friends: that thought is blissful. I think we participated in that event at least three or four years in a row, typically on a team of six or eight members.

Inevitably, I'd assign you to the first leg of the race year after year. Everyone other than you dreaded even the thought of running that leg: 3.1 miles uphill, absent of even a pause to catch your breath. You were a *maniac*.

I loved running that leg with you in preparation for the event. I think it might have been your favorite run.

You always hoped to see a bear back in those woods. I'll never forget the day that dream of yours was fulfilled (the day I thought my heart was going to jump straight out of my chest!).

Snapshot of our 2003 Tussey mOUnTaiNBACK Team, B-unit

In any case, to this day I can still vividly see you running that leg. You always had a specific time in your mind that you intended to break. With a perfect running stride, you charged from the start all the way to the finish. You treated those 3.1 miles just like a 400m sprint. Once you got to the top, you'd put out your hand, anticipating our high fives. I'd laugh, throw you a five and commend you on a job well done. But until I told you your time, gave you my approval, and dragged your ass to the car you wouldn't stop asking, "How did I do?"

Some of my favorite memories were spent in the car during those many runnings of that race: goofing around, telling jokes, listening to loud music, ridiculously cheering on our teammates, engaging in friendly competitive talk, eating food, and making runs to the barbeque stand down the road for a feast of fried chicken.

Yes, in the middle of that fifty-mile long relay. We were all nuts.

Not sure I'll ever be able to do that race ever again...

That day in Virginia was one of the best days of my life. The scenery was out of this world; your company was long overdue. We all hated that you'd moved all the way to Virginia, and it was nice to see you in person and not simply listen to your voice over the phone. None of us wanted to return home. Not without you in our car.

Before we left, you took us rafting down the New River. I remember how I harassed you because the first part of that ride was merely a float. "I thought there were supposed to be rapids?"

With a grin you responded, "Just you wait!"

We completed the last half mile of that course possibly eight times. I had a blast.

I want to return to that day. I want to return to all those days when you were in existence, in the physical sense. But I cannot, so I will have to make the best of this day, today, and its ever frigid air.

You didn't mind the cold even the slightest. You could have survived comfortably skiing in a jacket with nothing more than a t-shirt underneath. When you ran outside during the winter months, you were comfortable wearing the same apparel you wore during the summer. If it was unbearably cold out you'd throw on a pair of wind pants and a long-sleeved cotton t-shirt.

You weren't a complainer. It seems you got caught up in whatever it was you were doing and didn't let anything else bother you, not the weather, not anything.

These days, what I hate most about the cold isn't that it makes me uncomfortable. I hate it because you are dead.

This is certainly gruesome but if there is something I've learned about death it is that thoughts like this are not unnatural or abnormal. Before your death, if someone would have confided in me the thoughts that arrive in my mind now, I would have thought they'd lost their mind.

I now know better.

I never would have thought of things like this before, not in the context of my most bizarre dreams, but now I cannot seem to remove myself from these despicable thoughts.

I think about you lying in that box, in the ground freezing cold. I worry for you. I hope you are not claustrophobic.

I'm not being cynical here, nor sarcastic. These are simply things I think about, and not just during a blue moon, but all of the time. These thoughts cross my mind at least once daily.

I know that your body is deteriorating, decomposing, and decaying. Your mind has to be elsewhere (if even it still exists). Your nervous tissue is no longer functioning. Yet, still I worry. You've got to be cold. Stuck within that awful box, you must be horrified.

I realize you can't be. You are dead.

Even when I was standing in that dire funeral home staring at your corpse, I said aloud over and over again as if I were a broken record, "This is not Jeremy. Jeremy is elsewhere. He is not here. He is somewhere else. I really should go and find him, he must be so lonely."

Therefore, I knew from the get-go you were not that corpse; it may have remotely looked like you, but it wasn't you. Your soul had left. And a body is just that without a soul — just a shell.

I just can't help but worry that you might currently feel stuck in that box: alone, cold, wet, hot, oxygen deprived, my list of concerns could go on for pages.

So, I hate the cold.

Just like I never hated the cold like I hate it now, I never was bothered by cemeteries before. I wasn't the type to think of these places as haunted. When the other kids made a fuss about going to a cemetery in the middle of the night (on Halloween) I didn't mind. I'd walk around the grounds softly, being careful to avoid stepping on top of a person, read the names of the dead engraved on their tombstones and silently pray for their souls while the rest of my group ran around screaming like idiots.

The tables have now turned. When I walk through any cemetery gate, I can feel the presence of the souls whose earthly bodies are buried there.

My perception of the dead is now very much different. Within the cemetery setting I see not just you, but all of the dead inside of boxes. I see a cross section of each and every single one of you lying in those caskets. Cut transversely, I see your bodies lying still in that box, covered first in white blankets, then layers of dirt, and finally grass placed on the top. Your faces stare blankly into the wood. All eyes are shut.

This image refuses to cease from haunting me.

When I stare at your grave, I fall deep into a trance imagining what your world may be like. To think of how many cold, decomposed bodies are present there compared with how many warm bodies exist on our earth, I have to somehow think your numbers outweigh ours.

I hate to think of all of you as nothing other than dead and forgotten. So many of our friends, family, loved ones, and ancestors are in the same position as you are now. There must be a better place out there. I just wish I could find it; understand it.

This wasn't going to happen today, not at McDonald's. Therefore, I was brought back to the imminent. As I finished my hot tea, I was shocked by the time. It was nearly half past nine. Obviously, once again I got lost in my thoughts. It was time to get moving. We had to deal with the cold, and possibly the wind. Oh, the prevailing westerlies!

I threw on my PVC-coated gloves, hopped on my bike, clipped my feet into my pedals and started pedaling in the direction of our destination: somewhere west of Gunnison; somewhere far warmer.

Freezing, we began our day with a "small" climb up to Cerro Summit. My theory is that the intention of this climb was to warm us up just enough so we would at least (as a result of deception) initiate the ten-mile or more descent into Montrose.

And yes, that descent proved to be bitter cold.

Montrose was a fairly large community (16,486 as of July 2006): one of the most populated towns we've traveled through as of late. Like Salida, it previously served as a railroad community. I would guess it's filled with significant history. More importantly (for me), it was a hell of a lot warmer than Gunnison and Cimarron!

When we arrived somewhere around noon the thermometer read 84°F, at which time I shed off nearly all of my clothes. My hands were drenched in sweat from the PVC-coated gloves, which allow little room for breathing.

Disregarding the cold, the ride today was one of the most memorable so far. On our way to Montrose, we saw striking lakes filled with

Scenic blue lake, Colorado, June 2008 ~ Photograph taken by Stephanie Herbstritt

crystal clear water tinted with a hint of blue, the most noteworthy of which was named the Blue Mesa Reservoir. Located between Gunnison and Montrose, this is supposedly the largest body of water in Colorado (so say the locals). And if you ask me, it couldn't have been placed in a more perfect location. With my gloves still on at that time, and my body enacting every possible attempt my mind could come up with to keep myself warm, from yelling and singing, to wiggling my torso back and forth on my bike as if I were dancing on top of it, the beauty of this lake certainly helped to distract me away from the climate.

The water was a perfect shade of sapphire at 7,500 or so feet of elevation. Who would have thought?

After Montrose and Cimarron, we traveled toward Ridgeway crossing the Dallas Divide just a few miles outside of town. This pass (located on State Highway 62) links Ridgeway with Telluride. It takes its name from the Dallas Creek that drains its basin into the Uncompahgre River.[19] We followed this river throughout most of the latter portion of our ride today.

The Dallas Divide may be considered a "low" pass through the Rockies (and I was definitely fooled by the elevation charts myself) but it certainly was not a gentle ascent. This climb proved to possess the steepest grades out of all of our climbs through the Rockies thus far. The summit might not have been marked, but the grade was so steep that when I arrived I was certainly aware I'd finished the job. I didn't need a marker.

After we completed this climb, we merely had to challenge our legs to one additional minor ascent (the smallest out of today's three) and then we took an approximately three-mile dive into Telluride.

We were mostly surrounded by large trees, remarkable scenery and exquisiteness today. Nevertheless, biking up the Dallas Divide did yield one very large scare.

As we struggled toward the summit, an oversized man driving a black Tahoe passed us by relatively quickly. He nearly pushed me off the (rather wide) shoulder of the road. At the time, oncoming traffic was lacking, and although the road traveled a fairly windy path, throughout this particular section blind curves were absent, so I can't say why he found it necessary to travel to the right of the white line directly into our paths.

We were biking to the right of the white line: abiding by the law. Frankly, he seemed to be on a mission to take out a few bikers.

As he rapidly sped by, I heard something obscene come out of his mouth. All I could make out of his nonsense was something of this nature: "If you don't get off of the road—" I couldn't make out the rest.

Before I had a chance to catch my breath following this near disastrous situation, this man made an abrupt U-turn in the road, slowing down as he neared in on us a second time.

This time, he laid onto the horn of his truck long enough for its echo to return to me from the valley below. With his head out his window and his vehicle swerving across the center line, he had to have vocalized every single vulgarity known to man.

But this wasn't good enough for him; he returned for a third attempt at ruining our ride or injuring us. I was petrified and biking as fast as I possibly could toward the top, less than a mile away. I knew Joe was awaiting our arrival there, but if this man decided to do something worse than scream at us there was no way we'd be able to out-bike him.

My mind raced with what Mom and Dad would do if something happened to us on this trip. How would they ever survive the loss of you *and* that of their remaining children?

Fortunately, this man never returned, yet once again I was reminded that our mostly benevolent world certainly does house evil.

We biked nearly 140 miles today to Telluride where I am writing you now. Yes, "to hell" I biked today!

This is one of the most spectacular towns I've set my eyes on yet (I know I say this about them all).

A ski town nestled in the middle of the Rocky Mountains; this is exactly what I expected Colorado to look like. I never pictured Colorado to look like Pueblo, although (in its own way) Pueblo was beautiful.

We are staying with a friend of a friend here.

We did not meet Nick until today, yet thus far he has treated us as if we're his long lost best friends. He allowed us to use his washer and dryer, laundry detergent, and dryer sheets as soon as we arrived. He was quick to offer us all warm showers, clean towels, and personal hygiene products. He even gave us full access to his kitchen for the next twenty-four hours and made a special trip to the grocery store to load up on necessities such as milk, eggs, and yogurt.

For dinner, he took us out to eat at one of his favorite restaurants in town, Fat Allies. Here, he introduced us to his friends.

During our walk to Fat Allies, Nick gave us a tour of the town, talked to us as if he had known us for years, asked about our trip and adventures, and mentioned how he would "be honored" to bike over Lizard Head Pass with us tomorrow.

During dinner, conversation wasn't hard to find, and after our meal was completed he insisted that all of us try both of the desserts available on the menu (pecan pie and a warm peach cobbler *à la mode*).

Fat Allies served the best food of this trip to date, point blank. I have never had french fries so delicious and my pork barbeque sandwich was divine, perfectly smothered in a very rich sauce. I would go back to this town just for the food! Honestly!

Nick was one of the most hospitable, kindhearted people I've met in my life. A genuine soul, he reminded me of you. An honest person who really does care to hear a response to the classic question: "How are you?"

It's people like him who keep your memory alive.

Good night, Jeremy.

All my love,
Jennifer

Black Canyon, Colorado
(Gunnison National Park), June 2008

Yes, in the middle of June icy conditions do exist here in the West! In fact, on June 7 Monarch Pass was impassable due to a snowstorm! Photograph taken by Stephanie Herbstritt.

Steph (back) and Brad walking their bikes toward the Telluride post office, Telluride, Colorado, June 10, 2008

Jen (l) and Steph (r) at Mountain Village ski resort after riding the gondola from Telluride, Colorado, June 2008.

With sophistication and speed, Steph dismounts the gondola, Telluride, Colorado, June 10, 2008.

28. Mesa Verde
Telluride to Delores, Colorado

"To the soul, there is hardly anything more healing than friendship."
~Thomas Moore

June 10, 2008

Jeremy,

Telluride has to be on my list of *"Top 10 Favorite Towns"* we've visited thus far. Approximately 2,300 people reside here year round. My guess is most of the residents work for a ski resort, Mountain Village, located on the opposite side of the mountain as the town. The mountain that separates the two communities has to peak at over 10,000 feet in elevation. It is one of the most beautiful sites I've seen in America.

Telluride is an environmentalist's paradise (as it's incredibly eco-friendly). There were very few cars noticeable, as the town operates a gondola as its primary form of public transportation. Chain restaurants are absent as are gas stations with bright marquees marketing cigarette specials and gas priced at over $4 a gallon.

Anyone, including tourists, can ride the gondola free of charge. The ride lasts about twelve minutes (and takes one from Telluride to Mountain Village or vice versa). From the views, I'd guess Mountain Village must house some incredible slopes. Employees of this resort have priority over skiers for use of the gondola. Therefore, I get the sense most of them take advantage of this perk. According to Nick, people carry their bikes with them in the mornings on the gondola and ride leisurely over their lunch hour up to Lizard Head Pass.

I don't think anyone in this community is overweight, nor out of shape. Certainly the fact that people walk or bike everywhere plays a contributing role in this statement.

You would have loved this town.

During my gondola ride, I hoped it would never end as the view out of that glass box was out of this world. As I went up and over the mountain's peak, I could see for miles and miles in the distance. My palms were undoubtedly sweating (due to my fear of heights) but I just couldn't look away from the view. It was simply that captivating.

I could see 14,000-foot peaks covered with snow encompassing me in all directions. Just the same, (at lower elevations) mountains of ponderosa pines stood tall.

As we neared the peak, the Victorian houses and clapboard storefronts of Telluride below shrunk to the size of miniature dollhouses.

Tears filled my eyes at the prospect of leaving such an incredible town. I wanted to expand on the memories formed in this lovely quaint village; still, I knew it was my time to leave. I'm not in a state to stay anywhere too long these days.

Getting off the lift was an adventure, given my usual clumsiness. It wasn't easy to shove two bikes into that glass box and, just the same, it wasn't all that simple of a task getting them out. As I rushed to get out safely, I recalled a day of skiing with you and one of your dear friends from college. We were riding the ski lift at Holiday Valley. I was sitting in the middle; you and Scott were situated to my left and right respectively. As we approached the top, we exited the lift. Unfortunately, in the process of doing so your right ski crossed my left. Simultaneously, Scott's left crossed my right. My legs spread effortlessly into a split. Then, on the way down that slope, I unintentionally and unexpectedly hit a thick patch of ice, landed on my back, and knocked the wind right out of me.

What a mess that run was! Still, I'd do anything to return to that particular day, or any other "rough" day for that matter.

Nick and Jen, Lizard Head Pass, Colorado, June 2008

I wonder if you'll recognize me fifty years down the road.

If I live to be eighty-five, I'll certainly look much different than at twenty-five. Assuming heaven exists, is how I look at death how I'll appear for all of eternity? I know I'll still recognize you because in my mind you will always be twenty-seven. But will you recognize *me*? And what happens if one ages in heaven? Will I still recognize you? Do we recognize a person because of his/her physical appearance or is it because of the spirit? Will you just know me because I am me, the spirit of Jennifer, or will you fail to know me because I am me, the body of Jennifer, age eighty-five, ninety-three, or what have you?

Death has posed far too many questions for me.

Returning to today…

Nick did meet us at the gondola and then we biked up over Lizard Head Pass together. Our own personal tour guide, he knew this ride like the back of his hand.

Telluride, Colorado, June 10, 2008

"Just a few more twists in the road...

"One half mile and you'll be to the top...

"The grade increases just slightly here."

Lizard Head Pass is located twelve miles south of Telluride on Route 145. Unlike some of our other climbs that have spanned over thirty miles, this approximately twelve-mile climb seemed to be fairly short.

The road wound gradually up grades not too horribly steep. We climbed approximately 2,500 feet to an elevation of 10,222 feet at the summit. Due to the scenery and Nick's gracious company, it didn't seem as if I'd spent an ounce of energy enduring that climb.

With all the twists in the road and canyons beneath, the wind seemed to spiral uncontrollably at times like tiny tornados surrounding us in every direction. For some reason its presence didn't seem to bother me so much today. Possibly I have surrendered to my enemy.

We'll see what I have to say about my nemesis tomorrow!

Just as we were about to reach the summit, I was able to find the prominent nearby peak that is said to look like the head of a lizard from which the name Lizard Head Pass originates.

From the summit, we traveled on toward Delores. Following our farewells, Nick returned to work at Mountain Village.

As this leg of the journey has passed, I am certain I will never again see Nick, not in this life. My heart is filled with hope for him, though; that his life is filled with happiness, prosperity, good fortune, and love. He's a good soul who deserves nothing less. As were you...

In this moment, my heart aches for you and what was stolen away from you that awful, gloomy April morning. My heart will never heal.

I am sad for myself, because I will never have you back here in this life with me ever again. I'll miss out on an infinite number of potential experiences with you: birthdays, weddings, outings, marathons ...experiences I haven't even imagined yet. Times in the future when I will be in the midst of something wonderful and suddenly realize you are not there to share it with me!

Snow-capped Rocky Mountains seen aside an abrupt twist in the road,
Colorado, June 2008 ~ Photograph taken by Stephanie Herbstritt

But worse, I am heartbroken for what *you* have been robbed of. I am still here on this earth, able to experience the joys of our earthly existence (take this bike ride, for example) and you are gone, possibly nothing other than decayed bones absent of any thought processes whatsoever.

I'm so sorry for what was done to you.

Our ride to Delores (where I am now sitting in dim light inside of a laundromat) was all downhill.

No joke: I think we might have traveled for forty-five to fifty miles downhill. I felt as if we were traveling into the depths of the earth. We just kept decreasing farther and farther down in elevation.

The roads were perfectly shaded with tall trees of pine. They were windy enough, but not too much that I had to be overly cautious. There were tons of wildflowers with colors from light blue to all shades of yellows present in the fields surrounding the road. This decline was the type of descent I've been hoping for all along on this trip. I didn't freeze, either.

See, really, I'm quite simple to please.

When we arrived in Delores, we took some time to relax and enjoy the town. We stopped at a book fair at the library and ate at the local "Ponderosa," which I must mention was not one of the chain restaurants. It was simply a locally owned diner. It was here that I learned the definition of a ponderosa. As per the waitress's definition, "These are tall pine trees mostly found here in the West with thick bark and dark green needles appearing in bunches." They appear like giant Christmas trees if you ask me. The ride to Delores was filled with these trees and it seemed only fitting to eat lunch at a restaurant with such a name.

This diner boasted a salad bar just like the chain restaurants do. Better yet, it provided us with the opportunity to taste yet another lunch special. For a measly $5 per plate we were each served a beef sandwich, french fries, salad, iced tea and dessert. Now that is a steal!

After this filling meal, we spent the remainder of the day traveling to Mesa Verde National Park.

From a historic perspective, it was enchanting. From a visual perspective, it was picturesque.

Mesa Verde, a city of rock formations, canyons and plateaus (some) covered in ponderosa pines, was home to the Ancestral Pueblo people.[20] Between 600 AD and 1300 AD they resided in the walls of cliffs and rocky canyons here.[21] From what I learned during my visit, it seems these people would farm, hunt and obtain their water from the plateaus, yet live within the cliffs set beneath. I still cannot begin to figure out exactly how they made their ways into these cliffs without falling into the deep ravines beneath their dwellings, but somehow they did.

Some of the structures that they lived in, to this date, are still standing. Seven *hundred* years later they are still standing! Now, *that* is incredible!

From across the canyon, a number of these houses and buildings compiled together to look like one solitary miniature toy castle. Yet when I zoomed in (with Steph's camera) on these structures, I could see each piece to the village. Possibly hundreds of people resided, performed jobs, went to school, cooked, cleaned, and lived in these now-abandoned communities.

One day people will look at our houses just as I looked at these, with awe and curiosity.

Tribes resided within different canyons. From what I read, mostly they kept their distance from one another. I suspect they invited one another to special events and perhaps engaged in their own fair share of quarrels.

These structures withstood centuries of natural disasters, storms, forest fires, and blizzards. You would have been amazed to see this place; to experience firsthand the history presented. Of course, I was as well, but also petrified due to the seemingly bottomless nature of these canyons. If only I could overcome this ridiculous fear of heights of mine. If only I had your sense of adventure.

A forest fire had swept through a large portion of the park. In this section most trees were barren and black. The sight was incredibly ominous.

Almost immediately as thoughts of darkness and death entered my mind, wild horses appeared to my right. Tall built and black, their coats were shiny and their statures were strong.

I thought to myself: a sign from above? Wild horses in the middle of a charcoaled plateau! The sight couldn't have been any more beautiful. This is land that should be preserved for all generations to see.

With that our visit drew to a close.

We didn't pick out a tent site (here in Delores) until nearly ten o'clock. By then it was dark and the camp owner was already in bed.

Because of our late arrival, we are sleeping in the very last campsite available, on gravel. Thank goodness for our sleeping pads. Somehow I think we'll all have sore backs tomorrow.

Twisted tree trunk, Colorado, June 2008 ~ Photograph taken by Stephanie Herbstritt

Ancestral Pueblo home, Mesa Verde National Park, Colorado, June 2008

Cliff dwellings of the Ancestral Pueblo people, Mesa Verde National Park, Colorado, June 10, 2008

Historic coal mining site, Rico, Colorado, June 10, 2008

The weather is certainly starting to warm up. Tonight it must still be in the high sixties, low seventies. I'm hoping we don't experience another morning like the one back in Gunnison. If I had my way, we'd have blue skies from here on out.

I am reminded we haven't seen rain in days. Actually, I don't think we have seen rain since we left Pueblo. Regardless, I better pull out this laundry, fold it up, repack and head to bed. It's getting late.

Funny how my bed now consists of a sleeping bag and the floor of a tent! From time-to-time we get a bit possessive of our sleeping bags. As for our pillows, the story is the same. Joe has a big pillow; the rest of us use travel-sized ones. What a sight it is to see when Steph "accidentally" falls asleep with her head placed on top of Joe's pillow.

I'm learning that a home isn't a structure: it is simply a term we use to describe a place where we feel safe, are surrounded by family, friends, and loved ones; a place where we can come back to no matter what, and will be accepted no matter what we have done, or said, who we have hurt, or how much we hurt.

My tent is my home, for now. In it, I fall asleep to the pitter-patter of rain when it is present, to the song of birds, the crackle of a camp-fire, the howling of coyotes, the hooting of owls, croaking of frogs and the plentiful chirping of crickets, all beneath the natural night-light of the moon and the comfort of the constellations above me, which give me hope that there is something else out there other than this beautiful, yet horrible, world itself.

I miss you.

Goodnight Jeremy.

With love,

Jennifer

Left to right: Jen, Brad, and Steph benefiting from a midmorning snack eaten on the side of the road, Colorado, June 2008 ~ Photograph taken by Joseph Herbstritt

Jen swallowed with exhaustion, Colorado, June 2008
Photograph taken by Brad Updegrove

29. Natural Bridge
Delores, Colorado, to Natural Bridges Monument, Utah

"Faith is taking the first step, even when you don't see the whole staircase."
~Martin Luther King Jr.

June 11, 2008

Jeremy,

*T*oday we made it to Utah. We have ridden our bicycles from Virginia to Utah — our seventh state!

Honestly, when we started out on this trip, I didn't know how far we'd make it. I didn't know what to expect. For all I knew we could have found ourselves stuck in Virginia…forever.

To now think we've ridden our bikes to Utah is simply incomprehensible.

I've given my best shot at this trip for you and your memory. I'm learning what it feels like to have left Virginia behind. She'll always hold a piece of my heart, but she can't have it all. I won't let her.

My life is still worth living. Your memory is still worth keeping alive.

Utah looks like another planet, an archeologist's paradise. I had no clue America looked like this. Unbelievable.

The quality of the road surfaces in Colorado was far from first-rate. To be completely frank, I think the roads have worsened considerably the farther west we've traveled. I am convinced this is a result of insufficient funding available nowadays for such projects.

Welcome to Utah sign, June 11, 2008

In any case, I was hoping, against all odds, that when we crossed the Utah border one of two things would occur. First and foremost, I anticipated the wind would calm down. This certainly didn't happen. I believe I need to surrender to the wind and accept the fact that I am traveling east to west and therefore directly into the prevailing westerlies (I know, you thought I surrendered a few days ago — I just can't give in).

Second, I trusted that the road surfaces would improve. I got just the opposite. As soon as we crossed the border into Utah, we entered a construction zone where, for approximately fifteen miles, we traveled with skinny bike tires on thick mounds of gravel pellets while eighteen-wheeler trucks flew by. I thought for certain I would fall directly into the path of one of these massive vehicles. By the grace of God, this did not happen.

After we reached Monticello the roads returned to the same quality as those present in Colorado. From here on out, I guarantee you I'll be grateful for roads like these, for if I have to pedal another inch on gravel surfaces like that, I believe I will be walking for the remainder of this trip.

Monticello was my first experience in Utah. At the time of our arrival, the entire town appeared to be under construction. It was a pleasant town with friendly people, just hard to appreciate with all of the commotion created by construction crews drilling, cracking concrete, laying pipes, and resurfacing roads.

We stopped for lunch at the only pizzeria whose storefront was still intact. The waitress was kind and served some of the best pizza I've tasted in my life. Its crust was thin, yet soft, covered in ample amounts of cheese and drenched in oil: a cardiologist's nightmare, yet the perfect treat after riding on that miserable surface of road for far too long a period of time.

From Monticello, we traveled on Highway 191 for approximately twenty miles to another small town, slightly larger than Monticello called Blanding. Then, for the next forty miles of our ride we traveled on Utah 95 into a different world, one I have never seen before.

Natural Bridges National Monument (or "Natural Bridge" as I refer to it) was our destination, located approximately forty miles west of Blanding and ninety miles east of Hanksville on Utah 95. (We are hoping to make it to Hanksville by tomorrow night.)

From the time we left Blanding until we reached Natural Bridge, there was absolutely nothing around us except for massive, brilliant red-rock formations housed on mounds of sand with minimal vegetation. The only feature Natural Bridge provided other than this was a campground with latrines.

From here on out towns will be scarce (spread far and wide). We will not see another town, gas station or water stop until we reach Hanksville tomorrow evening. To me, this is both electrifying and terrifying at the same time.

The rocks we passed by sat in "open" cattle ranges. Yellow signs depicted the presence of these cows reading "open range" every twenty miles or so along Highway 95 warning travelers of these large, but innocent, animals.

Throughout the past few weeks we've crossed through other open ranges, particularly in sections of eastern Colorado, but none of them compared to what I saw today. There were no fences in sight. I assume that the cattle must come from ranches separated by seventy or more miles of desert. A very lengthy fence must enclose the perimeter of the property with the main road running through the center of the square. These cattle were roaming the land utterly free with no suggestion of a home for them anywhere in sight. Where they find water, I couldn't tell you.

Before we spotted the first open-range cows of the day, I was fortunate enough to get my third flat tire of the trip. It seems that *I* am the only member of our group prone to running over invisible, sharp objects which puncture bike tires and tubes. Egaads!

As Brad fixed my flat, I realized there was no sign of human existence anywhere. The sound surrounding me was that of total silence. The heat coming from the sun was intense and I could smell the lack of water. I worried Brad wouldn't be able to change the tube and we'd be stuck in the desert without water or food, possibly for hours. My anxiety made the task seem to take all that much longer.

As he fumbled around making three attempts at changing the tube, no cars crossed our path. By good luck, in what seemed like hours but of course wasn't, Brad was able to change the tire successfully. We returned to the ride as if nothing had happened…

Yet, once I started biking my tire just didn't feel as if it was rotating smoothly. I kept looking back to confirm it was inflated. It appeared to be, but I wasn't satisfied. I got off my bike a few times to examine the situation as I thought possibly my view of the tire from my seat wasn't satisfactory. Surely, Brad hadn't done a good enough job repairing the tire. (I'm sure you can imagine how well that line of thinking went over.)

I became obsessed with looking back at my tire to confirm its status of air.

"Jen, for the thirtieth time, it is fine! Let it go."

As you know, I've always been a bit finicky regarding most aspects of my life. Looking back, for once, this aspect of my personality seemed to have been an advantage as my persistent anxiety kept our little troupe's minds busy while we made our way uphill.

Brad was about ready to rip off my head and throw my bike into the ravine. Had Steph not been off sightseeing with Joe in that moment, she probably would have done the same with the both of us. I think I was descending before my brain registered the fact that I'd made it past the summit.

Fussy, fussy, fussy! I must have driven our parent's nuts as a kid. Nothing was wrong with that tire: nothing!

So, now we were approximately ten miles east of Natural Bridge (just shortly after we reached the summit of what will forever be known as "Flat Tire Pass") and came across our first open range cows of Utah — two nearly emaciated Black Angus steers standing on the right side of the road. They were tall and thin, so thin that I could actually see the outline of their skeletons penetrating through their shiny black coats.

Initially, these cows appeared in view about a half mile away from us. At first sight I thought they were wild bears, a mother and her cub, and so I stopped abruptly, afraid for my safety.

Possibly the sun distorted my perception. *Bears* in the middle of the desert? What was I thinking?

Regardless, (after I petrified Brad) we waited on the side of the road until a man in a 1980-something, run-down, light-blue pickup truck drove by. I waved him down, inquired if he knew what type of animals these were, and he started laughing. He said I'd see many of these "friendly" creatures throughout my journey across southern Utah. They were nothing to be afraid of —they were merely cows.

Slightly embarrassed, my face turned red.

In the distance, they really *did* look like bears. He told me we didn't need to worry about seeing bears in this area of the country, only snakes, scorpions and mountain lions, the latter of which tend to avoid people as they are very secretive animals who come out *only at night*. He told me to set my fears aside and enjoy the ride.

While biking through one of Utah's many open ranges,
this friendly cow caught our attention, June 2008

With a face now the hue of a tomato, I rode my bike past these fearless creatures, gave out a little "moo" and headed downhill toward Natural Bridge.

I was petrified during the majority of our ride because as soon as we exited Monticello we lost all cell phone reception. My battery actually died along the way as it was "searching for service" devoid of my knowledge. This worried me tremendously because the roads we traveled on led us through truly desolate terrain. Ranches were not simply five miles apart like they were in Kansas where even the towns were no more than twenty or thirty miles apart. Instead, there was nothing to even depict a ranch along the road.

Rumor has it (from here on out) towns will be placed an entire day's ride apart. Ranches will not be any closer. If one of us gets hurt, I won't simply be able to run to someone's front door and beg for help. Ranches will be fifty to seventy miles apart, situated miles off the main road. All I will be able to see of these ranches will be a sandy

Above: Jen, Steph, and Brad biking in Utah, June 2008

Below: Cow skull marking Utah ghost town, June 2008

Photographs on this page taken by Joseph Herbstritt.

Hitching post ~ Utah, June 2008
Photograph by Joseph Herbstritt

Above: Circular rock formations, Utah, June 2008

Below: Decaying tree atop cavernous ravine, Utah, June 2008

Photographs on this page taken by Stephanie Herbstritt.

dirt road leading to what will appear to be nowhere. There will be no houses or fences, and there certainly will not be any water other than that present in our bottles.

If we were traveling unsupported, I am not sure we'd be able to make it across this state. It is horribly hot here, not terribly humid, but the heat of the sun is scorching and without ample water I doubt we'd make it a day in this environment, especially with our level of exertion.

I don't think it has rained here in days, let alone months. Even if I wanted to, I couldn't drink the water from the streams that surround the roads because all of the steams are now completely dry. Under rickety, poorly constructed bridges, many positioned at a slant on an incline or winding around a curve: these streams look like nothing other than desert sand.

And if for some reason I grew ill and needed to rest alongside of the road, shade would be very difficult to find. The only shade I saw today was that present when I rode my bike through what appeared to be a natural tunnel, devoid of a roof, made out of two massive rock formations paralleling one another on opposite sides of the road.

If something happens to any of us throughout this ride across Utah I honestly don't know what we will do. We certainly won't be very successful with hitchhiking, and calling Joe to the rescue will be impossible: cell phones don't work here. And Joe is notorious for adventuring on his own excursions throughout the days while we are biking. At times he travels an hour or so off of our route so as to visit a certain site.

The only cars I saw in operation today were those that were present in Monticello, Blanding, and directly outside of these communities. As luck would have it, we also saw that pickup right by the "bears." If the rumors I've been told are true, which I'm sure that they are, I expect that over the course of the next few days I will be able to count the number of cars that pass by our paths each day on one hand.

As it was nearing nightfall we still hadn't made it to our destination, and I was in fear of the animals that might come out.

That darn man in the pickup. I know he told me not to worry, but his mention of mountain lions created a multitude of scenarios in my mind.

I am used to using the term "rural" to define our hometown of Bellefonte. I am embarrassed by this statement as I now realize Bellefonte is a city compared to the areas I traveled through today.

I can't say I didn't like the escape today's ride provided. It was nice to be alone with my thoughts without any distraction. Nevertheless, the environment was very novel and undeniably fear-provoking.

As the ride culminated, my odometer read 120 miles. Not bad for just under twelve hours. By this time all of us, including Joe, were justifiably fatigued. We ate dinner, washed our dishes, set up our tent, and brushed our teeth, and I think all of us were having trouble keeping our eyes opened.

While we were eating our dinner of mountain pies and canned raviolis, an elderly couple camping directly across from us initiated a conversation. They were from northern Utah, Salt Lake to be specific. Of course, they were very kind and appeared to be about the age of Grandma and Grandpa Herbstritt (probably in their mid to late seventies). They were having trouble inflating an air mattress so we assisted them with the task. They provided us with some valuable insight on Utah's many national parks. They told us of their favorites and attempted to persuade us to visit such.

I learned that none of the national parks here have showers. In my mind, this demonstrates how scarce water actually is here. Most of the bathrooms will be latrines (devoid even of sinks), just like the ones available here at Natural Bridge. It seems antibacterial hand rinse will have to suffice.

It looks like we won't be showering until we get to Nevada! Something tells me water will be just as scarce there. So, for those who are fortunate enough to smell us (or our tent, for that matter) over the course of the next few weeks, I wish them the best!

Our conversation was pleasant, full of stories of families, friends, children, grandchildren, and Utah. This couple encouraged us to visit Salt Lake City on our journey home. I hope we do.

Because we arrived here so late tonight I didn't have a chance, nor did I have the energy to see the Natural Bridges. Tomorrow morning, as the sun is about to rise, I will attempt to get a glimpse at these three believed gorgeous (but rare) natural bridges, supposedly formed from running water.

You, being a civil engineer inspired by natural works of art such as this, would have loved these particular structures. I have no doubt.

All of these red rocks make my imagination run wild. I see massive birds, lions, cats, balancing rocks, and creatures of all sorts surrounding me in their designs. Their presence makes me question if these natural wonders were formed solely by erosion alone. Part of me has to believe that a higher power had a hand in this. I hope this is so, for if it is, by now, I'm certain, you've met the Creator.

After dinner was completed, we all carefully cleaned up. From here on out accidentally dropping table scraps on the ground could yield a fatal mistake. We have definitely entered mountain lion country. Warning signs are present in all of the bathrooms. The last thing I want to be faced with in the middle of the night (when I am walking to the latrine) is a ferocious mountain lion hunting for his prey!

As I unzipped the tent and placed my weary, salt-covered body into my sleeping bag, I looked around me at all of the guests in this park. As remote as we are from civilization, there certainly are a number of "Cruise across America" RVs present here. These RVs frighten the heck out of me while I am biking, due to my suspicion that most of the drivers have a significant lack of experience driving these substantial vehicles.

By the way, did I ever mention to you my run-in with the taxi cab driver?

That's for tomorrow.

I would bet that this park is filled to capacity tonight. I'm surprised by this as I was told Natural Bridges National Monument is not as popular of a tourist destination as some of the national parks present here in Utah, such as Bryce Canyon and Zion. I hope that we are able to land a spot to sleep at each of our destinations, as once we get to a location it will have to suffice. There will be no being picky or finicky, for towns and parks from here on out are a full day's ride apart.

My mind needs to settle. I need sleep. This is a beautiful section of our country. We will certainly take our time biking through this land. I pray you are here with us enjoying every minute of this breathtaking place.

Darkness has long past approached.

Goodnight.

Jenny

Bryce Canyon National Park, Utah, June 2008
Photograph by Stephanie Herbstritt

One of Utah's many red rock formations almost
always seen beneath a bright blue sky,
Utah, June 2008
Photograph by Stephanie Herbstritt

30. Fresh Fruit
Natural Bridges National Monument to Capitol Reef, Utah

"I respect faith, but doubt is what gets you an education."
~Wilson Mizner

June 12, 2008

Jeremy,

One of the final straws that led to this trip was not the taxi cab driver, but the local media.

Sometime around late December 2007 and early January 2008, a few friends and I were walking in downtown State College around one in the morning. We were heading to the Tavern to have a few drinks. (None of us had touched even an ounce of alcohol at the time this event played out.)

I was trying to take back control of my life: do something typical: go out for drinks with the girls.

It was snowing hard; the roads were snow-covered and slick. As my friends and I walked down Calder Way in the vicinity of Rapid Transit Shoes, I slipped on the ice. As I did so, a local taxi cab driver was pulling his mini-van to a stop. Somehow, I fell (with my legs crossed) straddling the back passenger tire of his vehicle, still in motion. As the tires rotated, his vehicle ran over first my left foot. Then, as the driver panicked, he backed up and ran over (again) that foot, as well as my right.

Sliding underneath the wheels of his vehicle, I panicked but was in too much shock to scream aloud. As my friends hit his vehicle while yelling frantically, he slammed on the brakes.

A cop driving behind him witnessed the entire event. After throwing some sort of wool blanket on top of me, she immediately called for an ambulance. Freezing, while I laid on the ground awaiting the ambulance's arrival, I sat in silence. I could have been killed. But I wasn't. I was barely even injured. My feet were just fine, thanks to an incredibly firm-soled pair of shoes.

After I was discharged from the Emergency Room, my friends and I howled with laughter. Only me!

Unfortunately, because a police report was filed, though no one was at fault, the local newspaper and radio stations got hold of this information. The next day's headlines read something like this: "GRIEVING SISTER GETS RUN OVER NOT ONCE, BUT TWICE, BY LOCAL TAXI CAB."

To think, *I* was the best news available.

I thought that story might give you a laugh. After it happened, I wanted nothing other than to call you and tell you all about it.

I can hear your laughter now, in this moment.

Today's ride took us on Utah 95 from Natural Bridge through Hanksville to Capitol Reef National Park.

I have so much to tell you, yet somehow I am short for words.

My surroundings are breath-taking, full of vertical cliffs, cavernous canyons, red-rock structures and sand arrangements all claimed to be created by erosion alone. The make-up of this place truly is magical. It's better than Disney World and Sea World combined. I wouldn't know, but really, this has to be better than any drug on the planet. If I didn't know any better, I would have thought I'd died myself and gone straight to heaven.

Here, there are many tourists roaming around, many more so than were present at yesterday's destination, but I feel as if I am alone, alone with my thoughts, alone surrounded by nothing but unimaginable beauty.

Steph walking atop a sea of red rock in Canyonlands National Park, Utah, June 2008

I wonder how these rocks actually formed. Millions of years must have been required in order for these creations to have reached such perfection.

There is no way, in my mind, that erosion configured this sediment into the most perfect of pictures, shapes, sizes, and colors, alone, by itself. I wonder how we, as humans, came to the conclusion that erosion alone was the sole architect of this design.

If these formations do take millions of years to construct, how can we be certain that erosion was the only hand that played a role in this complex process? We were not here in the beginning. Not one of us on this earth today existed at that time. Surely records of old have faded, been shred, and are now unrecognizable. Where is our proof?

In life, is there anything we can be certain of other than death?

I desire to achieve faith in a god, honestly I do. I want to believe in a supreme being who represents good, reigns over evil, keeps all of his promises, and has a place set aside for each and every single one of us that is far better than this world, far better than even my current surroundings, which in this moment, to me, make up the most spectacular backdrop on the planet.

I want to believe, my yearning is evident, but something is prohibiting me. I cannot identify the entity at this time, maybe I never will.

It presently is entirely too complicated for me to believe when for all of my life I placed my trust in a god who simply thwarted me. I was taught that he answered prayers, but I found out, all too unjustly, that he doesn't answer mine. I was taught he would protect me from evil, but he didn't protect you, and in turn, he abandoned me. I was taught when I needed him most he wouldn't simply stand tall by my side with a thrash in his hand. Instead, he would carry me, be my legs, my guide and my strength. He wouldn't bestow upon me anything I couldn't handle.

My god has turned out to be a fraud and, to me, it seems that for all of my existence he has been on retreat. Is it true that when the boy down the street was diagnosed with cancer and his family prayed assiduously day in and day out that his god answered his family's prayers but mine neglected our family's when we prayed helplessly, on bended knee, that you somehow would call and say you were alive, safe, in a hospital, in shock, scared, but breathing, heart beating and alive?

You see, I want to believe. It is the only way for me to continue on: to know that one day, even through all of this pain and suffering, we will be reunited and live eternally together in peace.

I want to believe that a higher power had a role in the splendor of my current residence, yet somehow, through all of the anger and the pain, I cannot believe.

I wonder if I ever will.

A red Jeep: I must have been locked in my thoughts as I almost pedaled into it while riding my bike away from our campsite toward a large fruit orchard located near the entrance of this park. Here, one can pick a variety of fresh fruit free of charge. From what I hear, you can seize all you like (in kind moderation).

Unfortunately, upon my arrival to this lovely orchard I learned we are but a few weeks shy of the harvest season: the fruit is not yet quite ripe.

I was disappointed, but not for long, as my eyes soon focused in on a deer. He was standing upright on his hind legs, eating unripe fruit dangling from the trees above his head. Upon noticing my presence, he glanced briefly at me and then returned to his meal. The deer here must be incredibly tame for he wasn't bothered by my presence whatsoever.

I chuckled out loud, then drew for my camera only to realize I didn't have it. What's the sense in owning a camera if you never have it with you when you need it? Disheartened, I rode my bike back to our campsite.

Just in time for dinner. Joe and Steph had prepared a smorgasbord of mountain pies, PB&J sandwiches, and SpaghettiOs. At the sight

Incredibly tame deer snacking on unripe apples, Capitol Reef National Park, Utah, June 12, 2008 ~ Photograph by Brad Updegrove

of this food placed out on the picnic table, my stomach began to growl and my mouth started to water. It was nearly seven o'clock at night. We had biked exactly 140 miles and my tank was running on empty. Today's scenery had been beautiful but the grades were tough. The pavement was black and saturated with the heat of the sun. My enormous appetite was well-earned, don't you think?

When we awoke this morning at Natural Bridge the air felt cool. But by the time midmorning rolled around, the temperature must have been nearing 100°F. Fortunately, there was minimal humidity present so it was tolerable.

The scenery wasn't much of a contrast from yesterday's, nor was the activity. Traffic didn't unexpectedly increase and the streams didn't suddenly begin to flow. Cows were still oddly present, enclosed in open ranges, and "Cruise across America" drivers still failed to leave ample space on the side of the road for my body and bike when passing by.

If anything, my surroundings became much more desolate today. From Natural Bridge to Hanksville, I saw absolutely no suggestion of human existence.

As I rode my bike, I couldn't help but adore the sun's creation of an art show, formed by reflecting its own light at different angles off the oversized rocks which (intermittently) formed a topless tunnel surrounding the road. The picture was striking. As the sun changed direction, was masked by clouds then uncovered, as the road wound and as the scenery morphed, the show became more and more invigorating to watch. I was taken back in time millions, if not billions, of years ago to the age of the dinosaurs. I could picture these creatures walking amongst these colossal rocks, stepping on top of them as if they were pieces of tile placed upon a kitchen floor.

Soon enough we arrived in Hanksville. If I hadn't been paying attention I could have easily missed the town, as it was made up of nothing more than a few gas stations situated on a half-mile curve in the road.

Size isn't everything, as this town served the absolute best ice cream available in the universe. In fact, it was better than the Berkey Creamery's. (I know, I should be rid of my Penn State diploma for writing these words.) For sixty-nine cents, I was served a large vanilla soft-serve waffle cone at a placed called Blondies. Honestly, from the bottom of the cone all the way to the top it had to have spanned ten inches, and I am not exaggerating!

Initially our intention was to spend the night in this sweet tooth's paradise, located ninety miles west of Natural Bridge on Utah 95. But after I finished my cone and looked at my watch, I realized it was only mid-afternoon. My taste buds craved the opportunity for fresh fruit at Capitol Reef. Therefore, we ventured on the extra fifty miles (only to discover the fruit is still premature…ugh).

From Hanksville to Capitol Reef all I saw were fields of sand piled in mounds. In these mounds, I noticed what appeared to be heavily travelled motorcycle tracks. The exhilaration these vehicles must provide in this environment has to be out of this world.

Upon entering the national park, we had to bike ten additional miles before arriving at our campsite. Throughout, the wind provided a multitude of tantrums.

We were biking along a windy road that appeared to have been created by chiseling out a narrow canal through the center of two adjacent gigantic rocks. A stream flowed to our right within this tunnel.

This channel pleasantly shielded us from the sun's warmth. Nevertheless, it also created profuse, violent gusts of wind that were disgustingly unpredictable. As the wind squalled, stream water blew onto the road sprinkling us with what felt like ice. Dust from the road sprayed our eyes, temporarily blinding us (then, causing tears to release). During a few of these blasts I was nearly pushed off my bicycle due to the strength of the breeze.

Foolishly, due to its magnificence, I kept my eyes on the steam as I biked by. The water flowed hastily with class-three and -four rapids spanning its entire length. Trying your hand at white-water rafting here, Jeremy, would have been your desire.

By ten o'clock my bedtime was drawing near. It was pitch dark out and my body was physically drained. Nevertheless, I couldn't get my mind off of the threatening content of a sign that I noticed hanging on the bathroom wall earlier in the evening.

That man in that pickup!

If you are attacked by a mountain lion: "…make yourself big, fight back and make noise." They are "more apt to attack children," rather than adults. "Don't leave your children out of your sight.

"They are more comfortable fighting creatures of their own size. Worry for the children, not for yourself!"

At the time I took notice of this sign, I was washing my face. I had a premonition its presence might make it difficult for me to fall asleep.

And my prediction was right!

As I snuggle up in my sleeping bag, surrounded by Joe, Steph, and Brad, I am attempting to fall asleep "surrounded by the comfort of chirping crickets, hooting owls, and singing birds, all which surround me like a figurine in a glass ball."

This fantasy is absolutely *not* working. I'm convinced those cats are going to eat me… And, after thirty minutes of listening to nature and counting sheep, I'm still unsuccessful.

With all of this thinking, I just realized I failed to brush my teeth. Seems I'll be returning to the bathroom to complete this task.

The sky is now black, but clear and colossal, filled with what appear to be a million stars positioned ever so flawlessly upon its expanse. A full-moon lights up the rock formations that surround me. The smell of the air is fresh and the sound of crickets chirping is hypnotizing. I do not hear anything that even remotely resembles the noise I suspect a pack of mountain lions would produce.

It's far past my bedtime. My teeth are now brushed. I am putting down the pen!

Goodnight!

Love always,
Jennifer

31. A Staircase
Capitol Reef to Escalante, Utah

*"Make wisdom your provision for the journey from youth to old age,
for it is a more certain support than all other possessions."*
~Bias

June 13, 2008

Jeremy,

Many of the towns in Utah which we've biked through span merely a curve in the road…if that. The town may consist of a gas station, restaurant, and possibly a hotel and/or campground.

Because a hundred miles may stretch between gas stations, people are forced to pay a steep price — nearly $5 a gallon. Grocery stores are, more often than not, absent. Internet service is meager and cell phone coverage is scattered. Oftentimes, I fail to even locate a post office within these towns.

I am unsure where the people of these communities reside: perhaps on ranches in the distance. There are minimal houses, if any, within the actual towns, and until we made it here to Escalante and actually saw a high school, I was beginning to question whether or not the children of these communities attended public school.

We began our ride with a scenic climb into Torrey, located approximately ten miles west of Capitol Reef. The road there was enveloped with soaring canyons painted infinite shades of reds and orange. The rocks which made up these canyons were laden with cracks. Some contained so many, I thought the entire structure might collapse if only I touched it in the wrong way.

After this small but invigorating climb, we stopped to rest at a local convenience store.

Ten miles into our ride! From the beginning we all knew today was going to be a long day!

Torrey was the first town we've passed through in days that actually had cell phone reception. I called Mom and Dad to update them on our progress. Brad made a call to his brother begging him to mail us additional inner tubes. Since I have been so fortunate to run over three invisible (yet sharp) objects that have repetitively punctured my back tire, we are now down to our last spare tube. If we get more than one flat tire today, we'll have no other choice but to catch a ride with Joe to the closest town and wait for this package to arrive.

In Torrey, we met three people: a couple in their early to mid sixties who are carrying their dog in a baby carrier-like trailer, and a young man whom they met up with (coincidentally) somewhere in the confines of the Nevada desert. They'd been traveling together ever since. Unlike us, they are traveling west to east. I'm slightly jealous of their position!

The older couple told us they are carrying some four hundred pounds packed in their trailer. I've been besieged by these hills with nothing on my bike other than my very own weight.

They joked with us that we are "cheating," not carrying our gear in panniers or in a trailer just as they are. I was slightly offended as my intention all along has not been to break any world records or win any competitions. I have simply been trying to get away, find peace, spend time with you, enjoy America and find good in this world. I forced myself to laugh and tried not to be bothered by this remark. I gave them credit for their accomplishments. Personally, I like our supported trip.

Our conversation continued as they told us about a man rollerblading across the country. An African American minister and his son are biking across as well. They're just a few days behind this threesome. We should cross paths within the next few days. There supposedly is also a middle-aged man traveling across. He is fairly overweight, so they say, but for him this trip is not about losing weight; it is a celebration of fifty years spent on this earth. They expect we will see him soon, as well.

As they spoke my excitement built with the prospect of continuing to run into other travelers. Some of these individuals will inevitably have a similar mindset as I do. Some will not. But all will be trying to complete the same task as we are: that is to make it across America on two wheels powered by nothing more than the strength of our legs.

All of the people whom this couple mentioned are traveling west to east. They have just started their journey; ours will come to an end in just a few short weeks. I do not want this trip to conclude. Just as I wasn't ready for your death, I'm not ready for this trip to come to an end. I like the peace, the distraction, the happiness, and the unknown this trip has provided to me.

The young man accompanying this couple must have been in his mid to late twenties. He told me just an hour ago he was informed via cell phone his childhood dog was diagnosed with cancer. He left her behind just two weeks ago. A friend of his who is caring for the dog noticed a raised area of discoloration on the dog's nose last night. In turn, she took her in for evaluation by the vet today. Indeed, this area proved to be malignant and according to the vet the cancer is evident elsewhere within the dog's body. The vet recommended the animal be "put down" and so it was scheduled to be done later today pending the permission of this man who was (now) understandably distraught.

I could see it in his eyes, even before he shared this fragile, horrible news with me. He needed a sympathetic ear to listen to his sorrows.

Throughout our conversation, he spoke of how "we cannot foresee when will be the last time we see one another" and how "unjust this world is." He questioned "why death was even created." I felt as if he were reading my every thought. He mentioned he had a premonition when he said farewell to his dog that he would never see her again. I thought it was ironic I felt the same way when you left Bellefonte following Christmas break.

I wondered if we as humans are able to sense the presence of death, not on the surface, but subconsciously, deep in our gut. This conversation brought me back to one of my many concerns: whether or not you knew that morning when you awoke it'd be the last time you'd do so. I hope you didn't, for I thought about how scared you would have been. I deduct I will never know until I face death myself.

I could relate to this man's pain in a certain fashion. Of course, I didn't know exactly what he was feeling at that time and in that moment. But I do know what it is like to lose someone whom I truly loved. My heart broke for him and his dog. So, following our farewells (and best wishes) I closed my eyes and said a prayer to a god I still do not know for this man and his dog.

After an enlightening conversation with a few Harley guys about Utah, the Mormon religion, biking, and life, we continued on our way. Just as an aside, some of the best conversationalists I've met on this trip thus far have been motorcycle riders and truck drivers.

From Torrey we traveled west toward Escalante on Scenic Byway 12 "Utah's First All-American Road," but not without a few struggles and stops along the way. We endured a very large climb outside of Torrey over Boulder Mountain. As we biked for miles and miles uphill, ascending some very steep grades, we encountered many secluded mountain lakes and streams. I was fortunate enough to observe a few rainbow trout housed within these waters. It was accordingly impressive to see lakes at such high elevations once again.

Boulder Mountain seemed to have what I thought were at least three summits, each one tricking me into believing that I had accomplished my goal. I would get to what I thought was the crest of the mountain, stare into the valley beneath out a scenic lookout, then, start to travel downhill, only to start climbing again. Ironically enough, I wasn't bothered by these pranks. The ride was fun and filled with awe. Numerous trees were present for shade, a large contrast to the past few days' rides, which have been void of shade except when traveling through those narrow, chiseled-out canyons.

Biking away from Boulder, Utah, June 13, 2008

Once we finally did arrive at the peak, we began our descent into Boulder. The ride downhill was terribly frigid but nowhere near as cold as that morning in Gunnison. I had to dismount my bike several times to warm myself up. I was shivering, dressed in black leg- and arm-warmers with long-fingered gloves, and two long-sleeved shirts layered on top of my arm warmers, yet, due to the change in elevation, I was still cold.

We stopped for lunch at a diner in Boulder. I drank two oversized mugs of scolding hot tea and was still frozen. Eventually the scenery abruptly changed and my body began to warm. Once again, I remembered, nothing lasts forever.

After we passed over Boulder Mountain and departed from this diner, the landscape returned to desert terrain just as quickly as we left it this morning with mounds of dry, gigantic, red rocks. This was what surrounded me for the remainder of the ride; this and a scorching-hot desert sun. I felt like Mario or Luigi in World 2 of Super Mario Brothers, Desert World, with the sun chasing after me, minus the quicksand!

*From left to right: Steph, Jen, Brad and Joe atop an initially believed-to-be summit
en route to Boulder, Utah, June 12, 2008*

As we continued our descent toward Escalante, we biked across a
three-mile section between Boulder and Escalante named the
Hogback. Immediately before entering this section of road, a sign
appeared that read something like this: "Steep Grades, Sharp Curves,
No Guardrail." In this segment, for three miles straight there were
absolutely no guardrails on either side of the road to "protect" us from
the sharp drop-offs into the deep, sweeping canyons on both sides of
the road. These canyons extended for miles in the distance. The experience was comparable to riding across a narrow bridge without any
railings, above a river bed some three quarters of a mile beneath,
absent of any water or current, with nothing around but the sound
of the wind.

Thankfully, we were traveling downhill, so this span of road disappeared relatively quickly. If it weren't for my fear of heights, I would
have wished for the experience to last a bit longer. The height of the
drop-offs surrounding me terrified me to a point of nearly inducing
an out-of-body experience. Nevertheless, this strictly must have been
the most memorable aspect of the trip thus far. I felt as if I were on

*Brad in his groove, biking surrounded by nothing but blue skies, red rock and earth,
Utah, June 2008*

the edge of the world. The only thing separating me from the canyons that encompassed me in every direction was a thin slice of road. My heart raced from a combination of excitement, thrill, anxiety, and awe.

As we approached the end of the Hogback, Joe, Steph, Brad, and I stopped our bikes (and car) right in the middle of the road. Time paused while we got lost in the view. As my body quivered and I laughed uncontrollably, Joe and Steph screamed into the distance, "I am on top of the world!" A smile covered Brad's face.

For miles and miles in the distance, in front of me, below me, behind me, and above me, all I could see was earth. No manmade structures — just earth. It was as if I'd been removed from the present time and placed into the era of dinosaurs. The only ingredient missing was the dinosaur. It was the most amazing sensation I've felt in my life.

Utah's Scenic Byway 12 is something I certainly deem all people should experience at least once in their lives. From here we biked mostly downhill to Escalante.

We saw such a vast multiplicity of topography today from desert with rock and sand formations to mountains with fields of green leaf and pine cone covered trees buried deep with crystal clear mountain lakes. I certainly love Utah.

Once again, we are sleeping in a national park. We began our journey through Utah with the National Monument of Natural Bridges, then headed to Capitol Reef and now we are sitting in the Grand Escalante Staircase where we have been told we might come across petrified wood and dinosaur bones along some of the hiking trails. I am not sure I will have the energy to go hiking later on in the day, as today's ride was truly extraordinarily exhausting. Nevertheless, I can certainly picture the terrestrial dinosaur's massive feet pounding on the grounds of this national park leaving footprints in the sand.

I hope one hundred years from now your footprints (and mine as well) are remembered.

Dinner awaits me! (Yep, it's raviolis. Or will it be SpaghettiOs?)

Jen

32. Panguitch
Escalante to Panguitch, Utah

"Grief teaches the steadiest minds to waver." –Sophocles

June 14, 2008

Jeremy,

This morning we left Escalante and biked to Panguitch, Utah. Between Escalante and Panguitch we endured two climbs, both spanning fifteen to twenty miles in length on the inclines as well as the declines. The peak of each summit was approximately 2,500 feet higher than the valley between. Both Escalante and Panguitch sat at the same elevation as this valley. On an elevation chart, the two climbs appeared like similar cones.

The climbs contained some challenging grades, particularly as each summit approached. With each peak we reached, the descents that followed were thoroughly enjoyable. For a second occasion, when I made the decline, the temperature was bearable. Granted, the summits were lower in elevation than those in the Rockies, but goose-bumps and chattering teeth were certainly absent. I believe the highest we climbed today was 7,777 feet. We took a picture as we thought this exact elevation a bit bizarre. In nature, anything is possible.

In any case, this is approximately 4,000-feet lower than Monarch Pass. Nevertheless, climbing 2,500 feet in elevation is just that. It isn't an easy task to perform once in a solitary day, let alone twice. Fortunately, after doing so I wasn't as cold as I remembered I was following my ascents up through the Rockies. Today, a gentle wind was blowing in my face and the sun was beating warmly on my back. Possibly only for today, I liked biking downhill!

The terrain remained very much that of a sandy desert filled with rock formations, canyons, cliffs, and very few residents. Seldom did I see a vehicle traveling the roads except, of course, for the "Cruise across America" RVs, which were quite prominent around the touristy destinations such as Bryce Canyon. It seems as if a lot of people rent these vehicles to endeavor on tours of national parks located mainly within the western United States.

For being a desert, the temperature this morning was incredibly cool. Two hours later I would have disagreed. This makes sense being that we slept at approximately 5,800 feet of elevation last night. As a matter of fact, higher elevations encourage temperatures to drop significantly at nightfall and increase no sooner than midmorning. The wind seems to follow this same trend, taking a break from its fits at night in order to gain back its strength for the following day. It appears to awake around ten o'clock each morning, about the same time that the RVs start to appear.

Jen secretively delighted to be biking on the opposite side of the road as this "Cruise Across America" RV, Utah, June 2008

Our first climb of the morning started as soon as we waved goodbye to Joe, still slumbering inside the tent.

Out of Escalante we traveled up and over our first summit to Henrieville, through Cannonville, and then to Tropic. All of these towns were dispersed going into, amongst and out of (respectively) a very large valley approximately thirty-five miles east of Panguitch.

Tropic sat slightly higher in elevation than Cannonville. It didn't appear very "tropical." Rather, it appeared very much like a desert with minimal vegetation.

Between Cannonville and Tropic the area became greatly more populated. Houses were prominent and there was even a convenience store located at the city limits of Tropic. There was a campground in town where I suspected multitudes of tourists stayed at last night due to the town's close proximity to Bryce Canyon.

Regardless, once we reached Tropic we began our second and final climb of the day. We climbed vigorously until we reached a left-hand turn that led toward Bryce Canyon. This was approximately the summit of the climb. Cars were abundant in this particular section.

From here, our route bypassed Bryce Canyon and traversed down-hill for approximately fifteen to twenty additional miles until we reached Panguitch.

About two miles after reaching the summit, we were mandated to follow a bike path for approximately six miles, as portions of the road became very narrow and were heavily traveled by tourists. It was a beautiful bike path, perfectly crafted without potholes or cracks. Its course was windy and narrow and certainly not heavily traveled when compared with the road (at least during our ride today).

It was comical to see a bike path in the middle of the desert, as I'm used to seeing paths of this type outside of cities or on the outskirts of State College surrounding Penn State University. It was fun to maneuver, and I caught myself pretending to be a participant in some sort of race, taking the curves as fast as I could. It was a wonder I didn't clip a pedal on one of those curves!

The road that we were not permitted to bike on traveled through narrow tunnels of red rock. I was disappointed I was unable to go beneath these as I'm sure the sight would have been awesome. I understood the safety reasons behind the rule; nevertheless, if it weren't for the presence of police on the side of the road prior to the bike path's entrance, I probably would have disobeyed the law and taken the risk.

The ride today was short: only about seventy miles in length. These miles flew by and to my surprise I was soon reading signs for The Dixie National Forest and Red Canyon, both located directly outside of Panguitch. As I got a glimpse of these brilliant red canyons from a distance I had to pause, pull over to the side of the road, and purely digest the beauty.

Utah truly has to be a gift from above.

By the time we completed our mileage for the day, it was merely time for lunch. I believe this is the earliest we've finished biking for the day all month long.

At Panguitch, we ate lunch with Joe at a local fifties-style burger shop then drove toward the northern rim of the Grand Canyon in Arizona. During our drive, we traveled through desert to forest in a matter of miles. Upon entering Arizona, in the distance we saw lovely pink sand dunes and then we abruptly entered a large forest of pine.

We are staying forty-five miles north of the Grand Canyon, as I assumed that if we wanted to stay directly at the Grand Canyon we should have booked a campsite at least a year in advance. Lately, I wouldn't describe myself as a planner, although two years ago I would have. Our campground will suffice.

Tomorrow we will tour the Grand Canyon during the day and then drive back to Panguitch late in the night where we will spend the night tomorrow. Our biking journey will continue the following day. This will be our third and possible final "vacation" of the trip before arriving in San Francisco!

The campground that we are staying at fell victim to a forest fire just one year ago. Though drinking water is hard to come by, the owners encourage all guests to take a few gallons of complimentary water upon arrival to put out one's campfire before he/she heads to bed. They mention they will come around to each site around sunset to ensure all fires are completely out.

Window of red rock peering into a sea of ponderosa pines, Bryce Canyon National Park, Utah, June 14, 2008 ~ Photograph taken by Joseph Herbstritt

Bryce Canyon National Park, Utah, June 14, 2008
Photograph taken by Stephanie Herbstritt

The ground here is incredibly dry. As I mentioned earlier, we haven't seen rain in days and it appears that this section of Arizona hasn't seen rain in the same amount of time either, possibly longer.

I think about the fear these people must have faced during that forest fire back one year ago. I cannot fathom this. I doubt one can feasibly drive away toward safety faster than a fire can spread. And even if one could, I can't imagine the horror in leaving and knowing that when you return, more likely than not, everything you own will be nothing but ash. We will surely be vigilant with our fire tonight.

Oh, heavens! Brad, Joe, and Steph certainly are going to make me nuts. Currently, Steph is strengthening her abs while lying on a picnic table flat on her back slowly lowering and raising her legs held straight together repetitively. Meanwhile, Joe and Brad have formed the absolute largest fire I think I have seen in my life. It looks like a bonfire fit for a tribe of warriors ready to light the tree branches not far from its highest flame on fire.

I'm running for water!

"Steph, help me!"

Thank goodness. Their fire is now of a reasonable size. You should know, the two claim they didn't create such a beast of a fire on purpose. The kindling here is simply that dry. Frightening, I'd have to say.

Joe, Steph, and I just got finished videotaping our very off-key rendition of the *Lion Sleeps Tonight* while dancing ridiculously like factious tribesmen and -women around our campfire.

I can't catch my breath; I'm laughing too hard. Literally — I'm rolling on the ground. Brad couldn't be any more humiliated. He's thinking, *And that's my girlfriend! Yep, she's twenty-six years old.*

Sleep may not come at all tonight. After experiencing the Hogback and Escalante's Grand Staircase, I can't imagine how vast the Grand Canyon will be!

Love always,

Jen

Steph jumping with animation above this mile deep crater,
Grand Canyon National Park, June 15, 2008

Joe thrilled to be standing on the edge of the earth, northern rim of the
Grand Canyon National Park, June 15, 2008

33. Arizona and the Grand Canyon

*"There's the country of America, which you have to defend,
but there's also the idea of America. America is more than just a
country, it's an idea. An idea that's supposed to be contagious."*
~Bono

June 15, 2008

Jeremy,

Okay, so they don't call it the Grand Canyon for nothing. What a place! I could have spent days here. Someday I will. There are so many trails to hike, sites to see and lookouts that took my breath away. The canyon is a mile deep and it must span hundreds of miles in length. It is the most remarkable natural piece of art I have seen in my life. And yes, I know I say that about all of them, but this time I mean it!

I was able to see for hundreds of miles in front of me. I could even see the San Franciscan mountain range located in California some 150 miles away. The air quality was that perfect. We were fortunate enough to have arrived here on a day with clear skies, the view couldn't have been any more superior.

Over the course of the past month, I have been taken back by the vast array of splendor which our country has to offer. From the Atlantic to the Pacific (we're almost there!), the foothills of the Appalachians to the snow-covered peaks of the Rockies, the great high plains of the Midwest to this spectacular view of the largest crater on earth, America certainly has it all!

We are a hospitable people who have withstood financial hardships, social injustice, racial prejudice, and war. We are the face of

America, you and I, striving to make this world a better place. For just a second today, while standing out on the edge of the earth, amidst the beauty of this canyon surrounding me in practically all dimensions, I was able to accept that you have gone on to a better place, one even more beautiful than this Grand Canyon, where you no longer feel pain, endure suffering, injustice, or cruelty. For just one second I was able to accept this. I will take what I can.

The northern rim of the Grand Canyon was filled with seas of trees. From what I understand, the southern rim is composed of more rock formations such as those that we've seen throughout our journey through Utah.

Most tourists tend to visit the southern rim. It was not hectic here whatsoever so I was able to enjoy the beauty of this place without the noise or commotion of a multitude of other tourists. This was nice.

We walked out onto a path narrower than the Hogback, with cliffs engulfing us from all directions. While standing on this path I was able to gaze into the canyon below and plainly get lost in time. The ravines were incredibly deep. I was absolutely petrified, yet I felt as if I were on top of this world. My hands were sweating throughout the entire experience and my heart wouldn't slow down its beat. I was less than an inch from falling off of the world. This was the most amazing feeling I've experienced. I yearned for your ability to see this place, one of the most spectacular views I have witnessed in my life.

Once again, I was taken back by the fact that erosion and sedimentation were the sole contributors to the creation of this natural wonder. I want to believe that a more supreme, higher being had his hand in this, just like Natural Bridge, Escalante, and Capitol Reef. Just as the body is too delicate and intricate, at least in my mind, to have evolved from simple microorganisms of the sea, and the universe is too complex to have morphed simply from the combustion of a primeval atom, I somehow can absolutely not comprehend how this massive, breath-taking canyon could have formed simply by the displacement of sediment.

Dead tree perched above the largest crater on earth, northern rim of the Grand Canyon National Park, Arizona, June 15, 2008 ~ Photograph taken by Joseph Herbstritt

Northern rim of the Grand Canyon National Park, Arizona, June 15, 2008

In this moment, I consider myself an agnostic. I am doubtful of the existence of God and/or the afterlife, or of any supreme being, for that matter. But somehow this canyon has created a sense of assurance in me. It's very hard to believe this world was created by luck alone.

Today I have hope that one day, with time, my faith will return and that eventually I will learn to live in a world without you physically in it. I may not like it this way, but I will learn to accept what I cannot control.

We have a long drive back to Panguitch. Until tomorrow: good-night.

Love,

Jennifer

Brad and Jen posing above the northern rim of the Grand Canyon, June 15, 2008
Photograph taken by Joseph Herbstritt

34. Celebrating Your Life
Panguitch to Milford, Utah

"We make a living by what we get. We make a life by what we give."
~Winston Churchill

June 16, 2008

Jeremy,

We stayed at a KOA in Panguitch last night.* We were able to shower and do laundry — certainly a blessing for all of those who came in contact with us today.

From Panguitch we biked through Cedar City to Milford, Utah.

Prior to the culmination of our day here in Milford we stopped in Cedar City. This had to have been the largest city we traveled through in Utah. Indeed, it had a Walmart. It was comical to see because the girls who served us our ice-cream back at Blondie's, in Hanksville, told us this would be the closest place to "civilization" we'd find in days. Well, we certainly found it. Cedar City was beautiful. I ate the most scrumptious oriental chicken salad at a cute little Irish diner (I know, weird huh?), next to a bike shop, where the owner so graciously re-aligned my chain for a measly $15. The buildings were brick. The business district was vibrant with an authentic downtown square integral with a post office, numerous churches, restaurants, bookstores, and boutiques.

It was clearly a university town, home to Southern Utah University, with college students populating the downtown streets and their emblem prevalent on storefronts. The town reminded me of home

---

*   *June 14: We biked to Panguitch in the morning and then drove to a campground by the Grand Canyon in the evening.*
        June 15: Saw Grand Canyon during the day, drove back to Panguitch in the evening.
        June 16: Woke up in Panguitch and biked west.

and our beloved Nittany Lions. It looked more like a community than many of the towns we have passed through during this trip, with streets in a grid, developments and a centralized downtown section where I assumed we would have been greeted by name had we been locals.

We took our time touring the town, chatting with the locals, and supporting their businesses. All too soon, we biked on farther west to Milford.

As we biked, I realized the date: June 16, 2008, the fourteen-month anniversary of your death. Rather than dwell on the circumstances surrounding your murder, today I decided to reflect on a few of the many fond memories I have of you in celebration of your life.

I'll begin with that infamous first kayak trip you took me on. I'll never forget how I panicked shortly after we came upon that fork in the stream. In case you've forgotten, we decided to traverse the left side of that "Y" only to realize upon doing so that a very large tree had fallen over and was obstructing our passage farther downstream. Unable to steer myself and my kayak to shore due to the strength of the rapids in this narrow section of water, I landed myself directly into that tree. As I hugged it begging for mercy, my kayak actually jolted beneath and proceeded to rapidly maneuver downstream unattended. I lost my paddles, my shorts and even your cell phone and keys, which were supposed to be protected in my kayak's rear waterproof container. The rapids had trapped me in a position I couldn't get out of, curling the tree. I didn't have enough strength in my arms to pull my body up on top of that very thick limb. Thankfully, you were there. You cautiously darted across that branch as if it were a balance beam, then hurriedly pulled me to safety. After we collected my kayak, which was now a mile or so downstream, found your keys, dismantled cell phone and my shorts now covered in mud, we rolled in our kayaks just laughing hysterically.

Swimming in your Cardinal Court community pool, doing cannon balls in succession competing with one another as to who could create the biggest splash — that was fun.

How you casually negotiated the purchasing price of my Pathfinder for me. How you and Dad unintentionally burnt down an entire alfalfa field one summer while burning brush then inadvertently called an elderly man rather than the fire department for assistance in controlling the fire, "Sir, I'd love to help you out, but for God's sake, I'm eighty years old!"

Proudly picking and selling bushels of home-grown sweet corn together at the bottom of our lane each summer long into our high school years. Cutting firewood with you and Dad. Altar serving with you. The way your complexion slowly turned green following 3-D motion rides. Your animated expression approaching and then following the first roller coaster you rode as an adult.

Your response to my weekly Sunday post-mass inquiry regarding my piano playing performance, "No one pays attention enough to notice [your mistakes]!" The nicknames you gave us — Janey-kins for me and Ranger Ruby-doo of the Ruby-doo Detective Agency for Steph. Your goofy humor is truly missed.

Our cousin's absolute favorite Jeremy story — "Jason, seriously, when a cow dies you just pick up the phone and dial 1-800-DEADCOW. Within a day, a guy driving an 18-wheeler will be over to pick it up and discard of it for you." At this time, you'd start laughing uncontrollably, as would all of our cousins. You'd be laughing because you knew this story was true (as in the past you had to call the number yourself), but you'd also be laughing because it seemed so unlikely to be true and you knew our cousins thought you were pulling their legs.

If you remember, this story evolved following the rescue of our neighbor's steer. He had been on the loose for nearly six weeks when the local police called Elda to report yet another "sighting." That day when Elda flew up our driveway, violently honking the horn of her Geo Tracker, you and I both eagerly hopped in hoping to assist in finally making the catch. On what was probably our fifteenth attempt, we finally did catch the steer that afternoon only to see him die the following morning. He must have grown ill while out in the wilderness. Another neighbor who owned the dairy farm you worked at recommended calling this number so as to sanitarily discard of his remains.

I could go on. How you'd drop anything you were doing at the drop of a hat so as to help an uncle, aunt, grandparent, neighbor, or friend. I can see you at our neighbor's farm house-sitting, throwing bales of hay into the sheep's pen while simultaneously talking to their dogs. Weeding our elderly neighbor Mrs. Dolan's flower garden. Plowing neighbor's driveways after the first snowfall of winter. Working on the construction of Uncle Chuck's house. You were that guy everyone and anyone could count on. When a neighbor's lawn mower or tractor broke — you'd fix it for them. When friends were relocating — you helped them out. You were one of the most selfless people I know.

Too often, I'm "too tired" to do this or that — "I'll do it tomorrow." You didn't make excuses. I yearn to live by your example.

On that note, tonight marks our fifth city park. Somehow I feel as if time has rewound and we're back in the Midwest. Although absent on the outskirts of town where a fine film of dust seemed to penetrate the air, the grass here in Milford is surprisingly green. The ground is flat (at least that present in my current view atop this plateau) and the people here remind me of those we met all throughout Kansas.

This area of Utah seems to be surprisingly more populated than some of the other sections we've biked through. As the sun's rays were absolutely scorching today I was pleased to see gas stations with fountain drink machines and talkative staff every fifteen to twenty miles. Each time our eyes narrowed in on such an approaching store, Brad, Steph, and I would awake from the trance the rhythm of our pedal strokes placed us in and start pedaling as if a dog were on our tail. We couldn't have been any more exuberant for the chill of ice pellets against our skin and on the roofs of our mouths!

Of course once we arrived here at the park we set our tent up beneath a metal pavilion, ate raviolis cooked on your propane grill, and went for an ice-cream run. We ended up sharing a half gallon of neapolitan while simultaneously watching a little league baseball game and engaging in conversation with a group of young parents.

As we spoke to these folks about their quaint Utah town I pictured us in a similar moment some twenty years prior — we were once those children dressed in uniform playing ball. Our parents were once the ones sitting on the sidelines cheering us on with proud grins hiding their faces.

We were once those innocent children — giggling, laughing, and daydreaming up childhood games while picking daisies in the outfield. Our parents were those parents — striving for a better life for you and for me, one filled with prosperity, good fortune and happiness.

In that moment in time my heart worried for the futures of these agreeable families — may life be good to each one of them.

And just like that the players from each team filed into a line to shake their opponents' hands — "Good game!"

Beneath our awning we actually have a stovetop, refrigerator, and sink all for our use. Although absent of lighting, clean public bathrooms are found approximately one-hundred feet away from our tent. Add in good company and I'd have to give this city park a solid five stars!

It's a little before eleven and the vast Utah sky is just now black. A group of junior high school-aged students are just now organizing what I suspect is a nightly game of flashlight tag. I'm not surprised as most of the houses that surround this park are still very well lit. I suspect this is a lively town.

The children just pelleted the roof above our heads with possibly twelve handfuls of rock. Looks like tonight might be a long night.

Still, I absolutely love this magnificent, manifold state.

From Utah, Goodnight!

All my love,
Jennifer

Brilliant rock formations, Utah, June 2008

Random RV spotted in the vast Utah desert, June 2008
Photographs on this page taken by Stephanie Herbstritt.

35. Great Basin National Park
Milford, Utah, to Baker, Nevada

"Many men can make a fortune but very few can build a family."
~J. S. Bryan

June, 17 2008

Dear Jeremy,

*B*rad claims he didn't sleep a minute last night. I wouldn't know as I was sound asleep but according to him the children playing tag didn't leave the park until 3 A.M.! Needless to say, Brad, Joe, and Steph are all a bit tired this morning. I couldn't be any more awake!

From Milford we biked to Baker where I am sitting right now on a picnic table outside of our tent set up at Great Basin National Park in Nevada. Indeed, we have ridden our bikes to Nevada! We've hit the Pacific Time Zone!

The scenery has changed tremendously from that in Utah. We are only approximately five miles into Nevada but the contrast is striking. We are now in the midst of what I would consider to be a proper desert. There is nothing around us (outside of this national park) other than sand and sagebrush. All of the rock formations which were present in Utah abruptly disappeared once we crossed the state line and this is all that remains!

In only a few short days we will approach the Sierra Nevadas, where we will cross over Carson Pass and enter into California. Before we reach the Golden State there will be a repetition of basins and ranges present here in Nevada that we will have to surmount.

Nevada is one of the driest states in the country, if not the driest. Therefore, we will have to be extraordinarily cautious over the course of the next few days to ensure proper hydration. I would hate to run out of water at any given time. Water here will be far dearer than it was even in Utah.

There will be no gas stations to purchase water from in between towns. Therefore, if we run out, we will be parched until the next town, which could be an entire day's ride away. We have filled up a cooler with water jugs, and I am hoping this is sufficient as we cannot be certain our next destination will have drinkable water. Fortunately, Brad brought purifying tablets along. I'm hoping we don't have to use these.

Towns will be dispersed some seventy or more miles apart and there will be nothing (and I do mean absolutely nothing) in between these towns. If you can believe it, there will be less between these towns than there was in Utah. There, although the towns were spread just as far from one another, at least I was able to look in awe at the rock formations as I passed by. Here, there will be absolutely no rocks, shade, water, or even evidence that a stream previously existed. The scenery will be constant: sand and sagebrush. Cell phone reception will be just as deficient.

We'll be traveling on U.S. Route 50, the "Loneliest Highway in America." Tourists will be scarce.

We will have to make certain to depart early in the mornings and not "accidentally" sleep in, as the sun will become dreadfully blistering by midmorning and the wind will pick up heavily by noon. We are heading directly into the face of the wind so this could become problematic if we are not careful.

I am incredibly eager for the experiences that await us over the course of the next few days. Thus far, this Western Express route is absolutely amazing!

Baker is the closest town to Great Basin. Situated at 5,310 feet, it is located five miles south of Great Basin (downhill). The climb from Baker up to Great Basin is definitely a climb!

Baker is desolate. There is barely anything in the town except for a hotel, a restaurant or two, and a self-service gas station with a shower for truckers and those passing through to use for a small fee.

When we arrived in Baker, we met another man biking across. He was heading east and had traveled down the Pacific Coast before picking up the Western Express. He has gone on two other cross-country trips and hopes after this trip to go touring overseas. There's something about an unprompted departure, saying goodbye to your routine life, picking up and starting over fresh, entering the unknown where no one knows your name... It is plainly refreshing, rejuvenating. I am inspired by this man.

He reminded me how much I *don't* want this trip to end. I could easily see myself continuing to bike, possibly down along the Pacific Coast. After this I might head over to Europe or Asia and do the same: bike across. I want to see all that I can. Certainly, I want to make an impact on society. I don't minimally want to live selfishly, obtaining wisdom, knowledge, and experience only for my own personal gain, but I could see myself biking here, there, and everywhere — the same as this man. It sure is addictive. This trip was the best thing I could have done for myself. Thank you, Jeremy, for giving me the courage to follow my dreams! I do believe you had your hand in this idea.

I was sad to leave Utah. It had so much to offer from scenery to sun, with a great deal of substance in between. On our trip home we will drive through the northern section of the state, visit Salt Lake City and exit through Idaho into Wyoming. My mind is made up. I cannot wait to return. For now, I will enjoy Nevada.

Great Basin National Park is probably the fifth or sixth national park we have come across in the past week. I love being witness to all of these natural wonders our country has to offer. I am incredibly appreciative that our forefathers chose to preserve these lands.

We saw snow here today at this very park. Remember: it is the middle of June! It was abundant on top of Wheeler Peak, a roughly

Steph raising her bike in celebration of our fourth time-change of the trip,
Nevada state-line, June 17, 2008!

13,000-foot glacier.[22] The sights here were out of this world. We did
not hike to the top but Joe is considering doing so tomorrow while
we are off biking. After biking today, I simply did not have the energy
to endeavor on such a strenuous hike, although at some point in time
I will have to return to accomplish this feat.

Supposedly, there are absolutely no trees in Nevada but Great
Basin is filled with an abundance of bristlecone pine trees at elevations
greater than 8,000 feet. In the lower elevations, where we are camping
tonight (around 6,000–7,000 feet) the landscape appears more like a
desert. It is cooler up here than down in Baker. Deer are seen passing
in front of our campsite and I have noticed a number of snakes, no
rattlers, but I fear they may be near. This (again) is mountain lion
country, and I am thankful that the latrine is only a minute's walk
from our tent. There is water here, but only for drinking. No showering will take place tonight.

This place sure does have people in abundance, just like many of
the other national parks at which we stopped. I met a woman in the
bathroom situated by the Visitor's Center who noticed my bike shorts
and inquired if I was biking across the country. She said her and her

Standing tall at precisely 13,063 feet, Wheeler Peak is a magnificent sight not to be missed in Great Basin National Park, Nevada, June 17, 2008.

husband just returned from a bike tour overseas in Europe. It was the time of their life. I am happy for them, as it seems they are taking advantage of all opportunities available in this life.

I feel like so many of us are too eager to accept a nine-to-five job with two weeks of vacation in suburban America as soon as we exit college. Too few choose the road less traveled made up of adventures like this: touring America, learning of our heritage, traveling, seeing the world in its entirety, and postponing financial success over personal achievements. So many of us say we want to "see the world," "travel," and "live life to the fullest" — but how many of us actually do?

I was a person who was content with working long hours at a job I didn't feel passionate about, and rarely making time for the important aspects of life. Yet, you — you were willing to postpone financial success in exchange for a higher education, time with family and friends, kayaking, hiking, seeing the country, and so forth. I admire you dearly for this. You are now my professor. Your death has instilled in me the insight required to no longer take for granted the time I've been given, the people whom I love, and my place in this world.

Regrettably, it took your death for me to truly realize tomorrow may never come.

April 16, 2007 was your last tomorrow. I hate this. Because of your all-too-premature death I am trying to live each day I've been given on this earth to the fullest. I am subsequently happy to see others doing the same as well.

The sky is black; there are absolutely no lights present, even in the distance. I love this place.

Goodnight from the high desert of Baker and the pine forest of Great Basin! We've made it to state #8!

Jen

36. Isolation
Baker to Ely, Nevada

"May you live all the days of your life."
~Jonathan Swift

June 18, 2008

Jeremy,

W*hen you died, I thought: "If I can just make it six months, life will get better."* When October 2007 approached, I told myself to be patient. The pain would eventually lessen. By the time a year had passed, I still felt I had not yet learned to cope. My frustration grew.

Through your death I gained a tremendous amount of wisdom. Eventually, I realized that I was coping just fine. Functioning earned a new definition. I let go of all control and accepted that which I couldn't. I quickly began to understand that the pain that death had, without invitation, gifted me with wasn't something that would ever fade. It wasn't going to get "easier" and I couldn't "just move on."

Fourteen months and two days later, I am far wiser than the young woman I had been on the day of your death. Grief has transformed me. I am a better person. Nevertheless, I wish I'd remained the same, as I never wanted you to die.

In a sense, the pain that I, and all of your loved ones, feel today as a result of your death is the most human aspect of your being that remains here on this earth. Your body is nothing other than decomposition. I will never see your smile again, nor will anyone else. Your voice will never again be heard and the rhythm of your heart will never again be felt. Your clothes are in boxes that may never be opened.

Another person, whom we've never met, now lives in your apartment. Another graduate student has taken on your projects. The title of your car has been transferred into another's name, and your Social Security number has long ago expired.

Everything that defined you as a member of this society is now gone. You are gone from this earth, just like our forefathers.

Stories will be told, at least until the day that I die, and the memories I have formed of you will remain sketched in my mind until the end of my life.

The void that is present in my gut also defines you and your absence. Its presence will not fade, just as your face will never return.

I hate that I exist and you do not. My existence amongst your annihilation. Yet, I have no choice but to continue on.

Jeremy, I miss you so much.

This morning when I awoke for the 428th day in a row to the reality of your death, I experienced a more difficult start to this day than I have to some of the others. Some are more bearable than others. Today was one of the worst with a reason unknown to me. My spirits were low and hope was absent.

Around five-thirty this morning we traveled out of Great Basin to Ely, Nevada, a short seventy miles away. The morning air felt incredibly cool as we'd been sleeping in the high desert at nearly 7,000 feet of elevation. From glancing at the elevation chart on my map, it appears that the average elevation in the state is approximately 5,000 feet. We will often be sleeping in areas situated at much higher altitudes. Therefore, I'll have to ensure I dress appropriately warm each morning. Temperatures will rise by midmorning, so I'll also have to wear a jersey with back pockets spacious enough to carry all of my garments once I remove them following the sun's scorching appearance.

This morning, I actually wore every piece of winter wear remaining in my bag. By the time ten o'clock rolled around, I was roasting and covered in sweat. By then we were almost to Ely.

Around that time the wind awoke along with the sun. I have a premonition that the five-to-ten A.M. period will be the calm before the storm each day we're here in Nevada. No longer will sleeping in be permissable, for it will result in a blistering, turbulent ride.

Fortunately, as the sun rose today, so too did my spirits. Ten in the morning is by far the earliest we've finished biking all month long. I was quite enthusiastic regarding the prospect of spending nearly an entire day in an unknown town.

Since towns from here on out will be dispersed so vastly and the sun and wind will become so intense by midmorning, our rides will be "short" for the next few days, at least until we reach the California border. For example, today we were given two options. Either we could have biked seventy miles here to Ely or 140 to Eureka. There

The barren Nevada desert: a lesson on the art of perspective drawing, Nevada, June 2008
Photograph taken by Stephanie Herbstritt

was nothing in between either, except for the side of the road, which (of course) is void of water. The choice was obvious. There was no way I was about to subject myself to riding my bike in the middle of a scorching desert, with winds that have been known to throw motor-cyclists off of their bikes, in mid-afternoon knowing I had a fine place to stay here in Ely. All members of our group agreed. Tomorrow, we'll head to Eureka.

We started out the morning with an approximately ten-mile climb to our first summit within this desert. Then, we biked downhill for approximately the same distance of road, into a basin, where we rode on flat ground for a short period of time until it was time to repeat the cycle: up, down, flat, up, down, flat.

The only object I could see around me (other than sand and sage-brush) was the pavement of the road, that of which we were following. I could see its path in front of me for miles and miles in the distance. Miles ahead of me, it appeared like a tiny black dot. Although, I felt as if we were biking in a straight line, the road appeared to curve slightly as its path progressed farther away from me and into the horizon.

The view ahead reminded me of middle school art class where we were taught perspective drawing with the emphasis placed on the vanishing point. As can be expected, this scene provided the opportunity for an infinite number of optical illusions to surface. At times I became incredibly frustrated. I felt as if I was exerting incredible amounts of energy to travel downhill when in reality I was ascending. It was an uncanny sensation.

Joe had an epiphany today while sitting on the side of the road for the (what?) thirtieth day in a row playing his guitar while simultaneously eating cereal drenched in possibly stale milk. He's "homeless." He couldn't have been any more excited by this thought.

You should have seen Steph's eyes light up when he verbalized this realization. She came across just the same thought while sitting on the seat of her bike today in this desert.

As I heard them converse, I couldn't help but laugh. Excluding the sickening reason we landed ourselves here, we're the luckiest people on earth. Living on the road is to die for!

I hope we're all giving you a good laugh, Jeremy!

Upon arriving in town, we ate lunch at a locally owned Chinese buffet. I didn't need this meal, but it certainly was tasty. I'm sure you could relate.

Following our stop for lunch we returned to a KOA on the eastern side of town. We had bypassed this earlier in the day in order to get to the restaurant.

The campground is beautiful with freshly cut green grass, sanitary bathrooms with warm showers and even a dog walk. Even though it is lovely, I honestly could care less about the looks of this place. I am plainly happy to have purified water and functioning electricity.

After checking in and waiting for the grass to dry (the sprinklers had drenched the grounds…it seems Ely is very well irrigated), Joe and Brad made a few more adjustments to the alignment of my chain.

I've been having trouble with it for days, and although it initially seemed to work perfectly after the tune-up performed at the bike shop in Cedar City, it started to repetitively de-rail once again today. You know how finicky I can be. It's making me crazy.

I've been paranoid regarding the possibility of a scenario where my chain de-rails (just as it did back in the Ozarks of Missouri) and I fall off of my bike and land flat on the ground still attached to my pedals. Fortunately Joe and Brad seemed to have addressed the problem.

After this tune-up performance was complete, we played a few rounds of tetherball in the park. Time surely does fly, for before long it was time for dinner. Our appetites are immense.

Around this time, a previously empty campground now flourished with guests. Over PB&J sandwiches and meatless spaghetti, we encountered some lovely company. As much as I enjoy spending time by myself focusing on my thoughts, it is nice to engage in conversation with another every once in awhile…or should I say, every chance I get.

Our company included an incredible couple. The man was a retired national park ranger and his wife's career was that of a psychiatrist. At the time of our visit, their permanent residence was in upstate Arizona. They were riding their motorcycle from one national park to another with no set agenda.

The ranger used to work at both Yosemite and Yellowstone National Parks. Ironically enough we've intended on stopping at both of these parks on our way home since long before we left on this trip. He gave us recommendations as to the best segments to visit in each.

As the sky became dark he built a very large campfire, enclosed in a metal ring, which we all sat around while telling stories of our journeys, friends made, and loved ones at home. The man shared a multitude of memories from his days as a park ranger. We heard of rattlers, crazed wild animals, outrageous guests and the like. I'm sure a few of his stories will make it difficult for me to fall sleep! Oh, the rattlers!

We ate s'mores, drank hot chocolate, coffee, and tea while sitting around this campfire amidst the cool air of this Nevada desert.

As the night became far from young, I said farewell to our new-found friends. Tomorrow, just like us, they will continue their journey without a care in the world.

Just like many of my most recent goodbyes, this will most likely be my first and final intended for these very fine folks. I wished them all my best.

As I laid my head down on the only green grass present thus far in Nevada, I was surrounded by the company of caring people in a tent "next door."

Under the light of the Little Dipper above me, my mind filled with dreams of the American Pony Express and young men on horses delivering pertinent messages some one hundred years ago, while ridding the desert of rattlers and scorpions.

Nevada is nice.

From Ely: Goodnight.

Jennifer

Above: Small Nevada town disguised by sagebrush, sand, and a mountain range seen within the horizon, June 2008. Below: Desolate Nevada desert painted with sagebrush and sand.

Photographs on this page by Stephanie Herbstritt.

Above: Descending toward an intermountain basin, Nevada, June 2008
Below: Railroad bridge, Nevada, June 2008

Sign displayed in Eureka storefront encouraging those passing by to apply for their "I survived Highway 50" buttons, Eureka, Nevada, June 19, 2008

Sand "tornado," Nevada, June 2008 ~ Photograph taken by Stephanie Herbstritt

37. Red Jeeps on the Loneliest Highway
Ely to Eureka, Nevada

"A journey of a thousand miles begins with a single step."
~Lao-tzu

June 19, 2008

Jeremy,

NYC, *December 29, 2004: I remember that trip like it was yesterday.* At the time, I was still in graduate school. You were on "holiday," attempting to figure out your purpose in life. You and your friend Jim organized this outing. The four of us siblings were to leave late Friday night, sleep at Jim's for a few hours, and then tour the city the following day. We were to return home late Sunday night.

Unfortunately, our trip itinerary didn't pan out as we had hoped.

You ended up traveling to Jim's earlier in the week. For some reason, I couldn't leave when you desired.

Joe and I drove up during the wee hours of Saturday morning. and Mom insisted Steph was too young to come along.

From Trenton, we took the New Jersey transit into Penn Station. We spent the entire day on our feet, touring the city from Second Street all the way up to Seventy-second (or there abouts).

That night, Joe and I drove back home to Bellefonte long after one o'clock in the morning. You were irate as I refused to spend the night at Jim's upon our return. "You've been awake for over twenty-four hours — you're bound to wreck that car!" At the time, I was training for something. God forbid I miss a training run.

The day couldn't have been more perfect (that is, until I left against your better advice and we both exchanged our fair share of angry words). Siblings!

If I remember correctly, we didn't eat lunch in the city as we were too busy glimpsing the sites. Dinner was held at a small, locally owned Irish pub.

The temperature was frigid all day long. The city was busy, exploding with people. Losing a member of our group (while walking the sidewalks) became customary due to the crowds.

The tree was incredible: a perfect green with dazzling lights and oversized ornamental balls. We'd hoped to go skating in the Rockefeller Center ice rink but the line seemed to span nearly a half mile. Time was costly so we skipped it.

Times Square was jam-packed with tourists. I couldn't imagine the site on New Year's Eve.

You always hoped to return to NYC for the apple's collapse, but you never had the chance.

I return to the memories of that day often in my mind. I replay them like a broken record. I'd go back in a heartbeat, if only I could.

Late August 2004
My graduate school apartment, Clearfield, Pennsylvania.
The town of Clearfield wasn't filled with a great deal of activity during my stay there, but the weekend of the Clearfield County Fair sticks out vividly in my mind today.

You, Jim, Joe, and Stephanie arrived for a visit. That evening, the five of us walked from my apartment to the fair, maybe two miles.

Then, we toured the gated animals, like gluttons ate cotton candy and overflowing barbequed pulled pork sandwiches, teased the carnival workers, and spent entirely too much money attempting to win a stuffed Bart Simpson doll.

If I remember correctly, despite our skepticism for their safety, we even rode a number of the rides.

We regressed to our childhoods that night. While you were asleep, Jim, Joe, and Steph rested your hand in a cold glass of water in hopes of tricking you into "peeing your pants."

The evening reminded me of our younger days at the Grange Fair. Our summers were spent anxiously preparing. The fair couldn't approach quickly enough. We'd travel there each autumn for ten consecutive days, jammed into one of Dad's old trucks, arriving no later than seven each morning.

Upon our arrival for the year, we'd move into the sheep barn what appeared like all our possessions. From at least four water buckets stuffed with a set of electric shears, countless curry comes, hoof clippers, and rags, to bags of feed, bales of hay, two shearing stands and a tub for bathing our lambs, the move-in process was always action-packed.

We would spend countless hours within the walls of that sheep barn preparing our lambs to look their best. We bathed them repetitively, trimmed their hooves, cleaned their ears, and sheared them to our satisfaction.

Finally, after days spent completing these tasks, we would proudly present our lambs in the arena to a judge. We'd do this twice, once for the 4-H show and a second time for the open show.

We never had the privilege of owning a grand champion lamb, but the time spent at that fair was enough for us.

When we weren't in the barn sitting high up in the lofts with our feet dangling into our lamb's pens beneath us socializing with the guests touring the barn, we'd run around the fairgrounds like wild children: riding carnival rides, telling jokes, eating hotdogs and ice cream cones, walking the streets with friends (and our sheep at times) and visiting neighbors at their tents.

With tents set up in blocks like a city of houses, some with Christmas lights, most with front and back porches, it certainly was a special place.

One I'll never forget. Sometimes I worry death may have taken from you these memories I consider to be so precious. I wonder if you and Shirley (Centre County 4-H Sheep Club leader, deceased) are smiling down on us as you read these letters together right now. It's hard to believe she's been gone almost a decade. By leading our sheep club, she instilled in us a tremendous amount of knowledge and grace.

The fitting and showmanship contest was my favorite activity at the Grange Fair. Supplied with wild lambs, straight out of the field, never once touched by human hands, we were expected to transform them into a presentable fashion in no more than an hour's time with only a ten-minute break, time enough to enjoy a Coke. After this, we were expected to show the insubordinate little tykes in an arena to a judge, keeping them in line.

In any regard, I'm off on a tangent.

After we left the 2004 Clearfield County Fair you, Jim, our cousin Jess, and I all journeyed to a local bar. If I remember correctly, Joe and Steph were underage, so they joined our cousin Kevin for a game of hide-and-seek in the dark. Looking back, I think Jess was too young as well!

We all met up afterward for a slumber party at my place.

That apartment in Clearfield brings back many fond memories. You visited me there often, meeting me after class during the summer months, bringing your kayaks along at times for a stroll down the river and hoagies to replenish us following our tour.

You moved me into that space, and just the same, you moved me out.

I miss your humor. I miss your laughter, your smile, and your quirky remarks, phrases, sayings, and gestures. I miss your surprise visits. I miss your spontaneity. I miss your voice, but, frankly, most of all I miss you. My life will never be the same.

Why did he have to kill you? Why did he do it? Couldn't he have solely taken his own life? Your life wasn't supposed to end that day. No one's should have. How could he have been so selfish? So ignorant? So pitiable? If he'd chosen a different path, you could still be here. But he didn't and you are not.

I can't focus on these thoughts or I will go mad.

Red Jeeps on the Loneliest Highway

Ever since we crossed the state line, we've been biking on the "Loneliest Highway in America": Highway 50. It is my opinion that some of the state highways we traveled across in Utah were a great deal lonelier than this highway, but I'm not the one doing the naming. All the same, there aren't many cars. Most of the vehicles I saw today were motorcycles, tractor-trailers, or red Jeeps. I assume the motorcyclists are on a tour similar to that of my new friends from last night. The eighteen-wheelers clearly are delivering goods. The red Jeeps are a reminder of you.

Death makes us notice and remember objects and events we might never have considered before. An antelope running by my side is now "you." A man with a similar running stride as yours is a reminder of both your existence and your death. Buffalo wings and black olives occasionally make me tear up. I often speculate the driver of a red Jeep is you.

Throughout this trip I've seen more red Jeeps than I can count on both my hands and my feet.

Looking back in time, I often feel like this vehicle should have been treated as some form of an omen. During the spring of 2006 you were preparing to leave for school. You were so wound up about graduate school. Virginia Tech offered the perfect program. It had everything you wanted: a striking campus, ample funding, professors with common research interests, and best of all, it was your ticket out of Bellefonte.

You didn't have a lot of money as you had spent the majority of your life in school, so you sold your 1998 Chevy Blazer. I think you got $2500 or close to it, and then, out of the blue, Dad gave you the Jeep. (Just a few days prior I had been the one driving it, but then I bought a car of my own so I had no need for it.)

That Jeep made it back and forth between Bellefonte and Virginia numerous times. You took it to North Carolina where you spent a week performing research on the waters of the Roanoke River. It sat outside your apartment on Cardinal Court. When you died, it had your high-water boots in it, covered in mud, and I couldn't help but picture you in them.

I had that Jeep for close to five years. You had it for a little less than a year, but it turned out to be far more yours than mine. It was just one of those things, like this trip, that had "Jeremy" written all over it.

The Jeep drove you to a place where anything was possible, where you were to fulfill your dreams and aspirations, where no one knew you or your family, where you had a clean slate, where you were to become a promising civil and environmental engineer, consultant or professor, where you would one day run another marathon, find love and happiness, leave your mark on this world. It is a shame some lunatic had to destroy all of that. If only he had thought things through. If only he had a soul, a genuine soul like you.

Every solitary time I see a red Jeep, I think of you. I sometimes imagine you as the driver. I've contemplated following a few just to see if maybe you are inside. The realist in me knows you are in a place far away from that red Jeep, but the dreamer in me just wishes for a split second you could trade places with the actual driver, and I could have one last glimpse of you. I know I'm getting greedy, but better yet, I'd really like one last conversation. I'd like to know you are okay. I'd like to tell you how sorry I am for what happened, how sorry I am that I wasn't the best sister I could have been, and how much I love you and always will.

I don't want to forget, I don't want the pain to go away, because that, right now, to me, means that I am "moving on," and I don't want to move on. I just want the pain to go away for a split second, that's it. Somehow, I think to myself, if I could be 100% confident of your status, if I could know for certain that you are okay, that one day we'll see each other again, then, deep down in my heart, I'd be able to accept we'll all be okay.

As we're traveling west bound, the majority of the drivers move over into the left lane when passing by in order to provide us with ample room on the roadway. Just as I've noticed in every other state,

Nevada, June 2008

although they are the minority, a few drivers have not been so friendly. It seems these drivers make a game out of swerving in toward our direction, oftentimes literally pushing us off the side of the road. I have to pay careful attention for these drivers, as often they appear when I am lost in the context of a daydream.

The surroundings today were predictably desolate. All I could see for miles and miles around me was sand and sagebrush. Short of a few colorful snakes and quick, minuscule lizards, there were absolutely no animals in my view.

Once again, our ride was quick. Therefore, we beat the sun and the wind. We arrived in Eureka around ten. This provided us with a generous amount of time to tour the town.

We bought groceries at a local food market that sat in one of the downtown's historic buildings. Interestingly enough, it wasn't only the singular grocery store present for seventy miles in any direction;

Windmill marking historic pony express route stop, Nevada, June 2008

it also was an animal museum. I laughed at the exhibit. It was certainly educational, but seeing stuffed mountain lion heads, antelopes, prairie dogs, and every other animal under the sun which could even remotely be found in the desert displayed on the walls was more than just slightly comical. Short of a taxidermy shop, I have never seen such a place in my life.

We looked at the animals, bought our groceries for far more than I ever expected (orange juice was over $5 for a half gallon) and walked to the city park located behind and cattycorner to this store. We sat on a picnic table devouring some of the best fresh turkey, ham and cheese sandwiches I've had in days.

The park was covered with the only other green grass I'd noticed since we left the KOA in Ely early this morning. It was enclosed by an aluminum fence, in a rectangular fashion, with a wooden western movie stage set up on the far west side. It wasn't more than one acre in size, but as I ate, I could picture the entire town congregating here during the sizzling summer months, late at night, just as it is about to cool off, watching a play put on by the locals.

Soon enough, a group of local miners entered the aluminum gates. Today, they're hosting a picnic for their fellow work-mates. As I stared at their one and a half-inch-thick steaks with a mouth full of saliva, I engaged in conversation with these friendly, talkative middle-aged men and women. I learned a bit about their town's history. Obviously, it is a ranching and mining community.

Upon my inquiry of a cheap place to lay our heads, they recommended this park. They said that during the summer months it isn't unusual for bikers to spend a night here. A group was in town just the other night. They're heading eastbound. We must have just missed them.

They warned us that this park would be the only green grass we'd find in town. The park is known to be safe and its price is free. It has water, flushable toilets, and a tree for shade (yes, a tree in Nevada). We took them up on their advice; this park exceeded all of our expectations.

Immediately, I phoned the local police to confirm this offer. Once I was given the right of way, my posse and I returned to Eureka's downtown to complete our tour. We didn't feel it was appropriate to set up our camp when these people were still in the midst of their picnic.

Eureka is located at 6,500 feet of elevation in central Nevada (and yes, its elevation is posted on the city-limits sign). Highway 50 runs directly through the center of the town, which is bursting with history. First and foremost, it is situated just south of the historic Pony Express route. The downtown section looks just like one would expect an old western town to appear. There is an opera house, a courthouse, post office, numerous bars, casinos, restaurants, and shops, all with what appear to be the original brick storefronts. A number of these stores even have the classic western swinging doors.

We visited the Eureka Sentinel Museum, which housed the *Sentinel Newspaper* from 1879 to 1960. The original press room was actually still intact. I cherished seeing the original typewriters and reading the old newspapers that now appeared yellowed and discolored. This building was swollen with history. There were models dressed with the clothes of men and women from the late 1800s, china dishes, silverware, medication bottles, old uniforms, gas pumps, and so on. Anyone could tour this museum free of charge, and you can imagine we were very pleased regarding the price tag. It's not often you get to see something like this for free. We spent a good hour or more touring this building.

Before exiting we applied for our "I Survived Highway 50" pins. We haven't yet made it the entire way across the state, but I am convinced we will. I can't wait to get my pin (go ahead and laugh), provided by the Nevada Department of Transportation. I'm not sure what I'll do with it, but it will be enjoyable to receive in the mail a few months down the road: a reminder of this trip and the memories made.

We toured the courthouse and opera house. The opera house had a classic appearance with a horseshoe stage and long, dark maroon curtains. I could picture this as the social center for residents back in the 1880s. I could see the women dancing at balls in fancy dresses with puff sleeves, watching operas and, (later, during the 1950s), watching movies with their husbands.

I could see fights on horseback in front of the courthouse amongst the dusty air, men wearing stirrups and cowboy boots walking through the swinging doors of the downtown bars and tumbleweed bouncing across the road in front of them. I thought about how much fun it would have been to have grown up during this era.

I couldn't help but wonder what the high school kids of this community do for fun. There are no malls to go shopping in or stadiums to watch games at. To a certain extent I bet they enjoy similar activities as the people of the 1880s for entertainment: plays, music, sports, writing, and the company of friends and family. In the simplest forms, aren't these the types of activities we all partake in?

This section of our country may not be a booming metropolis, but I think it might have more to offer than some urban areas do. I am jealous of the residents and the high school seniors who just recently graduated. To live in a part of this world, so secluded from society, yet surrounded by such beauty — wow!

As we walked around town, we met two other bikers. They are traveling west to east (of course...who wouldn't?). They have been stuck in this beautiful little western town for the past three days waiting for the arrival of a package. They are staying at a hotel across the street and are obviously discouraged and frustrated. We befriended them, encouraged them, exchanged email addresses and wished them our best. As we engaged in conversation their package arrived. Soon enough they continued on toward Ely. The sun was about to set. I'm not sure why they were in such a rush to get out of town; regardless, I worried for their safe arrival.

After a long tour of the town we returned for a late afternoon nap and then dinner. As we ate our food, a few high school boys made laps around the park sounding the most ridiculously loud (and obnoxious I might add) music I think I've heard in years. I laughed at their sight. Taken back to the days of my own high school years when my friends and I would do just the same, only in State College in a friend's Ford Mustang convertible, I felt embarrassed of how I must have appeared. I remember being their age.

As the sun began to set, a local woman who doubled as the manager of the town's community pool greeted us saying she heard of our arrival. She welcomed us to use the town's pool and its showers. I was amazed at how incredibly friendly the people here seem to be. I felt as if I'd returned to the Midwest.

Nevada is splendid (except for the wind).

In a few days, Jeremy, we will be crossing over Carson Pass and entering California! We are almost to California and my excitement is building! I can't believe we are actually going to make it across. Right now, I am crying both tears of sadness and joy as I walk alone back to the grocery store for dessert.

You should be here.

It was birthday cake-flavored ice cream. The three of us finished a half gallon. I imagine I will dream well tonight.

From a town in Nevada marked with the hillside letter "E," goodnight!

Jennifer

Middlegate, Nevada, June 2008 ~ An oasis found in the midst of Nevada's barren desert.

Nevada, June 2008

38. Our Final Farewell
Eureka to Middlegate, Nevada (via Austin)

"Even with the best of maps and instruments,
we can never fully chart our journeys."
~Gail Pool

June 20, 2008

Jeremy,

I remember our last physical farewell as if it occurred yesterday. The vision is clear.

It was January 8, 2007. I had surgery that day, but never told you. It was a simple, outpatient procedure; still, I was too embarrassed to mention it.

You wanted to go running around noon, shortly after I returned from the doctor's. I invented a reason as to why I couldn't go along. (I'd given you a lame excuse about not wanting to waste gas.) You ended up running by yourself and lifting at the YMCA. Later in the evening, you drove over to my place.

You'd been annoyed that I'd refused to pick you up at Mom and Dad's house in Bellefonte. You mentioned something about being a "poor graduate student" who didn't have a lot of extra cash; yet I was worried about driving as I'd had sedation. It wouldn't have been safe for me to be on the road.

I should have been honest with you, swallowed my pride, and told you that I couldn't drive because of the surgery. If I'd told you beforehand, you probably would have offered to take me to the doctor's, and we could have spent the entire day together goofing around.

It was one of the only days I had off during that Christmas season because my office had refused to fulfill my time-off request. For practically a month during December 2006 and into January, you were at our parents' farm in Bellefonte with Steph, Joe, Mom, and Dad. They were all on vacation for winter break as well. I was jealous that I'd missed out on making cookies, decorating the house, cutting down the tree, and all the activities related to the holiday season.

Now, it was after New Year's and here I was with a day I could have spent with you, but I had too much pride to tell you what was going on with me that morning.

Anyway, once you arrived at my apartment that night, we drove over to a local restaurant in town to watch the BCS game: Ohio State vs. Florida State.

We left the restaurant a few minutes before it ended and headed back to my apartment where you and Brad watched the remainder of the game together while I went to bed. I had to work the following day and wanted to get to bed at a "reasonable hour," as I had an early morning ahead of me. I offered for you to spend the night; I was worried about you driving home so late. It was raining; the roads might be dangerous. But you said you would be fine. It was a warm 60°F out, and you'd only had one beer.

I will never forget how you lumbered up out of that burgundy leather chair in the corner of my living room to give me a hug goodbye. The chair was positioned cattycorner to the front door where I was standing ready to walk up the stairs to bed.

"I probably won't see you for awhile, Jen," you said and walked toward me to give me a hug. This was odd because we always did the high-five thing (which by the way hurt like heck) or the handshake-with-the-eye-wink maneuver. We really weren't a hugging family. We really weren't an "I love you" family either. It was just understood.

But that night you did give me a hug, and I couldn't help but harass you with a phrase such as, "Don't get soft on me."

Afterward, I thought that night was odd, and now I know why. It was the last time I'd ever see you alive.

That entire trip you'd made back to Pennsylvania that holiday season was simply out of the ordinary. You had come home for Christmas break, but the weather suggested otherwise. Temperatures were in the mid seventies, and there was absolutely no humidity present the entire time you were home. This was unseasonably warm for central Pennsylvania that time of the year. Heck, we were running in short-sleeved t-shirts and shorts.

I remember thinking so many times (and even saying aloud to Brad) how I wanted to spend as much time as possible with our family that Christmas season because it "would probably be our last Christmas together as a family." I had no idea how true those words were; yet they were almost like a premonition. I remember thinking how sad it was that we were all grown up.

Jeremy, if things would have turned out differently, I'm sure you would have soon found someone and married. After all, you were twenty-seven years old. At the time you had a girlfriend, and who knew what would have happened between the two of you? You could have been married in a year and, then you would have transformed into one-half of a couple: Jeremy and so and so.

I'd lose the opportunity to hang out with you alone. Holidays would never be quite the same. I'd have to share you with another girl who would tag along to everything, every event; and I might not even like her.

Okay, so I was slightly selfish.

Regardless, I wanted to cherish the time I had left with you as my single, unwed, big brother. I wanted to spend as much time as possible as a family (two parents and four children, sans spouses).

You'd gone to Philadelphia for New Year's, and I was mad you didn't stay home and run the First Night 5K with Joe, Steph, Dad, and me. Now, I am mad at myself that I didn't say the heck with the 5K (and work) and go to Philly with you. If only I knew then what I know now!

Before you left to return to school, you said to Dad, "I'm sorry we weren't able to finish the fence." You and the rest of our family had worked so diligently on that fence. It was complete; you just wanted to fence in yet another pasture. Dad said "no worries" — you could finish it that summer. A mere five or six months away…

Did you know something at that time that we didn't know?

If you didn't die, I would have thought of that Christmas and all of those events as just one more holiday. Now, I replay the sequence of events over and over again in my mind, reliving the regrets, as well as the memories, because, unfortunately, they are all I have left.

Since leaving Virginia, and with every mile between there and Nevada, I am learning to gain hope for my future. This doesn't mean I am living in the future. Actually, I'm living in today. I just have hope that tomorrow might be better. Possibly it won't (possibly it won't even come), but possibly it will, and I will take this as progress inspired by you.

The pain of losing you isn't going to go away, but there is beauty in this earth that I'm learning to appreciate. I'm going to see everything I can, and do everything I possibly can to the best of my ability, in your name, because you cannot.

This trip is the beginning of a gift I've created by accident, started at first in just the hope of getting away from it all. This gift of exploration and reflection is especially for you, in thanks for all you have done for me.

Today was one of the most exciting days of our trip.

A few days ago, when we met the middle-aged couple who was traveling across the United States from west to east pulling their dog behind them, we were given the recommendation to settle in a "town" called Middlegate, Nevada.

When we looked at our maps, we saw absolutely nothing between Austin and Carson City in regards to food, water, gas, lodging, and so forth. But our friends came across an oasis in the middle of the Nevada desert, here, and suggested we make it to this petite settlement simply for the experience.

We left Eureka early in the morning shortly before daybreak. Today, the sunrise was particularly stunning. I felt as if it became visible directly in front of my eyes, regardless of its concrete distance from earth. The colors were incredible with hues of yellows, reds, and even purples shining through. The air was cool with minimal humidity, and the wind was surprisingly calm, but only until about the time we reached Austin.

Then it threw a fit.

We were scheduled to receive our delivery of new bike tires and tubes. Our delivery was supposed to arrive around eleven o'clock at a campground in Austin. Yesterday, according to package tracking, our shipment was somewhere in the Midwest, delayed due to weather, en route to Salt Lake City. We were pessimistic as to its arrival as the Midwest has recently been distressed by a number of large storms and (subsequently) many sections have suffered horrible flooding. Its timely arrival appeared unlikely.

The ride into Austin was all downhill — that is after we endured three lengthy, steep climbs and two descents over the seventy-mile stretch between Eureka and Austin. Once we finally started to descend into Austin, I wasn't sure I'd be able to stop, as the downward slope was that steep.

Austin was a fairly developed community located in the middle of the desert, halfway up (or down, depending upon how you look at it) a mountain. Our ride there consisted of (you guessed it) sand, sage-brush in variable shades of blues, basins, dried up riverbeds, ranges, and countless optical illusions.

Although the terrain and scenery haven't changed much since our entrance into Nevada, this state intrigues me. We might not be surrounded by much in regards to physical structures, automobiles, people, mountains, valleys, and canyons, but for me, at this point in my life, simplicity, absence of chaos, and tranquility are all I desire.

Because the descent into town was so vertical and abrupt, I honestly passed by the campground we were supposed to stay at without even realizing it. I stopped at a local Baptist church where a man standing outside was performing some landscaping. Joe (awaiting our arrival) was pulled over, talking with him as he shoveled sand and laid mulch. Steph, Brad, and I joined in on the conversation. We talked about our trip, this lovely town called Austin located on the American Pony Express route, and California as lately my mind (as well as that of the others) spends a lot of time pondering this state and what we'll do when we finally arrive in San Francisco.

My plans are to drink a celebratory beer, cross the Golden Gate Bridge, ride over to Sausalito, eat some of the best, most authentic Chinese cuisine I've ever tasted, and simply sit in a blissful state of accomplishment!

He laughed when we inquired as to the location of our campground. "You biked right passed it. All of you bikers traveling west end up here. If it weren't for me, I'm not sure any of you would find your way to that campground!"

He really seemed to have an eye for the events and activities that took place within the confines of Austin. In fact, he even knew the delivery truck had already made its routine stop for the day (to our campground). "You better check on that package before someone else gets his hands on it!"

We thanked him for his company, obtained a succulent suggestion as to where to find inexpensive burgers for lunch, and then waved goodbye.

I probably never will see this man again in my life and am sad for this fact. I've met so many amazing people along this journey to the west, and most of them I will never come across again in my life. I take down many of these individual's addresses and make a mental picture of them in my mind. I promise I will keep in touch, but can't help but think their place in my mind (and in my heart) is that of a unique, exceptional person I came across along this trip, whose path I may never cross again and who doesn't know much more of me than that of my journey. In a way, I like their place in my heart.

We walked up to the campground only to discover our package had not yet arrived. It'll have to be re-routed to San Francisco.

Discouraged, we continued on toward the recommended diner, located roughly a half mile down the hill from the Baptist church.

There, I devoured one of the juiciest cheeseburgers I've tasted in my life, accompanied by salty french fries and a refreshing sweet tea.

Although I wasn't quite ready to call it quits for the day when we arrived in Austin, something tells me you might have spent some additional time there enjoying a beer while conversing with the locals. They were fascinating folk, each with a story to tell.

It was after lunch, around one in the afternoon, when I had the desire to continue on to Middlegate. I was anxious to experience this oasis in the middle of the desert.

Soon after we started biking west, I realized this decision was based on poor judgment. About ten miles outside of Austin the wind became fierce. We probably should have turned around, enjoyed a tail wind for once and turned back.

We didn't. I was too stubborn.

Selfishly, I persuaded the others to continue on. You see, I've grown accustomed to riding my bike a century a day and, as you know, I'm not one for change. For the past few days we'd cut that century short, and I just *needed* to get back into routine.

Instead, we earned the opportunity to *forever* swear off biking after noon. The strength of the wind was unbearable and the heat was intense! Happily, as my mind relaxed and my body adjusted to the conditions, I was able to focus in on my surroundings. A group of shirtless men were riding on horseback eastward toward Austin. They were traveling on the first road planted parallel to Highway 50 that I've yet been able to see. Their sight reminded me of the historic men of the Pony Express. After they passed us by, I was able to appreciate the beauty of heat lightning (without rain) flashing above perfectly *white* sand dunes present directly off the road.

As I let go of my frustration, I realized I had no choice but to continue what I'd set out to do. Taking breaks from the wind, we stopped every few miles at each of the original, authentic Pony Express stops (marked today for educational purposes with wooden posts). Here young men, younger than you and I, rode on horseback from St. Joseph, Missouri, to Sacramento, California for an all-too-short eighteen months between 1860 and 1861[23] delivering important messages and precious letters to loved ones like you.

I imagined what this territory looked like to them, back some 150 years ago when rattlers were abundant and roads were far from being developed. They created a path that we follow today. I can't imagine the land was much different then than it is now, as all that seems to grow in this area is sagebrush on sand; but at the same time I can't imagine how one would find his way across this desert without any roads in place when all the surroundings appear precisely the same.

I can't imagine the fear and the freight these young men faced. I have to thank their souls for what they gave to our country: important notifications, contact with family and friends, a mail system, exploration of the West, etc. To have experienced America as they did must have been quite an event, full of all sorts of emotions. I am admired by them and tell myself that no matter what, no matter how strong this wind blows, I will get as far west as I can on my bike, until I can't get any farther without jumping into the Pacific and swimming on.

And then, in the distance, I saw it (after the men, the sand dunes, heat lightning and numerous stops), I saw it: the infamous "shoe tree."

This was the first tree we'd seen in days outside of any developed town such as Eureka. It was large and old with untold branches bifurcating in all directions spanning upward toward the sky, and covered in shoes: the shoes of others passing by.

And then, not more than a mile in front of me and to my left, I saw it — Middlegate.

This truly is an oasis in the middle of the desert. There is a "motel" here: made up of approximately five double-wide trailers all connected together. There is a bar and a restaurant with the coolest water and the most luscious, fresh strawberry shortcake I've tasted in my life. There is wireless internet access, cell phone reception (in the middle of the desert!), laundry, running water, a shower, bathroom, and a pool.

And the price for bikers is *nothing*. All the owners ask for is good company.

I can understand why certain individuals choose to live in this community, powered by nothing other than generators, in the middle of the desert, isolated from the distractions of mainstream living. There is something special about this place. I'm not sure I will want to leave.

Today, two other groups of bikers came across this oasis as well. We befriended them. As well, we befriended a few older men, probably in their early to mid seventies, who are spending a few days here with their wives, riding four-wheelers through the mounds of sand, simply having the time of their lives.

Age is but a number, right?

While I sat at the bar late at night, the deliveryman from California made recommendations to me as to where he believes we absolutely should stop on our way home: Jackson Hole, Wyoming, Custer, South Dakota, and Chicago, Illinois (to name a few). We talked the night away; his energy excited me.

I really don't want to return home. Perhaps I never will…

Before we knew it, it was far past midnight. I said my goodbyes, collected my sleeping bag and pillow, unzipped our tent, and entered our home.

I wish you could see this place: an oasis in the middle of the Nevada desert. It's simply serene.

Goodnight.

Love,
Jennifer

39. Carson City
Middlegate through Fallon to Carson City, Nevada

"Character is what you have left
when you've lost everything you can lose."
~Evan Esar

June 21, 2008

Jeremy,

Today we left Middlegate, biked through Fallon, and into Carson City: the capital of Nevada and the last town in this state where we'll lay our heads. By tomorrow night we'll have made it to California.

The ride today provided us with a vast alteration in our surrounding scenery from that of the past few days. We saw very little sagebrush compared with the remainder of our journey through Nevada. Instead, we saw fields of white sand.

Initially, this was *all* we saw. Biking on a paved black surface, surrounded by flat, white fields of sand, both saturated by the sun's rays, is apt to provoke vertigo in anyone. I still don't feel right.

The flat fields didn't last forever. Soon enough, we passed numerous dunes. In fact, we even passed a place called "Sand Mountain," a 4,700-foot mountain located just east of Fallon, made up of sand as white as a dove's feathers.

We saw names scripted in sand, created by the positioning of rocks placed along the sides of the highway. Just as graffiti marks buildings, bridges and beautiful rocks along the coasts of this country, these individuals wrote their names and tales of their love with rocks placed in the sand on the side of the road. I must say, it was entertaining to read the inscriptions when there was nothing around me but fields of white sand.

Folks camping out in front of Sand Mountain located directly off U.S. Route 50,
20 miles east of Fallon, Nevada, June 2008 ~ Photograph by Stephanie Herbstritt

Although biking in the desert may sound boring, it actually isn't. Biking on a stationary bike or running on a treadmill is far worse. The mind is intelligent. It finds distractions easily, such as these written words and the flow of my thoughts.

Not too long after these writings started to appear, we passed through Fallon, an agricultural community, possibly slightly larger than Bellefonte. This area seemed fairly urban compared with the towns we'd most recently ventured through like Eureka, Ely, and Austin. In what felt like the blink of an eye, the ground turned to grass and fields of corn started to grow. It was evident this town was very well irrigated!

Grass in the middle of the desert: unbelievable!

As we passed by Fallon's Naval Air Station, I heard planes flying so near to the ground I felt as if they were surrounding me like a hive of bees.

This area seemed busy, a stark contrast from yesterday's visit to Middlegate.

Photographs on this page taken by Joseph Herbstritt.

After Fallon, we biked on to Carson City. As we approached the capital of Nevada, the area became abruptly overpopulated. Rapidly, we saw gas stations, strip malls of stores, expressways and activity: booming activity.

I was saddened to leave the desert so quickly. I liked being alone with my thoughts.

This metropolis of Carson City, Nevada, is practically on the border of California.

As we arrived into the city, we came across a few drops of rain. The wind picked up and I even heard a few bangs of thunder the minute I laid my eyes on the large white sign that marked this city's limits.

Fortunately (in my mind), this tiny storm didn't last long. By the time we arrived at our campsite it had long ago passed.

We are staying in an RV park situated in the middle of a city populated with nearly 50,000 people. It is fenced in. Our spot doesn't have grass. Instead, we are sleeping on fine gravel. We are still in the middle of a desert, regardless of popularity.

The bathrooms here are lovely, with individual shower stalls as big as a bathtub. We have a pool and even a hot tub. I feel we have moved from one extreme to the next: we've gone from primitive camping to luxury camping in less than twenty-four hours and one hundred miles. (I still prefer primitive.)

After dinner, we visited the downtown section of this community and realized our fortune to have arrived during "A Taste of Carson City." Unfortunately we had just eaten, and tickets cost something like $30 per person. Definitely out of our price range!

The aroma of the food smothered me as we walked through the streets of this city, filled to the brim with people, families, and friends, enjoying a variety of fine cuisines that represent this city.

As we walked, my foot began to hurt. The band of shiny tissue connecting my heel to my forefoot seems to be inflamed. I'm convinced this is a result of the overuse of this fascia for over a month now.

I sat on a street corner resting my foot and stretching my hands, the left of which is still numb and exceptionally weak from the grasping of my handlebars day in and day out (go figure). As I did so, I smiled at myself.

I'm not bothered by my ailments. I'm just happy to be here — almost to California. I was smiling because I knew you'd be proud. Heck, *I'm* proud.

I love this city of Carson, built in the middle of the desert where some 150 years ago nothing stood but minimal sagebrush, yet buildings were built, water was irrigated, trees were planted and here grew a city, the capital of Nevada, in the midst of a desert, where the wind blows strong and the sun never fails to shine.

Or so I think.

What a world we live in!

All my love,

Jenny

Steph (l) and Jen (r) at the summit of Carson Pass, June 22, 2008
Photograph taken by Brad Updegrove

40. The Sierra Nevadas and "Hangtown"
Carson City, Nevada, to Placerville, California

"Who would venture upon the journey of life,
if compelled to begin it at the end?"
~Madame de Maintenon

June 22, 2008

Jeremy,

Today we left the metropolis of Carson City in the early hours of the morning and climbed up and over Carson Pass following State Route 88 (Carson Pass Highway).

I swear to you, it felt as if we reached the summit twice before we actually did. Indeed, we biked over two "passes" with the first being Carson Pass, and the second Carson Spur. The climb was brutal, but this didn't deter us as we were up for the challenge. In the end, our efforts certainly were worthwhile as the scenery presented to us was out of this world.

This was our solitary pass through the Sierra Nevadas, the final mountain range which we were required to cross before meeting that infamous coast referred to as "the West."

We've made it through the Appalachians of Virginia and Kentucky, the Ozarks of Missouri, the Rockies of Colorado and Utah, and now we have crossed the Sierra Nevadas bringing us into that desirable territory of California.

This pass, named after Kit Carson was passed by Carson himself during the mid 1800s.[24] As we know from our history books, his exploration of this land was of great importance during the days of the California Gold Rush and the American Civil War. This was the primary route used for shipping vital resources from California eastward, during those days.[25]

It was nice to have the opportunity to follow this passageway myself. While biking, I felt as if I had stepped right on into the history books of my youth all over again. I wondered what this experience was like for Carson and his men. I couldn't imagine how they found their way through as far west as they did. I knew they had the help and guidance of the Washoe Indians who ventured through this section of the Sierra Nevadas themselves prior to Carson.[26] Nevertheless, I just couldn't imagine how either group found his way through these fields of green, in the dead of the winter, when everything certainly was barren and covered in snow. Food most surely must have been scarce, and the wind (I doubt) was far less than atrocious.

I am thankful they made it, as the ride that Carson Pass provided me with today was outright splendid. I wonder if you've had the opportunity to sit down with Carson and inquire about his historical journey. Possibly this thought is childish, but I crave the details which make up your world. I want to know if it truly exists.

As I neared in on the "first" summit, not far in the distance I could see snow-covered mountain peaks. When I peered into the valleys beneath me, I noticed they were filled with forests of green and volcanic rock formations. Crystal clear mountain streams were rapidly flowing into lakes at elevations nearing 9,000 feet. The roads were shaded perfectly with tall trees of green as they wound in circles up to the top.

Once we reached the final summit at 8,650 feet, I stared in awe at the valley floor beneath me. I was amazed at my accomplishment, at *our* accomplishment. I had climbed from Cason City, Nevada, through the lovely town of Woodfords, California, up and over Carson Pass. I had crossed the Sierra Nevadas. Below me, and around me, stood high the trees of the Eldorado National Forest. Around me, water was plentiful, a stark contrast from the desert surrounding Middlegate. And the grass surely was green. At this site, Joe and Steph rolled in it like dogs off the leash. None of us had seen such ample grass in days. We completed our final proper climb of this journey. In doing so, we made it to California, the "Golden State."

While gazing off that mountain peak in awe, I was unable to acknowledge my place in that moment. What this journey accomplished, I really couldn't put into words. I just knew we'd made it to California where our journey would culminate. Or, possibly, here it would just begin. My face was beaming, and my eyes were smiling, for the first time since your death.

After we crossed Carson Pass we took a less-traveled route into the valley floor beneath us. This route was the Mormon Emigrant Trail. We came across a group of nearly thirty motorcyclists who had the same idea as us. Neither of us were the first to discover this passageway, of course. A group of Mormons founded this corridor some many years ago. It was a wagon trail connecting an area called Sly Park with the Carson Valley.[27] It was additionally traveled by a multitude of miners whom I'm certain worked very long hours earning their keep for their families, traveling to and from work daily on this path, treading the soles of their shoes as well as their horses. I wondered if they witnessed the beauty of this place in the same sense that I did as I biked. I can't imagine that they didn't.

This thirty-mile section of road was almost entirely downhill except for the very first section which actually consisted of a few steep uphill grades (I guess these were required to warm me up, in case I wasn't warm enough from the ride up over Carson Pass!).

This trail was windy, perfectly paved, quiet, serene, and surrounded by trees. It appeared to be a deer's heaven and an artist's most perfect landscape. The wind was calm and the sun rested warmly on my back. Goosebumps were present, not due to cold-weather conditions, but because of a sense of awe that infused this singular experience.

As I rode my bike down into the valley approaching Placerville, California, I wished so deeply that you could have been with us to enjoy this accomplishment. I know this is impossible. I understand, at last, the permanence of your death.

Arriving at state number nine, 'Welcome to California,' June 22, 2008

From front to back, Jen, Brad, and Steph biking toward Carson Pass, June 22, 2008
Photograph taken by Joseph Herbstritt

🚲

Tonight we'll be laying our heads at the Placerville KOA.

This place is absolutely immaculate. I'm having a hard time believing we are actually camping, for it resembles a Caribbean resort far more than a campground. With electricity, warm water, a pool, the heat of the sun, green grass, soft ground, and numerous gazebos, I couldn't ask for much more.

Yet, I'm unsure I like the luxuries this place has to offer. I'm not one for change. I've fallen in love with simplicity.

The air here is warm, but the humidity is rising. I'm reminded these fair temperatures will not last for long, for in just a few days we will arrive in San Francisco where the weather will be cool and the breeze will blow strong, irrespective of the season.

As a Gold Rush town, Placerville obviously is overflowing with history. In 1848, when word got out that gold had been found in this area, people from all over the country came here, to this now quaint town, in search of not simply gold, but the American dream of wealth, prosperity, and dreams fulfilled partly by obtaining such.

Back when we were in Middlegate, a local couple told me the tale of this town's little nickname: "Hangtown." Not nearly a year after word spread regarding the presence of gold in this community, crime became prominent. The fate of three individuals accused of various crimes was placed in the hands of the public. When they yelled out "hang them," it was done. From this very incident, the town received its nickname: a name which people still know this town by to this very date. I never would have guessed the history of this settlement, but now that I do, I am happy for how this town has evolved.

The road to Placerville paved a path, winding in circles mainly downhill, creating such abrupt twists and angles in the road's surface that at times I thought I might clip a pedal. Tall trees draped over my head, just like a canopy, with the sun's rays peeking through.

This road showed promise and happiness. A smile filled my face as I rode my bike into town. This is America.

From the Placerville KOA: Goodnight. Hello, California!

All my love,

Janey-kins

Top: Jeremy, riding his bike in Ohio.
Bottom: Steph and Jen (carrying the backpack) touring the city, San Francisco, June 2008
Bottom photograph taken by Joseph Herbstritt

41. Nearly There
Placerville to Winters, California

"It is good to have an end to journey towards;
but it is the journey that matters in the end."
~Ursula K. LeGuin

June 23, 2008

Jeremy,

Today we all planned on sleeping in until at least seven. *Yep, that's sleeping in for us these days!*

But by the time five o'clock rolled around, my mind was simply too excited to sleep any longer. As Steph, Brad, and Joe slept, I lied awake imagining our arrival at the great city of San Francisco, California.

I thought about the emotions that would overcome me. Would I be happy or sad? Would I cry tears of joy, tears of sorrow, or wouldn't I even cry at all? Would I be satisfied with what this journey provided me with?

Before seven, we were on our way. I couldn't help but wake them (sorry guys!). Really, I'm picturing our arrival into San Francisco to be better than the best Christmas morning any kid could ever have! I'm *that* excited.

As I clipped my cleats into my pedals, I thought about the prospect of riding my bike one hundred miles to a quaint, yet sophisticated, town named Winters. The distance seemed so small.

My mind set has changed drastically since May 12 of just this year; hasn't it?

I knew once we reached this lovely town, we'd fall asleep on the sand of a campground located at Lake Solano. From Lack Solano, my prospective intention for all of us was to spend the following day biking fifty short miles to Vallejo. And from Vallejo, we were to take a ferry to Pier 1 in San Francisco.

Even if something terrible happened to any one of us, and we were unable to bike one hundred miles today, from Placerville we'd still have only 156 miles remaining before arriving at our final destination.

That fact itself was exhilarating!

The ride today was lovely. I love California. The scenery here is just unbelievable. I can now appreciate why California is one of the most populated states in the union.

The ride began as we biked out the gravel driveway of the Placerville KOA. From here, we biked for miles down windy, narrow roads, most of which were set on a decline with minimal shoulders. I told you it was all downhill from the Carson Pass summit, now didn't I?

All along, there was an ample amount of shade created by a collection of tall trees of green canopied over the road. The sun lit the road dimly as it flickered through the leaves. The scenery couldn't have been any more perfect.

One of the towns we passed though, Folsom, was a booming metropolis. Yet, even here the air felt serene. Once a major role-player in the days of the Gold Rush, I could feel its place in history as I biked past a multitude of rolling hills of gold surrounding the city. Historically, it is the sight of the first railroad of the West and, today, it is home to America's famous Folsom Prison, founded in 1880.

In Folsom, we departed from the main road arriving on a series of bike paths which we followed all the way to Davis. But before we were able to make it to Davis, we biked through the capital of California: Sacramento.

We picked up another bike path here. This path was much more heavily trafficked than the one we rode on through Folsom. Locals were riding their bikes for pleasure, as well as to and from work and classes. In all honestly, I think I might have seen more people on this

Above and below: Capitol Building, Sacramento, California, June 2008
Photograph by Joseph Herbstritt

Photograph by Stephanie Herbstritt

Tower Bridge crossing the Sacramento River linking West Sacramento to Sacramento;
Sacramento, California, June 2008 ~ Photograph by Stephanie Herbstritt

bike path and over the course of the path twenty-four hours than I have seen in the course of the past month. The sight of these people elated me.

I am about to complete an incredible journey.

Yet, you are still dead.

After exiting the bike path, we traveled for a short distance on a wooden walkway through the west side of the city. I was certain I would earn my fifth flat tire of the trip here. Fortunately, I didn't.

Soon enough we witnessed the home of the state's governor, the legendary Arnold Schwarzenegger, and I forgot about the very prospect of a flat. The building was under construction, therefore, we were not able to appreciate its sight in all totality, but as you've probably already predicted, I was equally enthused to have simply earned a glimpse of this most elaborate mansion.

I can predict Dad now, construing a joke about this mansion and somehow making an attempt to relate its condition to history:

"Hey Dad, why are there so many tarps covering the areas being remodeled?"

"Well, Joe, that's because every time Reagan entered a room he said, 'Gorbachev, Gorbachev tear down the walls.'"

That'd be our father!

We got lost in Davis and somehow returned back to the streets. Davis was clearly a college community with coffeehouses, organic markets, streets filled with bars, art galleries, and flavorful clothing boutiques. The streets were cluttered with students and professors walking and biking to and from their destinations. Traffic lights had special signals for bikers and pedestrians. The area appeared exactly how I expected California to emerge: eco-friendly, organic, and warm.

Just as we found our way back onto the bike path, it was time to leave. We returned to a series of roads reminiscent of western Kentucky. These roads followed a fairly straight path centered on the countryside. We traveled past vineyards and orchards lined with countless trees planted in rows. The air was fresh, pollution seemed absent and the warmth of the sun with only a light breeze was utterly refreshing against my now roughened skin.

Approximately five miles outside of Davis, and only about the same distance from Winters, we ran into construction. We waited in traffic for only a few minutes. Then, as the drivers of the other vehicles present in our line were forced to remain patient, we were waved on through. Biking sure does have its perks!

Soon enough we exited the construction zone and arrived in Winters, just in time for a late lunch.

If I relocated to this area, I think I'd choose to live in Winters. Located within the coastal mountains of California, it's not far from the Napa Valley (abundant with wineries and vineyards). Equally of importance, it is only thirteen miles from the University of California at Davis.

Even though Winters is located in such close proximity to more urban areas like Davis, Sacramento, and even Vallejo, it has the feel of a cozy small town. The streets are far from crowded and filled with local merchants. It reminds me of home.

After lunch, we returned to the seats of our bikes for yet another scenic ride: to Lake Solano. Being that this lake is located at the base of California's coastal mountains, this made the culmination of our ride today far from "downhill." As we entered the campground we encountered a number of quick, steep climbs, but nothing we weren't prepared to overcome.

I have no right to complain. Only fifty miles remain!

When we finally arrived here, the view was simply stunning. Amidst an environment of serenity, we are surrounded by rolling hills of gold and the most spectacular view of this crystal clear lake.

Our campsite is primitive. It will be our last campsite until our trip home as San Francisco doesn't offer primitive camping.

It is quiet here. I feel as if I am back in the middle of the desert. Very few other campers are present, and the air is calm…

The lake, located not more than a half-mile walk from our campsite, is filled with rainbow and brown trout. A few local fishermen (whom I ran into while wading my ankles into the water) informed me that Lake Solano offers some of the best fly-fishing around. I can certainly understand why. If I were a fish, I'd want to live here. Free of debris, this water is enticing. I could stay here all day. But I need food and I know Joe and Steph are busy cooking back at the campsite. They sure have become good chefs throughout this journey. Possibly it is simply my appetite.

Tomorrow we will leave this lovely lake and bike to Vallejo. In Vallejo we will board a ferry which will deliver us at Pier 1 in San Francisco. From Pier 1, we will bike six miles through the city to the Golden Gate Park. Here — I've discovered — is where my journey will just begin.

Yes, at that point in time all four of us will have made it as far west as we can, either by bike or by car. But this journey has simply set the stage for the remainder of our lives.

From tomorrow on, we will all have but two choices in life. We can follow one of two paths. We can return to the lives we previously lived and settle for routine. We can hold on to anger, resentment, distrust, hatred, and memories filled with violence, or we can accept the prospect of hope.

We now have an incredible opportunity. We can take the wisdom we've gained from this trip and fight: fight for what is right, for human dignity, mankind, a world full of promise, and one we surely lost sight of as a result of your death.

Or we can simply surrender, give up, and give in to the hatred, sorrow and horror.

The choice is ours to make.

I'm going to fight; and not just for my life but for yours and your legacy. This is why I've written this memoir.

I am proud of the physical accomplishments each of us has made. We have practically ridden our bikes across America! Tomorrow I'll be able to state this definitely with pride.

More importantly, I am proud of this journey. I'm proud of the fight I've put up along the way to remember your name and to learn to live life again.

I'll never move on. But I'm beginning to learn to live my life again.

Although the thought of living my life without you here on earth brings tears to my eyes, I've found peace in knowing that you will forever guide the spiritual journey I will travel the remainder of my days.

If only in memory, you'll always be by my side.

We all miss you, Jeremy. We *always* will.

For the rest of my days here on this earth I will choose to live, because you cannot. I won't just walk through the motions of life, I will live.

And tonight (as is now routine and will be for the remainder of my days) I will pray to my new god — a being I'm just beginning to understand — for you, your soul and our world.

From Lake Solano, California: Goodnight!

Tomorrow night, I will write you from San Francisco, California, where the streets will curve quickly and the hills will be steep, the wind will blow with all of its might, and the temperatures will be cool!

Sleep will be hard to come by tonight!

All my love,
Jennifer

Postcript:

*I ended my letter to Jeremy that night, and the next day
Steph, Brad, and I, with Joe following in the car, crossed
the San Pablo Bay, entered San Francisco, and pedaled
against the force of the wind past the Golden Gate Bridge
— seen in the horizon all the way to the Pacific Ocean —
where, in silence, we wrote "The End" in the sand. The
gentle waves took the words quickly, like our beloved
Jeremy was taken from us. But we had done it; we'd left
Virginia and made it all the way across this beautiful
country, from the foothills of the Appalachians past the
coastal hills of California all the way to the mesmerizing
sounds of this great body of water. No one could ever take
our memories from us: of this trip, or of our most dearly
loved brother.*

42. Two Weeks and Twenty Years
San Francisco, then east...

"Other things may change us, but we start and end with family."
~Anthony Brandt

November 6, 2008

Dear Jeremy,

*A*fter we arrived in San Francisco, we spent five days touring the city, strengthening our gluteal muscles (damn those San Franciscan hills), eating damn good Chinese food (prepared in some of the smallest and filthiest restaurants I've ever seen), walking along the piers, listening to the sea otters bark, and simply existing on the coast of California.

Dad and Brad exchanged places. Dad flew out to California joining Joe, Steph, and me for our journey home. Brad flew to New Jersey to begin a new job. Oh, the realities of everyday living!

Our reunion with Dad was emotional. As we drove up to his arrival gate at the Oakland airport, I saw in front of me a proud father. With a smile hiding his face and a jump in his step, upon sight of us he rushed toward the Pathfinder waving both his hands in the air. Before I had a chance to exit the car, he opened my door and embraced me securely. "You guys did it! You biked across America!" Tears of joy filled our eyes. Indeed, we did it!

Brad stayed with us for one final celebratory night before returning to the East Coast. Early the following morning he quietly loaded a small bag into an airport shuttle parked outside our hotel's front entrance. As he did so, I stood in silence watching his gait. A sense

Steph, Dad and Joe standing in front of the Powell and Mason Street Trolley,
San Francisco, June 2008

(From left to right) Brad, Jen and Steph at the Golden Gate Park, June 24, 2008
Photograph by Joseph Herbstritt

Jen locked inside a cell in Alcatraz, San Francisco, June 2008
Photograph taken by Stephanie Herbstritt

Colorful row-houses lining the streets of San Francisco (found in the vicinity of Haight and
Ashbury), June 2008 ~ Photograph taken by Joseph Herbstritt

Golden Gate Bridge, June 2008
Photograph taken by Joseph Herbstritt

View of San Francisco from the top of Coit Tower located on the crest of Telegraph Hill, San Francisco, June 2008

Many meals were eaten here during our stay, Chinatown, San Francisco, June 2008

Joe appreciating a scenic view along the Pacific Highway en route to Big Sur, June 2008

Dad at Big Sur, June 2008 ~ Photographs on this page taken by Stephanie Herbstritt

Sea otters, Big Sur, June 2008 ~ Photograph taken by Stephanie Herbstritt

Jen and Dad demonstrating the astonishing size of this sequoia trunk,
Sequoia National Forest, California, June 2008

Dad resting on a rock as he climbs up toward Bridal Veil Falls,
Yosemite National Park, June 2008
Photograph by Stephanie Herbstritt

of emptiness camouflaged his expression. Tears welled up in the corners of my eyes. Time doesn't pause. Actively searching for distraction from my thoughts, I frantically rummaged through my purse for some spare change to send along with him. All I had left, hidden in one of the many compartments of my bag, was a wrinkled twenty dollar bill I'd saved from the morning of April 16, 2007. I'd placed that bill in the pocket of my shorts for use just in case I wasn't able to finish the marathon: cab-fare. A piece of my past. I left the bill tucked away, tightly hugged Brad, and returned to the room.

Together, Joe, Steph, Dad and I spent in excess of two weeks traveling back to our roots.

After our stay in San Francisco, we ventured down the coast all the way to Big Sur. Here, we slept a mere three miles away from a (contained) massive wildfire. We slept under a sea of redwoods in the middle of the forest. We had hoped to fall asleep on a beach, but as law-abiding citizens we couldn't find a location that permitted camping on the coastline that wasn't already filled to capacity.

The next day we traveled to Yosemite where we saw the most magnificent waterfalls; one known as "Bridal Veil Falls" truly resembled the veil of a bride. We saw rock formations of variable shapes and sizes, canyons and ravines filled with some of God's most beautiful pieces of art. We saw sequoias with trunks wider than the length of my body, some larger than the length of our home. We saw families grouped together spending time vacationing and enjoying the company of one another.

From Yosemite we began our journey east back through the desert of Nevada, this time following US Interstate 80 rather than 50. This was the one and only time during the trip home that we drove on this road. We had wanted to see America, not an interstate. Now, however, we agreed not to experience the "Loneliest Highway in America" ever again (sorry Nevada).

No, that's not sand! Driving toward Salt Lake City surrounded by nothing but the Great Salt Lake, Utah, early July 2008

Jen paranoid that Sally (the eldest and most easy going horse guiding our group) will abruptly take off...that or slip off the edge of a cliff! Jackson Hole, Wyoming, July 2008

Three hundred-some-odd miles on I-80 through the desert turned out to be mentally straining (go figure). At times the wind was so harsh it nearly blew my car off the road. I had to remain diligent, my attention focused solely on the road.

Just as everything in life eventually is, soon enough that experience became the past.

We took I-80 to Fallon where we spent the night sleeping in our four-person, green tent set up behind a convenience store on a bed of surprisingly green grass (yes, in the middle of the desert).

That morning I woke up at the crack of dawn and ran fifteen laps around that store, if only to feel your presence.

From Fallon we ventured on to Salt Lake City where we toured the great historic Mormon buildings. We were not permitted to enter into the distinguished Tabernacle, being not of the Mormon faith, but we looked at it in awe.

A city like Salt Lake, located in the center of the desert, was a sight to see. Driving along the highway as we entered the city, surrounded

Dad sporting his American flag bandana accompanied by Steph sporting her
"May the forest be with you" t-shirt, Wyoming, July 2008

by nothing other than the Great Salt Lake, itself, was (as well) panoramic. It looked like sand, but I knew better. It was water, and water was all I could see for miles and miles in the distance. The only variable separating me from this great lake was the byway. I wondered how it was constructed.

And then, out of nowhere, abruptly the city appeared, like a cat hunting for its prey. It was amazing to see such life and prosperity amidst the dry, northern Utah desert.

From Salt Lake we traveled north through Idaho to Wyoming, where we stayed outside of Jackson Hole. It was here where we rode on horseback deep into the Rocky Mountains.

Dad kept his promise.

We saw the Great Grand Tetons (over 13,000 feet in elevation) and simply couldn't believe the vista of these snow-covered peaks.

As we traveled farther through Yellowstone National Park we saw buffalo in herds, at times crossing the road no quicker than a tortoise, each time causing a traffic jam of tourists. Animals here were unfenced. They lived freely within their natural living environments. While we beamed at the sight of the volcanic hot springs, a buffalo appeared so close to us that I could have honestly reached out my hand and touched his head without even stretching.

Moose dashing across the road less then twenty-five feet in front of the Pathfinder, Yellowstone National Park, July 2008 ~ Photograph by Michael Herbstritt

Dad spontaneously decided to take a few years off his physical appearance—this is him after thirteen washes, Jackson Hole, Wyoming, July 2008.

Jennifer, Stephanie, Dad, and Joe at the Crazy Horse Monument, July 2008

Snow-capped Rocky Mountains, Wyoming, July 2008

Indeed, I'm actually within feet of this Buffalo. Buffalo were found in masses within Yellowstone National Park, July 2008.

Jen standing in front of a Mount Rushmore replica including George Washington, Thomas Jefferson, Abraham Lincoln, and Theodore Roosevelt, July 2008

Mount Rushmore under hazy skies, July 2008

Brisk winds blowing Jen to the left while posing amid the Badlands of
South Dakota, July 2008 ~ Photograph taken by Stephanie Herbstritt

As a little boy, Jeremy loved trains.
On this particular day, this midwestern railroad reminded me of him.

We saw Old Faithful erupt. Additionally, we saw many other hot springs erupt.

Dad tricked Steph into wearing her bathing suit into the park: told her there would be "hot springs."

"I bet they'll surely loosen up your legs after all of that biking."

"Be sure to wear your suit."

Steph didn't realize these hot springs were actually volcanoes. I'm not sure if Dad initially realized this either. Regardless, none of us could stop laughing when we realized Dad's little trick (and Steph's gullibility).

We saw elk, white-tailed deer, bison, and even a moose. Indeed, we saw a moose jump a fence, walk ever so slowly across the road in front of us (no more than twenty-five feet away), and then jump the fence on the opposite side of the road. Joe recorded the entire escapade on video. I took twelve pictures (none of which turned out).

Dad picked up some hair dye outside of Jackson Hole. When I woke up on the morning of our departure from Yellowstone, I found our father painting his beard with some sort of brush. If only you could have seen his sight! You wouldn't have been able to catch your breath as you would have been laughing absolutely uncontrollably. The color was a bit dark, to say the least, and after left on his face for probably ninety minutes there was absolutely no getting that dye off of his head…not even after a full thirteen washes.

Steph couldn't have been any more humiliated due to the fact that we'd be meeting up with her boyfriend's family for the first time in just a few short days. Dad looked like he'd spent just a little too much time in the coal mines. He appeared covered in soot!

From Yellowstone, we traveled east to Cody, Wyoming, and then farther east to Custer, South Dakota. It was here that we saw the vision of Custer's last stand, saw fireworks on the Fourth of July and saw the Crazy Horse Monument and learned of his legacy. Here, Crazy Horse is currently being carved into the side of a mountain in the Black Hills of South Dakota. As I've learned, he was a respected war hero and member of the Lakota tribe, a man who fought for the preservation of Lakota traditions and this tribe's rights to reside within these sacred hills.[28] The circumstances of his murder in 1877,[29] I only vaguely understand. What I do know is that this man was, and still is, considered an Indian hero. His words, "My land is where my people lay buried," spoken proudly by the Lakota people still to this day, will forever be engrained within my mind.[30]

We traveled to Mount Rushmore and saw George Washington, Abraham Lincoln, Thomas Jefferson, and Theodore Roosevelt carved into the cliff of a mountain. Over the course of fourteen years Gutzon Borglum and four hundred-some other workers created this masterpiece located outside of the Badlands of South Dakota.

As we left Rushmore, tears filled my eyes. It was difficult for me to wave goodbye to the Rockies. Doing so meant we were traveling home.

Fortunately this sorrow didn't last long. Once we set our sights on the Badlands all gloom dissipated. I was not prepared for what I saw when we drove through these lands. I expected to see desert with nothing but sand: no sagebrush, trees, or even animals; nothing but desolate desert.

This is far from what I saw.

I saw the most mesmerizing erosions of rock. Sharp, narrow, jagged rocks clustered together in thousands compiling to form gigantic bizarrely shaped pinnacles, each painted a variety of rich shades of browns, orange and yellows. These lands to me seemed far from "bad." I understand the name, but to me this place was simply extravagant: undeniably worth preserving.

From the Badlands of South Dakota we returned to the heart of the Midwest. We traveled across Nebraska where I was handed my first speeding ticket of the trip. And yes, I got into an argument with the cop. And then Dad!

We slept in Sioux City, which lies within three states: Iowa, South Dakota, and Nebraska. We stayed in *South* Sioux City, Nebraska.

After Nebraska, we entered Iowa where my journey through life began. We stopped in Des Moines where we visited our old neighbors from Waterloo. They've relocated just as we have. It'd been twenty years since we'd been in contact with one another and all we needed to do was pick up the phone. We stopped by their new home and conversed as if we had just met over coffee yesterday. The reunion was heartwarming.

From there we visited Iowa State University in Ames. We spent the night there and then drove to our old home in Waterloo the following day. In Waterloo, I gazed at that red-and-yellow split-level house with eyes first glassy and then bloodshot. Memories unpeeled. I remembered the aluminum fence Dad and a neighbor constructed adjoining our yards. Its purpose was to prevent our disappearance during our active toddler years.

We knocked on this old neighbor's front door and his faced gleamed with excitement at the site of us. He recognized Dad in an instant. Old stories were shared. A friendship was rekindled between him and our Dad.

I remembered that back yard. I remembered our sandbox. I remembered our friends, the snow in the winters, sled-riding with Mom, falling off of my bike with training wheels, your John Deere tractors, Dad's business trips and the toys he brought back for us, the park down the road, and happiness — sheer bliss.

Dad took us over to his old place of work: John Deere. His old office is now nothing but dirt. The building has long been demolished, the victim of a recession.

He drove us to a park, the same one he used to bike to with you in the carriage on the back of his bike. You did this on Sunday afternoons while I stayed home with Mom.

He showed us the John Deere showroom where the two of you pretended to operate the machinery. True farmers you were to become one day. Tears filled his eyes as he fisted his chest, realizing yet again all that was taken from him, and from you, at your death.

We traveled to the hospital where Mom used to work. The building has changed immensely. Years ago it was destroyed during a tornado and/or flood. Since then, it's been rebuilt.

So much has changed in Waterloo, as would be expected in over twenty years, yet so many memories remain present in that town. The experience was bittersweet.

From Waterloo we drove to Madison, Wisconsin, then to Milwaukee, where we toured the Harley Davidson factory. Dad (being a smart you-know-what) told the workers he drove a Yamaha.

From there it was Chicago and a view of Wrigley Field from the top of the Sears Tower.

From Chicago to Yellow Springs, Ohio, then Girard, Ohio — a far distance from Girard, Kansas, where we had earlier met the truck driver who provided us with some of the very best advice of the trip: "Take extra time and enjoy what I have recommended."

From Girard it was home to Bellefonte, Pennsylvania. This part of our journey is finished.

Love from the beauty of our home in Bellefonte,

Jenny

Jeremy, Jen (center), and Steph outside Jeremy's row house apartment, Baltimore, Maryland, summer 2005

Joe (left) and Jeremy, Joe's high-school graduation, June 2006

Afterword

November 6, 2008

Dear Jeremy,

Since I arrived home in the middle of July 2008 a number of changes have occurred.

I recognized what you had realized earlier — in order to become the person whom I desire to be, I have to find my own way through this world.

For me, in order to do this I needed to leave what I'd known as home for nearly twenty years and form a new home; start fresh for myself. So, I relocated to New Jersey with Brad.

There are two aspects of my life worth mentioning that haven't changed. One is obvious. You are dead, still.

The other is the wisdom I've gained from my bike trip; from leaving Virginia and traveling to California, using nothing more than the power of my legs and the strength of my will — often encouraged, I know, by your spirit as well as the love of our family, including Brad. I will never lose sight of the knowledge and power provided to me by this journey.

I am not alone in the wisdom in which I gained through this experience. Earlier in the day I checked my email and found this note written by Dad. The subject was titled, "My final chapter." Within the body of the email Dad wrote: "What do you think?"

I find it interesting that he sent this particular note on this particular day: the day of your birth, November 6. He and I had recently participated in the Tussey mOUnTaiNBACK 50-mile relay. The purpose was primarily to live in your memory. Here is Dad's essay:

My Final Chapter

All too often my heart feels broken. The pain of Jeremy's death is persistent. Sometimes, it feels as though the hurt stops all reasons to continue on with life. At this point in life, I am weak and find it difficult to take another step, to look forward to another day, to plant another seed, or to imagine future plans.

Considering this, I looked to my final chapter, my final adventure, my final battle. I only discovered that the finale was not mine to predict. I found the words of St. Paul as I ran my leg of the 50-mile relay, or correspondingly my leg in life. "I have fought the good fight, I have finished the race. I have kept the faith. From now on there is reserved for me the crown of right-eousness, which the Lord, the righteous judge, will give me on that day, and not only to me but also to all who have longed for his appearing."

As I anticipated my desire to participate in the race, I was encouraged to train for such an endeavor. Jennifer (my daughter), whom I so often describe as my rock, encouraged me to find a team, to train, and to run the race. My emphasis was to run the race in memory of Jeremy. I was searching for a connection to him, a connection that I could feel, a connection that I could trust that was truly similar to something like feeling his handshake as I planned to cross the finish line.

As time approached the race date, my plans diminished as the team I was on disassembled and withdrew. Likewise, I withdrew from inside and had given in to the feelings of loneliness and despair.

Jennifer was my persistence, she found me another team, encouraged me to join, and taught me to continue.

Peg, my wife, has volunteered many of the previous races and was also a volunteer to this one. Correspondingly, she has volunteered in the race of my life. The evening before the race we watched a TV clip advertising the event from years past; there she was, checking off the runners as they handed off the baton. She kept track of their progress similar to how she has kept track of my progress in this life.

Here's to Dad finishing his 5.3 mile-long leg in honor of you.
Photograph taken by Kate Ryan, Nittany Valley Running Club member

I thought this could be such a climax, such a finish. I imagined as I crossed my finish line, Jeremy would be there with his outstretched arm, awaiting me to grab his hand and continue my journey into the next life. I imagined Peg to write down my time of finish, to look at my effort and desire, to record my passion in this lifetime so others could continue on in my place.

As I was running my 5.3-mile leg, I looked at the beauty of the forest. I found it unimaginable that such beauty was allowed to exist in relation to the horror that I have seen in the past few years of my life. I thought this would be the place for my demise: a man who only saw cruelty, horror, and despair to be left alone within a space filled with beauty, brightness, and hope.

As my legs began to lose strength, alongside of me came Peg in her car. She rooted me on as I asked how much longer. Peg said: "Only two or three more miles, Mike, but you will make it." I thought, *Two or three more miles? That will be nearly impossible; my legs are now in slow motion... I'm ready to stop.* Others encouraged me on, then a friend's vehicle arrived, their encouragement said, "You must continue, you must make it, you must endure." So, I knew, I must continue, I must because there at the finish would be Peg and my friends; I prayed there at the finish would also be Jeremy with his outstretched hand.

Joe (my other son) has so often explained his philosophy of life to me; he has taught me to see the reality and truth of what has happened and that we have no choice but to continue on.

Stephanie, my youngest daughter, told me the night before the race that she had run many miles that day. She told me that my leg in the race should be easy compared to the miles she had run. Indeed, correspondingly, my life in comparison is so much easier than hers. She is in her youth, so new to the struggles presented to us in this lifetime. She represents the future in more ways than I can see. She learns more each and every new day.

So, when she told me that my leg would be easy, I thought, *I need to prove her right, my leg would be easy*. I kept telling that to myself as my legs started to cramp and my hip joints started to pain, *Yeah, this is easy compared to our lives*.

Jen and Joe are also in their youth, they know the future is theirs, they know they are the ones who will determine the future. Peg and I have carried the torch; now, we see we will pass it on.

I crossed the finish line, taking longer than most thought I should have. I was overtaken by the cheers as I crossed.

I discovered that this was not the final chapter, that I must indeed continue my journey.

I witnessed the compassion in the lives of my teammates as we traveled in our van from leg to leg cheering one another on. They would talk about their families; they called their spouses and children to update them on their progress and showed their love.

I thought, *What path will I take?* I can never answer that question for I don't know the answer. Is the path we take predetermined or do we have the free will to continue on? There are so many influences in our lives, so many challenges, and so many decisions that can alter our paths.

For me, the final chapter was not written, nor will I be the one to write it. All I know is that some day, sometime, somewhere the final act will be there. Will I be judged on what I accomplished or will I be judged on what I have endured? I would like to read the final chapter. Maybe it never will come; maybe it's just a new beginning.

Continue the race, train for the race, pursue the finish, persist and never give in to defeat, take on all obstacles and overcome them with every ounce of strength left. As you pass others, encourage them; as they pass you, encourage them also. The race is your life. The race never ends.

Jeremy, I cried when I read this letter. Dad's pain is so real, as is all of ours. It won't ever go away. His sorrow won't diminish. Nor will any of ours. No matter how many times our brains are shocked, how many medications we swallow, or how much alcohol we drink, we'll always be sad.

We'll forever be sad that you were robbed of an opportunity at life. Thirty-two great souls were shafted, murdered, removed from this world prematurely, without warning, for a reason none of us will ever be able to even begin to understand.

You woke up that morning expecting to go to class, to study, to possibly go for a run. You didn't expect to die.

The journey through grief, as our family has reluctantly found, is incredibly painful. Our trip across America might have been both mentally and physically challenging (just as the Boston Marathon was for me back on April 16, 2007) but when I compare both to the struggles of grief, neither appears remarkable.

Despite its simplicity, this trip permitted not just me, but all of us, the opportunity to grieve. I never wanted this opportunity. But I needed it.

I know you'll never return, Jeremy. I know I'll never see you again, but with each mile I biked over those thirty-nine days, I gained a considerable amount of hope for my future and that for generations to come. Right now this is all I can hold on to: hope.

Today we should be celebrating your twenty-ninth birthday with you still here on this earth. Instead, our family will place flowers on your grave, a lot which is now marked with a finely crafted red marble stone engraved with your name, your birth date, and the date of your murder.

Numerous masses around the world will be held in your name as I think between Mom and Grandma they've hit up every congregation they can think of, including the Vatican.

Even though nearly nineteen months have passed since your death, the pain of your absence is still raw. It isn't any easier, nor do I expect it ever will be, and nor will I ever want it to be. It seems it was only yesterday when I last heard your voice, a voice I will never forget. In the same respect, it seems it was only yesterday when I was informed of the news of your death.

Every morning I awake to the same nightmare, and I will continue to do so until the day that I myself die.

I miss you tremendously. When I run, I still try to catch up with you. When I attend Mass, it is your hand I reach for during the reciting of the "Our Father." When I was looking for houses here in New Jersey, it was you whom I wanted to call and tell of what I found. I called, but all I got was your answering machine with an empty promise recited by your voice that you'd call back as soon as you could.

In the future, when I hear good news, like Joe or Stephanie is getting married or having a child, or Mom and Dad are buying a horse, or remodeling their kitchen for the umpteenth time, it will be your number I'll want to call to share my excitement with.

When your birthday comes around each November 6, it will be your number I will dial, that year and every year after. What I would give to wish you one more Happy Birthday! Instead, forever in my mind you will be twenty-seven.

On August 16, 2008, exactly sixteen months to the date following your death, we put on the second annual "Herbie's Hometown Loop." This event reminded me of the good that is present in this world amongst all of the chaos and havoc I have seen.

The night prior to the race, we hosted a pre-race pasta dinner. I swear to you it felt as if the entire town was in attendance. I had to hold back my tears as I witnessed the compassion that our community still has for us. Their compassion made me realize that you made an impact on all of their lives in some fashion or another in your short time on this earth.

You made such an impact on their lives that even though you'd been gone from this earth for over a year your face was still fresh in their minds. Even if they didn't know you, they will not forget your smile as seen in the newspapers. And if they did know you: your laugh, conversations held with you, times spent with you and the stories that you told will always be held dear within their hearts.

None of us will ever forget you.

As for the race we put on the next day, it was a total success. We worked diligently to make this race all about you. When you passed, I was horrified that you would never be able to experience some of the aspects of life that many of us take for granted: the ability to marry, have children, attend your younger brother and sister's twenty-first birthday celebrations, mow the yard one last time, finish that fence or even just say "Goodbye, I love you," just one more time. So I wanted to give you your day. I wanted to create an event for you, where the focus was you, a celebration of your life.

So on August 16, we put on a four-mile run, sixteen-mile bike ride and seven-mile kayak race, all separate events, in memory of you. This was a day meant to remember you. For those who attended and never knew of your name, we provided them with a small glimpse of you. For those who knew you, we asked them to remember. We featured all of your favorite foods from "fire in the hole" Buffalo wings from Bonfatto's to Eat n' Park cookies, pizza from your favorite local pizzerias, and some of the freshest, juiciest fruit in town, courtesy of a number of fine local farmers.

Thirty-two trees were given away with each one meant to memorialize either you or one of the other very fine people who were taken away all too prematurely in that same senseless act of violence on April 16, 2007. Attached to each was a memoir. Seeds were given to all who participated to plant and sow in your name as a remembrance of your love for gardening. Give-aways from local stores were provided and there were enough freebies so that every participant was able to leave with something held in their hands.

We featured the best quality race t-shirts around, as we all know why you loved to race! Kid's activities were flourishing; the Dairy Princess was present, as was a fire truck for the kids to tour. A kid's bike race was run; helmet fittings were performed, as were bike checks. There were cheerleaders performing face paintings and the Nittany Lion and Ike the Spike were both in attendance. Even an appearance by your favorite local bar band, the Phyrst Family, was made.

This day was all about you.

Margaret Herbstritt (Mom), baby Joe, and Jeremy, Boalsburg, circa 1987

Your best friends joined us. Many traveled great distances to remember you.

Your extended family was in attendance.

The only thing missing was you. I sensed your presence that day. Truly I did. I knew you would have been proud, but it wasn't enough. It never will be.

I choked up prior to the race when I presented a brief speech thanking everyone for attending and reminding them of why we were present. I choked up because after all of the work I'd put into that race you still were not there, at least not in the physical sense.

This world never will be the same without you in it, my big brother, Jeremy Michael Herbstritt, civil engineer, Penn State Alum, and the proud driver of a 1994 red Jeep Cherokee.

Every day that I wake up until the day that I take my last breath, in the face of darkness and horror, I will stand tall, hold back my tears, put a smile on my face and choose life. I will live for you, in your memory, simply because you so unfairly cannot. I will make it. I'll be a fighter, because you were, and because you'd want me to be.

On Christmas Eve, with tears pooling in the corner of my eyes, I'll march myself out into the blistering cold, through a foot of snow if I have to, cut down a fresh pine tree from the tree farm we used to support and I'll set up that tree, hang your stocking high, as we had done for so many years before, and say a prayer for your soul.

On Thanksgiving, I'll play backyard football at Grandma's. I'll be covered in snow, wet and cold, words will be hard to eject as I'll be holding back tears, but I will do this in your memory, if for nothing else, other than because you cannot.

I'll remember your smile. I'll remember your laugh. Sometimes I'll laugh out loud when I think of what you'd do or say in a situation I've been placed in.

I won't forget you — you can count on me for this.

You'll always be my big brother; no one will take your place. Everything I do in life, I'll do it for you. My life is now dedicated to you because you weren't given a fair chance at this life.

Jeremy Michael Herbstritt, you're still my hero, my best friend, and the only running partner I'll ever have. You'll always be the person I go to when I need advice. You'll be a shoulder to cry on and a gentle voice to calm my fears. You'll be an ear to listen, a heart to sympathize with and eyes to travel through life with me.

On a warm summer day, you'll be present in the cool breeze on my cheek and the cleansing of a loud banging thunderstorm following a hot humid day.

In the winter, the fresh snow on barren branches and the first snowfall of the season witnessed in darkness under the sparkle of the stars as I walk out of midnight Mass alone on Christmas Eve.

In the spring, you'll be a crisp flowing stream where water clashes up against strong rocks where fresh trout are swimming, and a baby fawn stumbles across with his mother by his side.

In fall, you'll be the autumn leaves on the trees as they change colors and start to fall.

But in the end, Jeremy Michael Herbstritt, you will always be my one and only big brother.

I am proud to have known you. I am proud to still have you as a part of my life. I am sorry for what happened.

I know what it is like to lose someone whom I truly love, for I have lost you.

I love you, Jeremy.

Thank you for all you've given to me. Thank you for helping me to learn to live life again.

Until we meet once more, for now, farewell.

All my love,

Jenny

Jen, Steph and Joe finding comfort in cuddling with Lizzy, late April 2007
Photograph taken by Evan Trowbridge

Endnotes:

1. City of St. Marys. Retrieved on September 27th, 2008 from
   http://www.cityofstmarys.com/history1.htm
2. Wikipedia. Retrieved December 8th, 2008, from
   http://en.wikipedia.org/wiki/Robert_E._Lee
3. Wikipedia. Retrieved December 9th, 2008, from
   http://en.wikipedia.org/wiki/Robert_E._Lee
4. Adventure Cycling Association. Retrieved on October 1st, 2008, from
   http://www.adventurecycling.org/routes/transamerica.cfm.
5. Berea College. Retrieved on September 14th, 2008, from
   http://www.berea.edu/about/
6. Berea College. Retrieved on September 15th, 2008, from
   http://www.berea.edu/about/
7. Kentucky Atlas and Gazetteer. Retrieved on October 11th, 2008, from
   http://www.uky.edu/KentuckyAtlas/kentucky.html
8. Merriam-Webster Online. Retrieved on October 12th, 2008, from
   http://www.merriam-webster.com/dictionary/providence.
9. U.S. Forest Service. Retrieved on October 14th, 2008, from
   http://www.fs.fed.us/r9/forests/shawnee/about/forest_facts/
10. City of Chester. Retrieved on October 17th, 2008, from
    http://www.chesterill.com/index.php?id=24
11. City of Chester. Retrieved on October 18th, 2008, from
    http://www.chesterill.com/index.php?id=24
12. Eminence, Missouri. Retrieved on October 21st, 2008 from
    http://www.eminencemo.com/springscaveshistoricsites.html
13. Eminence, Missouri. Retrieved on October 22nd, 2008 from
    http://www.eminencemo.com/springscaveshistoricsites.html
14. Marshfield Area Chamber of Commerce and Tourist Information Center.
    Retrieved on October 22nd, 2008, from
    http://www.marshfieldmochamberofcommerce.com
15. Kansas Collection. Retrieved on November 14th, 2008, from
    http://www.kancoll.org/khq/1957/57_3_unrau.htm
16. City of Pueblo, Colorado's Website. Retrieved November 17th, 2008, from
    http://www.pueblo.us/cgi-bin/gt/tpl_page.html,template=1&content=
    742&nav1=1&

17. Canon City, Colorado's Website. Retrieved on November 17th, 2008, from http://www.canoncitycolorado.com/

18. Royal Gorge Bridge and Park Website. Retrieved on November 17th, 2008, from http://www.royalgorgebridge.com/Bridge.aspx

19. Wikipedia (Dallas Divide). Retrieved on January 12th, 2009, from http://en.wikipedia.org/wiki/Dallas_Divide

20. National Park Service; U.S. Department of the Interior's Website. Retrieved on January 17th, 2009 from, http://www.nps.gov/meve/

21. National Park Service; U.S. Department of the Interior's Website. Retrieved on January 18th, 2009 from, http://www.nps.gov/meve/

22. National Park Service; U.S. Department of the Interior's Website. Retrieved on May 13th, 2009, from http://www.nps.gov/grba/index.htm

23. American West (Pony Express Information). Retrieved on January 19th, 2009 , from http://www.americanwest.com/trails/pages/ponyexp1.htm

24. Wikipedia. Retrieved on January 21st, 2009, from http://en.wikipedia.org/wiki/Carson_Pass

25. Wikipedia. Retrieved on January 22nd, 2009, from http://en.wikipedia.org/wiki/Carson_Pass

26. Wikipedia. Retrieved on January 23rd, 2009, from http://en.wikipedia.org/wiki/Carson_Pass

27. El-Dorado County Website (*Traveling the Mormon Emigrant Trail*). Retrieved on January 23rd, 2009, from http://www.co.el-dorado.ca.us/stories/mormon.html

28. Crazy Horse Memorial Website. Retrieved on May 13th, 2009, from http://www.crazyhorsememorial.org/

29. Crazy Horse Memorial Website. Retrieved on May 14th, 2009, from http://www.crazyhorsememorial.org/

30. Crazy Horse Memorial Website. Retrieved on May 15th, 2009, from http://www.crazyhorsememorial.org/

Acknowledgments

Sometimes all we need is for one person to believe in us,
To support us,
To point out our strengths rather than our imperfections,
Console our sorrow with laughter and delight,
Feed our grief with friendship,
Love us unconditionally,
And above all, remind us that there's still life out there worth living.
Sometimes all we need is just one person.

All in the same day, I remember anxiously, yet enthusiastically, submitting my manuscript to a publishing house based out of Athens, Ohio, going for a run to clear my head, and returning to a kind and gentle email crafted by a woman named Janice Phelps Williams. From our first communication, I felt Janice believed in me and the meaning behind my words. Her positive attitude, encouragement and keen interest for my project were the driving forces behind actually advancing with publishing my manuscript. If it weren't for her dedication, attention to detail and kind heart, *Leaving Virginia* never would have come to light in the sense that it has. I will forever be grateful for Janice's involvement as my editor, designer, mentor and friend.

Throughout my life, I've come to realize words can't suffice in certain scenarios. I find this to be one of them. Words of gratitude will never be enough to thank all who have listened to my heavy words, held me while I sobbed, called when it must have been easier to have set down the phone, shared holidays with me and my family, expressed simple gestures to show someone genuinely cares, and encouraged this bike ride, when it might have made more sense to disregard the idea and label it as abnormal grief. This type of support has fueled my momentum and determination to continue on for nearly three years now. So, forever I'll feel a debt to you: my friends, family, colleagues, coaches, teachers, neighbors, fellow running club members, Penn State, State College and Bellefonte communities, and so many others. You are loyal and dependable. I admire your generosity.

Life may not always seem fair, but I suspect if we reflect on our lives in these moments of despair, we'll find much better days worth mulling over. If we're lucky enough, as we look back, we'll come across a common set of people, whose paths have paralleled ours, who have stood by our sides through the thick and the thin, who often stand humbly unrecognized. When I look back on my life, I can easily point out a handful of people fitting this description. My boyfriend, Brad, is one of these commendable souls. No matter how bad life seemed to get, or how crazy I may have acted, he never walked away. And so, I feel honored to thank you, Brad, for giving up dreams of relaxing in Europe following graduate school graduation, to sit on the firm seat of a bicycle and ride across America with me, for loving me when I suspect it must have been difficult, and most importantly, for accepting my family as your own.

And to my dearest family — Mom, Dad, Jeremy, Joseph, and Stephanie — for teaching me that there is still life out there worth living, I thank you. You've helped me to appreciate again life's simple pleasures, and in doing so, restored my zest for life. I always hoped we'd live together forever as a family. I now know we will. Through the binding of our souls, we'll always be a family. For teaching me this, and so much more, I can't thank you enough. Not once did you doubt my determination to bike across America, write this memoir, fight for our family and for what I felt was right, or engage in life again. You've supported me and my decisions, no matter how ludicrous they may have seemed. You have stood proudly by my side through our darkest days. And despite all the hurt death has inflicted in us, when the curtains of this world are drawn to a close, I trust you'll still stand proudly by my side. You've taught me the joy of love, life and remembrance. I couldn't be any more honored to call you my own.

And especially to you, my big brother, Jeremy, for loving me unconditionally, inspiring me to be better, and paving in front of me a path for this new life — I'll forever be obliged. Thank you for teaching me the wonder of living life completely no matter where I'm at. Never will you be forgotten.

Author Q & A

How many miles did you bike? 3,643

How long did the trip take? Thirty-nine days of biking, forty-three days total to get across the country including a few site-seeing/vacation days, two months round-trip including our cross country drive home.

Where did you start/end? Yorktown, Virginia to San Francisco, California

How much planning was involved? Very little! For months I knew I needed to get away. I had lavish plans as to how I would escape. A few of my ideas included teaching English in China for a year, providing HIV/AIDS education to a community in Africa, and backpacking across Europe. One day Joe came across the Adventure Cycling Association's website and suggested I try to bike across the country. Little did he know that a few short weeks later we'd be attempting to do just what he'd suggested! Secretively, I immediately decided I was riding my bike across the country. For weeks, I built up the courage to resign from my job. Once I finally did (on March 30, 2008) a huge burden lifted from my shoulders. My last day of work was April 31, 2008. About a week prior, I ordered the TransAmerica Trail series of maps through Adventure Cycling. The two weeks prior to our departure on May 12 were spent researching the towns we'd pass through, picking out overnight towns, collecting borrowed camping gear from family and friends, practicing riding my recently purchased bike, and buying groceries for the next (tentative) two months. During those two weeks, I'd often take Brad out on bike rides. He was very doubtful this trip would ever take off as I had a terrible time figuring out how to unclip my cleats from the pedals. In fact, the first time we went out I fell over directly into him knocking him over as a red light was turning green amongst fairly heavy traffic. We didn't tell many people we were leaving, just a few close friends. That was it. It was quite spontaneous, just as Jeremy would have had it!

How did you pick your route? Originally, I thought I'd be able to map out a
route across the entire country myself. I must have been out of my
mind. Being that Joe came across Adventure Cycling's website, we
simply purchased their already made maps detailed with the location
and address for overnight towns, campsites, national parks, where to
find gas, bike shops, grocery stores, etc. Originally, we planned on
following the TransAmerica Trail all the way to Astoria, Oregon but
about two weeks into the trip we changed our route. We followed the
TransAmerica Trail to Pueblo, Colorado where we picked up the
Western Express Route and followed this to San Francisco, California.
My mom brought the Western Express maps down to Bowling Green,
Kentucky when she came to visit us there over Memorial Day weekend.

Who went along on the trip? At any given time Brad (my boyfriend), Joe
(my younger brother), Steph (my younger sister), Mike (my dad) and
Peg (my mom). Brad biked from Yorktown, Virginia to San Francisco
with me. Steph joined us in Bowling Green, Kentucky. Joe was our
driver (he drove all of our gear in the SAG wagon — my 2004 silver
Nissan Pathfinder). My dad joined us for the first and last two weeks of
the trip and my mom was with us just for a short vacation we took away
from biking in Bowling Green, Kentucky over Memorial Day weekend.

What kind of bike did each of you ride? I rode a dark purple 2006 Trek
Madone 5.2 road bike. Brad rode a blue Specialized Roubaix Elite road
bike. And Steph rode a gold Bianchi Volpe road bike.

What supplies did you carry/bring with you? More than we actually needed!

Bike gear	Camping gear	Other
Spare Tires	Tent	Skateboard
Spare Tubes	Sleeping bags	Guitar
Multipurpose tool	Pillows	Maps
Bike levers	Grill/pots/pans	Cameras
Bike pump	Cookware	Chairs
Air cartridges	Food/water/Gatorade	GPS
Lube	Toiletries	First aid kit
		Weather radio

What gear did you take with you when you rode? Per person: two water bottles, snacks, one spare tube, air cartridge, tire lever, multi-tool. And I had the bike GPS.

What do you wish you would have brought along? Pepper spray for animals that chased us! Aloe, more spare tubes, a larger variety of canned goods.

How many flat tires did you get? 4 (me), 1 (Brad), 0 (Steph).

What do you know now that you didn't know then? I honestly didn't realize the level of poverty present in some sections of our country previously. As well, I never actually appreciated geography as I learned to do during this trip. I couldn't have told you what the Ozarks were or where they were located for that matter. I didn't appreciate the vastness of the Nevada desert. I never knew how many national parks our country has to offer the curious eye. I was terrible at reading maps, pitiful at starting campfires and incompetent at putting up a tent.

Who was the most interesting person that you met? A man not much older than myself riding his bike around the world! Just the same, a curious, yet wise, truck driver from Girard, Kansas.

What was the most breathtaking sight you saw? Truly, it'd be unfair to pick just one; however, for me, if I had to pick I'd say the Hogback, a three-and-a-half mile narrow section of road absent of guardrails following the ridge line encompassed by nothing but red earth dropping off abruptly into cavernous ravines in all directions found in the middle of the Utah desert.

Did you ever think about quitting? There were times I thought we'd never finish. I'd be lying if I said I didn't think about quitting. But when I saw myself throwing in the towel and returning to the same life I'd left behind, I never was actually able to call it quits.

What would you have done differently? At the time in my life where I was at, nothing. Of course, I wish I would have ventured on this trip years ago with Jeremy by my side, but if I had to do it all over again given the same circumstances I wouldn't change a thing. Well…possibly I would have brought along the above mentioned items!

What was your favorite state? They were all great. California because of the diversity of scenery. From the vineyards to the rolling coastal hills, San Francisco's Chinatown, skyscrapers and of course, the Golden Gate Bridge. Utah because of its pristine beauty overflowing with red rock formations, erosive pinnacles, echoing canyons and national park hot spots. Kansas because of the hospitality of its people. Nevada because of its serenity. Missouri because of the physical challenge the Ozarks provided me with thereby distracting me at least partially from my grief. Colorado for its altitude and the sparkle its vast peaks returned to my eyes. Illinois because of the reminders it provided me of my precious childhood. Kentucky due to the humility it provided me with. And finally Virginia because of the open road it placed in front of me amongst such horror and devastation.

What was the best food of the trip? Hands down the pulled pork sandwich I devoured at Fat Ally's in Telluride, Colorado and the soft serve ice cream at Blondie's in Hanksville, Utah.

Where there any major arguments? Of course!

What was the scariest moment? On our first day in Utah Joe and Steph decided to venture off on an excursion of their own (as wasn't uncommon, at least for Joe). We didn't discuss evening plans as we figured we'd see them somewhere on our route later in the day. It was around dusk and we hadn't heard from them since earlier in the morning. We were about ten miles from the entrance to our next possible campsite, Natural Bridge. And the campgrounds for Natural Bridge were about five miles off the main road but forty miles from the next town. There was absolutely no cell phone reception. In fact, there was nothing around us but red rock and sky. We sat ourselves on the side of the road for about forty-five minutes until the sun started to set — still no Joe or Steph. Finally, we continued on toward the campsite. Just as we started to bike off the main road toward the campground my cell phone rang. Fortunately, in a five foot by five foot space my cell phone had reception! It was enough to inform Joe and Steph of our whereabouts and hear that they had just gotten caught up sightseeing.

What was the funniest moment? Hands down waking up to Dad dying his hair while seated on a picnic table at a KOA outside of Jackson Hole, Wyoming. As well, dancing around a flaming campfire while obnoxiously singing the *Lion Sleeps Tonight* after being splashed by a Port-o-John — this was, oddly enough, hysterical.

What was the saddest moment? Driving past Blacksburg, Virginia realizing Jeremy still wasn't there.

What was the best part of the trip? Biking away from the Yorktown Victory Monument on May 13, 2008.

Did you ever get lost? More times than I could ever recall! Oddly enough, we had a stack of maps, a GPS and even a compass, none of which prevented *me* from getting us lost!

What did Joe do all day long? Parked in farmer's fields, played his guitar, filmed us, wrote music, cheered us on, took down camp, set up camp, adventured on his own excursions, went grocery shopping, scouted out surrounding towns, to name a few things.

How did you cook? Either on the propane grill (often times set up in the middle of a parking lot) or above a campfire. Mountain pies, foil packs, pasta, and/or canned raviolis were typical meals. Hamburgers and corn on the cob were special treats. Ice cream was a nightly ritual as were burnt-to-a-crisp marshmallows.

Where did you sleep? For the most part, enclosed in a 4x4, four person tent, although, for the first two weeks of the trip we used 2-two person tents. These turned out to be a bit leaky — after waking up in the middle of the night in the midst of a torrential downpour only to find myself saturated in a pool of rain water I opted to purchase a more waterproof tent capable of fitting all of us. As well, we spent a few nights in hotels.

Did you know what you were doing when you finished the trip? No idea.

Would you do it again? Absolutely! Notice, I didn't even hesitate.

What was the most valuable lesson learned? Truly, there are too many to pick from but to name a few: Most of my material possessions are completely unnecessary. Some of the simplest aspects of life are what will be remembered forever: roasting marshmallows while sitting around a warm campfire in the midst of the high plains of Kansas, things like this will never be forgotten. Flat tires build character. From east to west, the topography of America continuously prepares one for what lies ahead. Most of us will never have the opportunity to meet some of the most noteworthy folks out there because we never took the time to explore what truly is in front of our eyes.

About the Author

Jennifer Herbstritt earned a Master's degree in Health Sciences/Physician Assistant Studies from the Lock Haven State University of Pennsylvania. Before the journey documented in *Leaving Virginia*, she worked as a Physician Assistant in State College, Pennsylvania. Following her bicycle trip across the United States, Jennifer relocated to Princeton, New Jersey, where she is currently employed as Adjunct Faculty in the Biology Department at Middlesex County College and as a part-time lecturer in the Exercise Science Department at Rutgers University.

An avid runner, Jennifer has completed nine marathons including the Boston Marathon in 2007. She enjoys participating in weekend 5K charity races and has helped organize Herbie's Hometown Loop, an annual 4-mile run, 16-mile bike and 7-mile kayak event held in memory of Jeremy. Within the next two years she hopes to complete her first ultra-marathon (the Tussey mOUnTaiNBACK), the course of which is set on some of her favorite running routes in Rothrock State Forest located on the outskirts of State College, Pennsylvania.

In addition of reading, running, writing and traveling, Jennifer enjoys spending time with family, friends, and her beloved childhood dog, Lizzy. Near-future plans include a trip to Asia and/or Australia and, of course, a second book.